# INTELLECTUAL PROPERTY

## PATENTS, TRADEMARKS, AND COPYRIGHT

## IN A NUTSHELL

### FOURTH EDITION

By

**ARTHUR R. MILLER**
Professor of Law
Harvard Law School

**MICHAEL H. DAVIS**
Professor of Law
Cleveland State University
Cleveland–Marshall College of Law

**THOMSON**
━━━━━✦━━━━━ ™
**WEST**

Mat #40330848

*Nutshell Series, In a Nutshell*, the Nutshell Logo and West Group are trademarks registered in the U.S. Patent and Trademark Office.

COPYRIGHT © 1983, 1990 WEST PUBLISHING CO.
© West, a Thomson business, 2000
© 2007 Thomson/West
　　　　610 Opperman Drive
　　　　P.O. Box 64526
　　　　St. Paul, MN 55164–0526
　　　　1–800–328–9352
Printed in the United States of America

**ISBN:** 978–0–314–15875–8

# ACKNOWLEDGMENTS

---

This is for Zoe and Izzie. The Fourth Edition, like the Third, owes its existence to Dana Neacşu who, still filled with provocative thoughts, retaught me the subversive fact that a good idea is its own incentive. Without her assistance, example, and love, I would not be able to thank my co-author once again for the continuing and increasing pleasure of working with him.

I also thank Jason LaSalle, my excellent student assistant who is already becoming an equally excellent practicing lawyer.

\*

# OUTLINE

---

# OUTLINE

VI

# OUTLINE

# PART III.   COPYRIGHT

*OUTLINE*

# TABLE OF CASES

**References are to Pages**

---

XV

# TABLE OF CASES

## TABLE OF CASES

# TABLE OF CASES

# INTELLECTUAL PROPERTY

## PATENTS, TRADEMARKS, AND COPYRIGHT

## IN A NUTSHELL

FOURTH EDITION

*

# INTRODUCTION

A book presenting the basics of intellectual property faces two difficulties. First, intellectual property traditionally includes the three legal areas of patents, trademarks, and copyrights. However, except for tradition and the fact that the three subjects are commonly taught together in one survey course, one might question why a single book should include these three divergent subjects. What they have in common is a relatively amorphous character and a highly abstract concept of property. Only two of them, patent and copyright, share a common constitutional source. That brings up the second difficulty. The "property" of intellectual property is not the concrete form that characterizes the area of real property, for instance. It has been said, with respect to tort law, and the supposed ease with which students grasp its basics, that anyone can recognize a punch in the nose. Unlike a punch in the nose, however, the force of intellectual property is more like that of the invisible beam of Buck Rogers' ray gun. "Patents and copyrights approach, nearer than any other class of cases belonging to forensic discussion to what may be called the metaphysics of the law, where the distinctions are, or at least may be, very subtle and refined, and, sometimes, almost evanescent." *Folsom v. Marsh* (1841)

1

(Story, J.). This abstract quality occasionally presents problems to beginners.

Two considerations, however, make our task easier. First, the areas of patent, trademark, and copyright, are substantially statutory. Although that means that the law cannot be understood without occasional reference to the statute, it also means that, with the statute, at least some "black letter" law is immediately available. With the recent explosion of intellectual property as a mainstay of national and international trade has come a concomitant explosion of statutory changes,. This presents a challenge to students and practitioners to stay up-to-date. Second, although intellectual property is relatively abstract, that is not to say that it is unfamiliar.

Trademark, for instance, is hopefully even more commonplace than a punch in the nose. We all have seen Xerox machines and the ads that manufacturer places periodically to reinforce the strength of its mark. We have used aspirin, which once was a trademark but is no longer. Likewise, although most people have not seen a patent document, we all have seen, used, and benefitted from patented items, processes, combinations, and the like. We have seen and used copyrighted materials, including this book, and enjoyed many of them. Without patented and copyrighted items, our lives would be quite different. The richness they bring to us is one of the justifications for these protective legal concepts (although one always should note that copyright was not necessary to inspire Shakespeare to write nor was the patent system necessary to encourage the first inventor of the wheel).

Finally, a basic book in any area cannot pretend to be the last word. As is true of all legal subjects, the field of intellectual property is hopelessly entangled with other legal areas, such as torts and property. It is inextricably bound up with antitrust and government regulation. It also is affected by concepts of federalism and the conflict created by simultaneous state and federal regulation of the same area. Although the basics are necessary for a good beginning, their mastery does not imply that the task is finished.

# PART I

# PATENTS

## CHAPTER 1

# THE FOUNDATIONS OF PATENT PROTECTION

### § 1.1 Origins and Development of United States Patent Law

It is possible to trace the development of American patent law back to ancient Greece. However, the accepted useful starting point is the Statute of Monopolies, adopted in England in 1623, an act that addressed a number of basic patent issues that remain relevant today.

Beginning in medieval times, certain segments of European commerce became centralized and exclusively controlled by various groups. The most notable of these were the early guilds, each of which controlled, at least partially, particular areas of commerce, such as leatherworking, glassmaking, and manufactured goods. These early "monopolies" were hardly like the modern exclusive rights granted for inventive developments. They were basically groups of artisans who, in a sense, had cornered the market.

In time, the right to control various sectors of the market became a royal privilege, granted by the monarch in return for various benefits. These early "patent" monopolies were not concerned with invention, but, rather, with commerce. Thus, the "importation patent" became very common: the monarch would grant the privilege to practice a particular art or manufacturing process to a foreigner who brought new technical skills into the jurisdiction. The patentee frequently would be required to train a number of citizens in the new art. The term of the patent was almost always for a certain number of years.

By the time of Queen Elizabeth I, the practice of royal patents had become a burden on free competition; this effect was heightened by the gradual transition from a feudal to a mercantile economy. Because the patents were not granted for new invention, the only people who really profited from the practice were the monarch and the patentee. In time, the rising powers of the common law courts enabled judges to declare unlawful the most serious abuses of this royal prerogative. However, these were selective and narrow efforts that did not succeed in effectively abolishing the monopolistic economic situation produced by the royal patents. Legislative action was the apparent answer.

Thus, in 1623, the Statute of Monopolies effectively ended the most serious monopolies, those affecting free trade and competition in staples and commodities. Although the Statute was not completely effective, it did halt the wholesale granting of monopolies by the Crown. Note that the Statute of Monopolies, the classical starting point in the development of patent law, was a reaction *against* the unrestricted grant of patent monopolies. This theme of antimonopolism is notable since the law does not favor monopolies generally and patents have a monopolistic character.

The English and common law tradition opposing monopolies must be balanced against the gradual development of an incentive theory of patents. Starting at least with the importation patents, it was recognized that the grant of an exclusive privilege to a person with a valuable talent would tend to confer benefits upon society if that privilege encouraged the person to practice his skill within the state. This was a useful tool in developing the industrialization of Europe by encouraging the importation of new technologies.

The common law reaction against monopolies was received in the New World and gradually the American colonies became perhaps more fiercely, although selectively, opposed to monopolies than their English counterparts. This selectivity was because of the distinction between inventive and importation patents. Even though it could be argued that a new technology already existing in a foreign country, if meritorious, would eventually be adopted here without a patent monopoly, the colonists recognized that the offer of an exclusive patent to someone who invented something new and useful would tend to encourage inventiveness.

By the time of the Revolution, virtually all of the colonies had granted patents. During the period of the Articles of Confederation, well-established state patent practices developed. Lacking a national procedure, there was, however, a serious problem because of the number of different states in which an inventor had to secure patents to achieve meaningful protection.

At the Constitutional Convention, in 1787, a measure was proposed to incorporate as one of the new federal powers the ability to secure, for limited times, patents and copyrights. The measure was adopted without debate. It reads:

> The Congress shall have power ... To promote the progress of ... useful arts, by securing for limited times to ... inventors the exclusive right to their ... discoveries. *U.S. Constitution,* Art. 1, § 8, cl. 8.

The existence of a constitutional patent power had and continues to have important consequences. For one thing, it is far more explicit in its goals and purposes than is the Commerce Clause, for instance, which undergirds trademark law, thus subjecting patent law to what at least appear to be more rigid constitutional constraints.

It can be seen from the Clause's words, then, that the constitutional character of the patent power immediately places apparent limits on Congress' ability to exercise that power by statute, although the Supreme Court has held that Congress has almost unquestionable discretion to do so within reasonable bounds. *Eldred v. Ashcroft* (2003). In addition to creating limits, the constitutional provision also makes the *scope* of Congress' patent power quite large. For instance, the trademark statute, unlike the patent laws, is founded upon the Interstate Commerce Clause and, as a result, federal trademark legislation must have some relationship to interstate commerce to be valid. The patent power, however, has no such interstate limitation. The strength of the explicitly worded Patent Clause also includes the potential to preempt state regulation. This, very briefly, means that there is a strong presumption in favor of federal regulation of this area. The consequence is that state regulation may be invalid if it interferes in any way with the objectives of the patent power. There is some support for the view that federal preemption is stronger in the case of a specific power, like the Patent Clause, than in the case of a less specific power, like the Interstate Commerce Clause.

Although it is the ultimate source of patent power, the constitutional Patent Clause, by itself, has no effect at all. Without a patent statute enacted by Congress, the Clause is just a potential source of power. The first patent statute was enacted in 1790. Since that statute there have been only three major revisions of the Patent Act: in 1793, 1836, and 1952. There have, of course, been changes to various sections of the present Act and, in fact, during the past ten years or so those changes, which are addressed later in this book, have often been profound.

A major reason why there have been so few changes in the Patent Act is that, until the last few years when technological change and globalization have become politically and scientifically important, patent law has not been a politically attractive or volatile issue. Thus, given a rapidly changing society and a relatively stable statute, changes in the patent area tended to come, if at all, from the courts. This, naturally, has caused controversy, with some commentators claiming that the courts illegitimately changed statutory requirements. That, they said, should be done only by Congress. During the past ten years or so, Congress has been more active and a marked judicial shift has occurred.

Until 1836, there was no general administrative body that examined the validity of patents. Since then, however, the Patent Office has been vested with the authority to examine patents and determine at the outset whether a patent application satisfies the requirements of the statute. Obviously, such an institution could not have developed absent a statute. In fact, in England, there was no equivalent office until 1905.

The present Patent Act, enacted in 1952, is completely codified in Title 35 of the United States Code. It includes design and plant patents and in logical progression describes the legal requirements and practical steps of patent application, grant, use, and challenge, produced through the statutory and judicial experience of the preceding century and a half.

## § 1.2 Patent Basics

The Patent Act requires that someone who wishes to obtain a patent satisfy certain requirements. Generally, a potential patentee must be prepared to demonstrate that she has developed a new, useful, and nonobvious process or product. 35 U.S.C.A. § 101. This demonstration is made by means of the patent application. The application contains a specification describing how the invention works. A second part of the patent application consists of "claims," under the preceding specification. They are the actual patentable features of the invention. The "claims" are the asserted new, useful, nonobvious advances beyond the prior state of the art of which the "invention" is a part. The relation between the specification and the claims is that the claims point out what it is that is patentable about the specification. A "provisional" application is a special application that is not examined by the Patent Office, has no claims, but gives the inventor a twelve-month grace period in which to file a normal, nonprovisional application. 35 U.S.C.A. § 111(b). Although the inventor gains domestic priority by virtue of the provisional application, the eventual twenty-year term of patent protection is measured not from the provisional, but from the filing date of the later, nonprovisional, application which might be filed as much as twelve months later.

One purpose of the patent system is to encourage the development of technology by making patent applications public documents, thereby disclosing to everyone information about new inventions. The goal of disclosure is served by the requirement that the specification contain a complete description of the new invention, revealing how it works and how to reproduce it. 35 U.S.C.A. § 111. This effectively discloses all advances in an art to those who practice it.

The patent application is submitted to the Patent Office but no rights immediately accrue. Unlike a copyrighted work, for instance, there is no monopoly right in an invention until a patent actually is issued by the Patent Office. (There may be other rights created by state common law, however, such as the law of trade secrets or unfair competition.) The Patent Office examines the application and conducts a search of past patents and of relevant technical literature to ascertain whether the claims are actually new, useful, and nonobvious—in other words, whether the new invention is patentable. The Patent Office examiner frequently denies patentability to some, or perhaps all, of the claims and the application may then be revised to meet the examiner's objections. Or, sometimes, the application is resubmitted with an explanation of why the examiner is mistaken, arguing that the application is suitable in its original state.

Frequently, this process goes back and forth several times until the patentee and the examiner are in agreement. The file of the patent application can become extraordinarily voluminous.

During the examination process, it may become apparent that one or more other patent applications either currently being considered, or granted within the preceding year, make similar or identical claims. An interference proceeding then will be commenced by the Patent Office with the objective of determining which applicant first conceived and reduced the invention to practice. This question of priority is decided before the Patent Office Board of Interference Proceedings.

Eventually, a patent may be granted effectively giving the patentee the exclusive right to make, use, offer to sell, or sell the invention to the absolute exclusion of others (technically the patentee only gains a right to exclude others from doing so but for most practical purposes, barring conflicting patent rights in some third party, this amounts to a monopoly right in the patentee to make, use, offer to sell, or sell) for a period of twenty years from the date of the original application. 35 U.S.C.A. § 154. However, because the marketing of certain patented inventions, such as drugs, medical devices, and additives, often is delayed by governmental regulatory requirements, their patent terms can be extended for up to five years upon certain conditions. When the delay is caused by the Patent Office itself, through no fault of the applicant, there is no five year limit on extensions. 35 U.S.C.A. § 156. In a counterpart provision, 35 U.S.C.A. § 271(e)(1), Congress exempted those who engage in regulatory review testing using patented drugs within the patent period from infringement. The Supreme Court has concluded that the exemption also applies to medical devices. *Eli Lilly & Co. v. Medtronic, Inc.* (1990). In addition, there are provisions that allow a similarly limited extension in the case of certain delays in the application prosecution and appeals process.

A patent cannot be renewed and, thus, after expiration, the once new development enters the "public domain." That simply means the patentee has lost the exclusive rights to the patent *and* that anyone else has the right to make, use, offer to sell, or sell the invention.

During the life of the patent, the owner has the complete right to determine who, if anybody, will have the right to use, make, offer to sell, or sell the patented item, 35 U.S.C.A. § 261, and to a more limited extent, how or where it will be initially exploited. It is important to understand that American law does not require the patentee to put the patent into use or to allow others to do so. The first requirement, of putting the device to use, is called "working" the patent, a requirement with some historical meaning and considerable foreign patent law significance. The second requirement, of allowing others to use the patent, is called "compulsory licensing." Like working, there is no absolute requirement in United States law of compulsory licensing (except, to a limited extent, for inventions achieved through government-funded research), but other aspects of the law, especially antitrust, may have the effect of obliging a patent owner to license others to use the patent. This rather absolute property right nature of patents has been somewhat eroded by *eBay, Inc. v. MercExchange* (2006), which held that the patent holder is not automaticaly entitled to enjoin infringers and may be required to accept damages instead, when the equities so dictate.

Although the patent owner is not required either to work the patent or to allow others to do so, he or she normally will find it counterproductive not to put the patent to use. Moreover, from a societal point of view, the exclusive right is supposed to be the incentive that the patent system offers the new patent owner to work the invention and make its benefits available to the public.

The patentee has different ways of using the patent, either himself or by allowing others to do so. The patent can be sold outright, by assigning all the rights to it, or others can be licensed to use it, either exclusively, by allowing only one other person to use the item and promising not to let others do so, or nonexclusively, by granting patent rights to a variety of persons. The patentee also has the right, expressly given by the Patent Act, to grant the patent privilege, through licensing or otherwise, on a geographic basis. 35 U.S.C.A. § 261. But there are antitrust implications in geographically limited licenses, and a patentee must not exceed the rights granted by the Patent Act to avoid committing an antitrust violation.

A patent owner may sue anyone he believes has been using part or all of the basis of the patent without authorization. 35 U.S.C.A. § 281. It is a

valid defense to a charge of infringement to show
that the grant of a patent somehow was unwarrant-
ed. The defendant must prove that the Patent Office was mistaken by establishing that the owner's
patent does not possess the required amount of
novelty, utility, or nonobviousness. 35 U.S.C.A.
§ 282. A challenge alternatively can be based on
some inequitable conduct by the patentee before or
after the patent grant. Alleged infringers have been
quite successful in attacking patents. In many United States Courts of Appeal, litigated patents were
found invalid more often than valid. That is one
reason the Court of Appeals for the Federal Circuit
was created, with exclusive jurisdiction over patent
appeals, with the effect, so far, of upholding the
validity of far more patents than was previously the
case.

An infringement suit is only one way that a
patent may be contested. Any person has the right
to ask the Patent Office to reexamine a patent; if
the Office grants the request, the patent application
will be subjected to a second, although drastically
more limited (in fact it is limited to the consideration of documents that were not considered initially), patent application examination. 35 U.S.C.A.
§ 302. A party who wishes to use a patent, believing
it to be invalid, also can ask a federal court for a
declaratory judgment that the patent is invalid. The
party seeking the declaration must demonstrate
that a real controversy about the patent exists—
which means that this remedy is only available to
competitors, for the most part, and certainly not to

the public at large—before the court will allow the suit and then must make the same showing as does a defendant in an infringement suit to avoid liability.

## § 1.3   The Two Theories of Patent Protection

There are two basic justifications for the patent system. The occasional controversies that erupt between "pro" and "anti" patent forces tend to involve fundamental disagreements about the legitimacy of the theories underlying these justifications. There is (1) the "bargain" or contract theory and (2) the "natural rights" theory.

The bargain theory starts with the premise that people will be encouraged to produce new inventions if there is some reward as an incentive. This theory, of course, is at least partially supported by the text of the Constitution itself, which enumerates the elements of the potential bargain: encouraging the useful arts by awarding an exclusive right to exploit the invention for a definite length of time. It also seems to be supported by common sense and the theory underlying the free enterprise system.

The natural rights theory has a very different emphasis. Under this theory, the product of mental labor is by right the property of the person who created it. Having all title to the invention, the inventor has no obligation to disclose anything and has every right to be compensated therefor. In order to obtain disclosure—and thus allow for other, later, inventors to build upon the earlier creation—

the government assures an exclusive right to profit from the invention. This theory, too, is supported at least in part by the Constitution, since it mentions the "rights" of inventors and states that the advancement of the useful arts is its goal, which can be best achieved through disclosure.

Both of these theories, of course, are partially incomplete. The bargain theory denies any absolute right of the inventor to his productivity—he must accept the government bargain or have no protection at all. Likewise, the natural rights theory is inconsistent with the idea of a limited monopoly since, if the inventor has complete rights to the invention, it is not clear how the government can declare the invention public property after the patent expires.

Nevertheless, both theories have great utility. The ideas of bargain and disclosure provide an explanation of the purpose of patent law that seems supported by both common sense and reason. Commentators have amassed data seeming to support the proposition that the American patent system has been extremely successful in furnishing the incentive to develop more and greater inventions. Countries having less developed and less sophisticated patent systems appear less successful in producing the number of patentable inventions than does the United States, although these studies are seriously undermined by the fact that those countries are almost invariably less economically developed, and a greater number of studies show a clearer correlation between economic, as opposed to legal, development and the ability to achieve technological innovation. The sheer overpowering number of American patents also supports the thesis that disclosure has enabled later inventors to build upon the base developed by earlier patents.

These policy arguments, of course, are very powerful forces against serious change of the patent laws. Suggestions that the patent system should be altered, perhaps by shortening the length of the grant, are met by objections that any lessening of incentives will create a society less conducive to invention and progress and therefore will be counterproductive to the aims of American society generally.

The theoretical arguments relating to natural rights also have great force in the continuing debate over the patent system. Critics argue that it serves only to increase the monopoly power of large corporations which receive the bulk of modern patents and that the government is failing to bargain sharply enough on behalf of its citizens. Supporters, however, pointing to the Constitution's reference to "rights" of inventors, argue that inventors have a natural right to their inventions and that to shorten periods of exclusive rights or to stiffen the test of inventiveness is akin to a taking of the inventor's property and is unjust.

None of these arguments is complete or persuasive by itself. Indeed, some of the points can lead to opposite conclusions. For example, just as some people point to the number of patents to support the idea that the patent system produces more inventions, others can say that the standard of patentability is so low that the number of patents is meaningless and that few patents really are for true inventions. Some critics point out that many of history's greatest inventions were created without patent rights at all. The printing press, early explosives, and the wheel, to name a few. Many patents are produced under government contracts with no absolute assurance of eventual exclusive rights. The atomic bomb and Einstein's work were produced without incentives of patent protection and Benjamin Franklin donated all of his inventive works to the public without ever attempting to patent them. Clearly there is no basis for concluding that one theory is more "effective" than the other or to make confident statements about what is the optimum amount of incentive to promote invention.

# CHAPTER 2

# THE SUBJECT MATTER OF PATENTS

## § 2.1 Ideas v. Applications

The Patent Act specifically enumerates the kinds of things that can be patented. Very briefly, these are basically either *products* or *processes*. Also included are any new and useful improvements thereof. There are also plant patents for living plants, and design patents for ornamental designs. To say that a product or process may qualify for patent protection, however, merely begins the inquiry because in addition to the inclusive definition (a product or process), there is also an exclusive and prohibitive one: ideas, generally, are not patentable. *Gottschalk v. Benson* (1972); *Parker v. Flook* (1978). It is the drawing of a line between products and processes on the one hand, and ideas on the other that presents significant difficulties.

The statutorily enumerated categories are quite broad and include most—but not all—new developments that commonly are referred to by laypersons as "inventions." But there is a definable category excluded from patentability. If a claimed invention resembles too closely the broad prohibited category of an abstract idea, rather than what could accurately be described as a product or process, it is not patentable.

Although ideas are ineligible subject matter for patent protection, the application of an idea is not. In fact, it is the distinction between the idea and its application that defines the area of patentability. Mere novelty, utility, or nonobviousness is not enough to gain protection for an idea. All of the specified subject matter is at least one step beyond the mere idea stage. Thus, for instance, Einstein's formula, $E = MC^2$, is a mere idea. It is not a particular concrete application of the principle of atomic energy, but the very idea itself. This is sometimes expressed as the "law of nature" doctrine. See *Gottschalk v. Benson* (1972); *Parker v. Flook* (1978), supra. A particular atomic power plant or a method of measuring atomic energy, or countless other applications based on this idea, might well be patentable. But the bare idea lies outside the scope of patentable subject matter.

## § 2.2   The Statutory Scheme

To be patentable, an invention must be something that is described in the Patent Act. Section 101 of the statute provides:

Whoever invents or discovers any new and useful process, machine, manufacture, or composition of matter, or any new and useful improvement thereof, may obtain a patent therefor, subject to the conditions and requirements of this title.

Those four categories exhaust the possible things for which a patent may be obtained. A "process" can be defined as a means to an end. The remaining three categories (machine, manufacture, or composition of matter) can be defined as ends in themselves—"products." Thus, there are, essentially, only two categories of patentable subject matter: processes and products. Products are physical entities—machines are perhaps the most obvious of the three subjects of the category. Manufactures are any fabricated products that otherwise satisfy the requirements of patentability. Finally, a composition of matter describes what most people imagine to be the goal of the typical laboratory inventor, since it is usually a new chemical invention, although it can be any composition of materials, not limited solely to chemicals.

Processes are more intangible and difficult to define than products. In a sense, they are a way of getting somewhere else from where one starts, and they may be either a way of getting to something inventive or they may be an inventive way of getting to something already known (or, at least, something noninventive). A typical process is the chemical one, which produces a compound through a series of steps that may be embodied in a particular machine in which case both the process and the machine may be patentable, although that is not always true.

In addition to the four categories of patentable subject matter, there is a blanket supplementary gloss that applies to all of them. This permits a patent to issue on "any new and useful improvement" on a process, machine, manufacture, or composition. Obviously, though, an improvement still will have to fit in one of the four categories first before it can be a new and useful improvement thereof.

Finally, courts often have articulated judicially created subject matter exceptions to patentability. These once included exceptions for printed matter, business methods, systems of bookkeeping, and methods of calculation. However, the Federal Circuit has purported to read the Supreme Court's decision in *Diamond v. Chakrabarty* (1980) to mean that it is improper for courts to read exceptions into a Patent Act that is worded as broadly as it is. *State Street Bank & Trust Co. v. Signature Financial Group, Inc.* (1998). Thus, except for the three categories of "laws of nature, natural phenomena, and abstract ideas," derived from *Diamond v. Diehr* (1981), (exceptions that the Federal Circuit somewhat inexplicably recognizes despite its rejection of judicial exceptions generally) many or most of the judicial exceptions are no longer valid. The rule seems to be that an exception, to survive, must be found in one of the three remaining categories. Exceptions, therefore, might well still include, however, naturally occurring substances, laws of nature, natural forces, and principles, *In re Taner* (1982), mere chemical formulas without more (as opposed to the chemical substance itself), *Petisi v. Rennhard* (1966), fundamental truths, original causes, motives, mental steps, *Gottschalk v. Benson* (1972), and, of course, ideas, but not necessarily methods of calculation and systems of bookkeeping, *Parker v. Flook* (1978), and certainly not business methods.

One rough benchmark is furnished by the principle that patents only can protect the *application* of an abstract principle. Consistent with the aim of patent law to give the patent owner his due without (1) giving more than he already has specified as his invention, and (2) removing from the public domain basic ideas that should be freely available, the limit on what is patentable subject matter apportions these interests between the public and the inventor in as sensible a way as is possible. To be patentable, an invention must be made by a human. The discoverer of a previously unknown naturally existing animal or naturally occurring plant cannot claim a patent in the discovery. (A *nonnaturally occurring* plant and a *humanly modified* living thing, however, subject to certain other requirements, may qualify. *Diamond v. Chakrabarty*, supra.)

For instance, although products of nature are unpatentable, not all natural products are unpatentable. The very concept of products of nature could easily swallow up all that does or will exist. With respect to chemical compounds, and perhaps new life forms, nothing is in reality completely made by human beings, for all things are fashioned out of naturally occurring substances. The category of products of nature cannot be defined so broadly. Therefore, courts have rejected the flat rule that products of nature are unpatentable. If a product of nature is new, useful, and nonobvious, it can be patented if somehow it has been fashioned by humans. *Diamond v. Chakrabarty*, supra.

Therefore, concentrated or purified products of nature are patentable if the resulting concentrate is the product of human intervention and if it does not occur naturally *in that form,* assuming it fulfills the other requirements of patentability in that state. *Merck & Co. v. Olin Mathieson Chem. Corp.* (1958). The borderline between that which is merely discovered in the wild and that which is created in the laboratory is not completely clear. Nevertheless, at least with respect to new chemical compounds, such as highly purified vitamins or drugs such as aspirin, the product-of-nature doctrine is no bar to patentability. With respect to truly naturally occurring things, however, the product-of-nature rule in fact just may be an oblique way of stating that the claimed invention lacks novelty or nonobviousness.

## § 2.3  Processes as Subject Matter Apart From Products

A process is a way of doing something. If it is a patentable process, it must be a new, useful, and nonobvious way of doing something. If the process is patentable, the result of that process—the something getting done—need not of itself be new, useful, nor nonobvious. In other words, the result of an inventive process need not be an invention itself. However, it might be especially valuable to have an inventive process that yields an inventive product. A patent on both the process and the product obviously would give virtually complete protection to the owner.

All subject matters, including processes, are subject to the rule forbidding patents on the proscribed areas of laws of nature, natural phenomena, and abstract ideas. Thus, a process patent cannot be so broad as to constitute the very idea of how to do something. It must be more specific. If a pants-presser, for instance, were claimed as new, the idea of pressing pants obviously could not be patented. A particular way of inserting creases, however, might be patentable because as a way of producing creases, the patent would cover the process and not the very idea of creases.

Thus, the patentability of the result or product of a process is not relevant to the patentability of the process. Clearly, pressed pants, the product of the process, could not be patented. Pressed pants, although useful, are neither novel nor nonobvious. But an ingenious way of producing creases certainly might qualify if it were novel, useful, and nonobvious.

A chemical process is a typical form of process patent. When new drugs are invented, the inventors may seek to patent the way in which the drugs are produced in the laboratory—the inventive process—as well as the drug. The drug may be held not inventive, perhaps because it is not new, or because it is an obvious derivative, or because it is not yet proved to be useful or effective in treating diseases. However, a patent on the process, if inventive, still may give the inventor substantial protection. (However, a process that yields a demonstrably nonuseful product will have just as much difficulty obtaining patent protection as will the product itself. See Chapter 4, Patentability—Utility.)

On the other hand, when a process is particularly abstract, for example, a mathematical method of converting binary numbers to digital numbers, it probably will not qualify for protection. *Gottschalk v. Benson* (1972). This is not because the process is not new, useful, or nonobvious. It is, instead, that the very nature of the process is that of an abstract idea, so general and basic that it is not something truly invented by the inventor. In a sense, it was there all along. This type of process may be barred from patentability because it is too much like laws of nature, natural phenomena, and abstract ideas. Thus, just as products may not be patentable because they are naturally occurring, a process may not be patentable because, although the inventor was the first to articulate the methodology, it is so basic as to be considered, in a sense, naturally occurring. A formula, program, or method, may be deemed to be out there all along, just like a mineral in the earth that the inventor merely found but did not invent. Or, an overly abstract process may be unpatentable because it effectively includes too much within its scope. A process becomes nonpatentable when it is such an abstract idea as to cover both known and unknown applications of the principle upon which it is based. *Parker v. Flook* (1978).

## § 2.4  The Boundaries of the Three Product Categories

It is not important that an invention might be correctly described in ways that fall within more than one product category. What is important is that it arguably fit *at least* one category. For instance, a composition of matter also may be deemed a manufacture or even a machine. As long as the product is inventive, it need not be definable only in terms of one of the three categories.

*Diamond v. Chakrabarty* (1980), involved new life forms, specifically bacteria genetically altered to digest petroleum waste material and spills. These new life forms, being both manmade, and combinations, even though complex ones, of natural materials, much like new chemicals, are described accurately both as manufactures and as compositions of matter. The Supreme Court did not bother to assign the bacteria to one or the other category of potential subject matter. Instead, it tacitly admitted that bacteria could belong to either, or both, categories. The Court stated that new life forms, although clearly bordering on the area of plant patents, and coming close to the impermissible area of naturally occurring substances, nevertheless are within the subject matter of patents. It held that new technologies, even though never imagined by Congress when the Patent Act was adopted, are eligible for patent protection. Specific mention of them within the subject matter section of the statute is unnecessary. Thus, if a new technology can be described as either a manufacture, composition of matter, or machine, it is potentially patentable despite the fact that Congress did not specifically describe it. Patent law and its requirement that inventions be novel and nonobvious invites new technologies, which therefore may fit unforeseen categories. Although *Chakrabarty*, on its face, simply said that various categories of inventions are not barred merely because they are not specifically mentioned in the statute, the Federal Circuit reads the case even more broadly. Standing *Chakrabarty* on its head, it seems, the Federal Circuit has held that if an invention is not barred by the statute, it is automatically eligible, despite earlier judicial exceptions to the contrary. *State Street Bank & Trust Co. v. Signature Financial Group, Inc.* (1998).

## § 2.5  Compositions of Matter

Compositions of matter, as one of three product categories, are *things*. By definition, they must be composed of other things. It is the composition that is the invention. Natural substances such as naturally occurring minerals are not patentable because they are not really "invented." Finders are not usually inventors. But if the inventor finds that she can compose a new substance from basic, "found," materials, and that substance is otherwise patentable, the new composition of matter may be eligible subject matter. *Schering Corp. v. Gilbert* (1946). Thus, an inventor can take the most basic and well-known things, such as carbon, hydrogen, and oxygen, and if she composes them in a particularly novel and nonobvious format, and it results in something useful, she may patent the resulting chemical. New chemicals are the paradigm examples of compositions of matter. It does not matter if the basic elements are natural. What is essential, as the Supreme Court has said, is that "[the inventor's] discovery is not nature's handiwork, but [the inventor's] own." *Diamond v. Chakrabarty* (1980).

## § 2.6  Manufacture

A manufacture is very simply any thing or article that is made by a human being. A manufacture is thus something "nonnatural," for a product of human effort is by definition something other than a product of nature. Not all manufactured products, however, are patentable. A printed form may be novel, nonobvious, and useful. But courts have held that printed materials, as such, are not patentable. *In re Russell* (1931). For printed matter to be patentable, there must be something about its structure, rather than its content, that is inventive.

A manufacture must have a definable structure that is claimed as its patentable characteristic. Manufactures are, after all, a category of product patents, and therefore must be "things," as opposed to ways or means. In summary, a patentable manufacture is any *human-made structure* that has inventive characteristics.

## § 2.7  Machines

A machine is an inventive *thing* that *does something*. The familiarity we all have with machines makes this product category seem relatively comprehensible but this apparent simplicity is deceptive. Because machines effectively embody an underlying process, there is a significant danger of overlap between those categories. As a result, limits on patentability that apply to processes also can apply to machines.

Just as a process may be nonpatentable if it is too general and abstract, a machine may be nonpatentable because it tries to capture such a process. To the extent that the inventor claims a very general series of steps as a machine, the machine could represent an attempt to patent something that, if claimed as a mere process, clearly would be unpatentable. Thus, for instance, an electronic computer may be a machine if it is otherwise inventive. But if its programming incorporates general laws or principles of nature or mathematics—for instance, basic arithmetic—to that extent it may raise the same two problems raised by attempts to patent abstract processes. First, they tend to monopolize what was already in existence. Second, they tend to incorporate too much within their scope. The patentability of machines, however, that include computers is beyond argument. See § 2.8, infra.

## § 2.8   Computer–Related Patents

One rule beyond dispute is that a law of nature, including its mathematical manifestations, is not patentable. This prohibition proceeds from the notion that such laws are the fundamental building blocks of science and should not be monopolized. The recent proliferation of computer software has forced the courts to define more precisely which inventions involving the use of computers or mathematical formulas (or "algorithms") are disqualified under section 101 of the Patent Act.

In 1972 the United States Supreme Court addressed squarely the issue of the patentability of computer related claims. In *Gottschalk v. Benson* (1972), the Court held that a process for converting binary-coded decimal (BCD) numerals into pure binary numerals could not be patented. The Court noted simply that the procedure was a type of algorithm and stated that if the formula were patented, the result would be a monopoly on a scientific truth. The Court did not allow a patent on the method because it felt that doing so would take the algorithm out of the public domain because *Benson*'s process was so abstract and broad that it covered all uses of the algorithm. The Court specifically stated that it had *not* held that all computer programs were nonpatentable subject matter.

In *Parker v. Flook* (1978), the Supreme Court held that a process utilizing a scientific principle is patentable only if the "process itself, not merely the mathematical algorithm, [is] new and useful."

Flook had applied for a patent on a method for updating an "alarm limit" in the catalytic conversion of hydrocarbons. Flook's process used a mathematical algorithm to accomplish this and contemplated use of a computer. The Court held the claim nonpatentable, explaining that "[a]ll that [the claim] provides is a formula for computing an updated alarm limit," and that the patent, if issued, would be on a law of nature. The Court stated as it had in *Benson* that the law did not allow a patent on an algorithm, but conceded that a process is not nonpatentable simply because an algorithm is involved. Rather, the Court required that the claim demonstrate novelty *independent* of the law of nature.

The uncertainty surrounding the patentability of claims that require the use of a mathematical formula, computer program, or computer led to the Supreme Court's consideration of *Diamond v. Diehr* (1981). Initially, the Court reiterated the *Benson* test for patentability of a process: "Transformation and reduction of an article 'to a different state or thing' is the clue to the patentability of a process claim that does not include particular machines," *Gottschalk v. Benson*, supra. The Court reasoned that respondent's method for curing rubber, described in detail from start to finish, involved just such a transformation. This simple but unassailable analysis led directly to the conclusion that the claim fell "within the § 101 categories of possibly patentable subject matter." The Court stressed that the use of a mathematical equation and programmed computer did not alter this conclusion.

The Court noted that there are limits on what may be patented under section 101, specifically the exclusion of laws of nature, physical phenomena, and abstract ideas. Both *Benson* and *Flook* were described as standing "for no more than these long-established principles." *Benson* was distinguishable, said the Court, because in that case the only way to use the algorithm was in connection with a computer. Since no one could have used the algorithm in a computer program without infringing Benson's patent, the Court explained, the grant of a patent in effect would have allowed a monopoly on an idea. Addressing *Flook,* the Court stated that the claim in that case was nothing more than a formula for computing an alarm limit, which, the Court declared, "is simply a number."

After *Diamond v. Diehr,* supra (in which the Supreme Court held that the mere presence of a computer in an otherwise patentable process does not render the invention unpatentable) and *State Street Bank & Trust Co. v. Signature Financial Group, Inc.* (1998) (in which the Federal Circuit held, *inter alia*, that a mathematical algorithm in the form of a computer program is patentable if it is applied in a useful way), although an isolated computer program that is not entwined in a specific statutory process will be labeled a mere method of calculation and, therefore, will not be patentable, see *In re Grams* (1989), *In re Iwahashi* (1989), an inventor need no longer avoid using a computer in a process or even product (as part of a machine) for fear that its presence will jeopardize the claim's status as patentable subject matter. In fact, it seems the Federal Circuit has attempted to make the presence of a computer or computer program an almost irrelevant fact, framing the issue in terms of practical application and concrete and tangible utility: is the computer or computer program—even if termed an algorithm—applied in a way that produces "a useful, concrete and tangible result?" *State Street Bank & Trust Co. v. Signature Financial Group, Inc.*, supra. As long as the result of an invention incorporating a computer or computer program is useful, concrete, and tangible, it seems that such incorporation is immaterial.

## § 2.9   Orphan Drug Act

The Orphan Drug Act, 21 U.S.C.A. §§ 360aa–360ee, provides an exclusive seven year right to market a drug that is necessary to treat a disease affecting less than 200,000 people (although that number can be exceeded when sales will not cover the costs of providing a drug). The Act applies when the FDA decides that absent the statute's exclusive rights, and other financial assistance the Act provides, the drug would not be made available to the patients needing it. Although the Act does not expressly grant a patent, the effects of its exclusive right often are indistinguishable from those of a patent. The Act applies irrespective of whether the drug is patented or even patentable. As such, it arguably suffers a serious constitutional defect, in that the equivalent of patent rights are granted to a noninventive product. Whether the Commerce Clause, for instance, can be an alternative source for Congressional power to grant what amounts to a patent is an unanswered question.

Some have argued that the Act does not grant true patent protection, because it only applies to the use of the drug for a specific disease and because the protection is vulnerable to the challenge that the marketer is not supplying the drug in sufficient quantities. See *Genentech, Inc. v. Bowen* (1987). However, many process patents are limited to quite specific applications, of course, and a challenge for failure to exploit is characteristic of all patent systems with a working requirement.

## § 2.10 Plant and Design Patents

In addition to utility patents, the Patent Act provides for plant patents, 35 U.S.C.A. § 161, and design patents, 35 U.S.C.A. § 171. Although the dynamics of both these fields substantially parallel the dynamics of utility patents, the particular elements are different because they substitute another requirement for utility as a prerequisite to legal protection.

The elements of plant patentability are not the same as for utility patents. Instead of novelty, utility, and nonobviousness, plant patentability requires novelty, distinctiveness, and nonobviousness. *Yoder Brothers, Inc. v. California–Florida Plant Corp.*

(1976). Patentable plants must be discovered in a cultivated state, not merely found in the wild, and may not be tubers such as potatoes or Jerusalem artichokes. Moreover, a plant patent can be obtained only to protect a new and distinct variety of asexually reproducing plant. Asexual reproduction is reproduction that does not involve the use of seeds, including such methods as grafting, budding, cutting, layering, or division. The protection offered by plant patents is the exclusive right to reproduce the plant.

Distinctiveness in the context of plant patents, therefore, is the analog to utility in general inventive patents. It is measured by examining the characteristics that make the plant clearly distinguishable from other existing plants. These characteristics include habit, health, soil, color, flavor, productivity, storability, odor, and form, among others. A plant need not be useful to be patentable; therefore, the distinctiveness of a plant need not be anything that makes the plant superior to others. All that is necessary is that it be distinctively different.

The nonobviousness of a newly developed or discovered plant is difficult to measure because plants are not developed for the same reasons as are utility inventions. Therefore, what would be obvious is not measured by the same standards. Nonobviousness for plant patents is determined by examining the degree to which the new plant represents an advance or variation over existing plants. Therefore, nonobviousness in plant patents tends to replay some of the themes of the distinctiveness requirement.

The major unresolved issues regarding plant patents involve the availability of protection for life forms of questionable plant status such as bacteria. See *In re Arzberger* (1940). Conversely, the utility patentability of new life forms had been clouded for many years by the very availability of plant patents. That issue, however, has been conclusively resolved by *Diamond v. Chakrabarty* (1980), which held that the plant patent system does not imply that other life forms cannot qualify for utility patent protection assuming the requirements of patentability are otherwise met.

A design patent can be obtained to protect a new, original, ornamental design for an article of manufacture. Instead of the novelty, utility, and nonobviousness requirements of general utility patents, design patents substitute the requirements of novelty, ornamentality, and nonobviousness. Since utility is replaced by ornamentality, the requirements of novelty and nonobviousness necessarily are transformed and deemphasized. Design novelty usually is determined by the "ordinary observer" test and nonobviousness by that of the designer with ordinary skill in the pertinent art, or the "ordinary designer." *In re Nalbandian* (1981). Some courts have defined nonobviousness for design patents as that which would be nonobvious to "the ordinary intelligent man." *Schwinn Bicycle Co. v. Goodyear Tire & Rubber Co.* (1970), citing *In re Laverne* (1966). Other courts have more demandingly defined the standard in a way analogous to that of utility patents as nonobviousness to the designer with ordinary skill in the pertinent art. *Fields v. Schuyler* (1972).

The major issue relating to design patents is that field's affect on copyright and utility patent law. Since the protection afforded design patents is against copying, it bears a striking resemblance to copyright. Similarly, because design patents by definition involve designs on articles of manufacture, they intersect with matters of utility patentability and threaten to protect by design that which may have a function otherwise nonpatentable under utility patent protection. As a result, a design patent cannot be obtained for an exclusively functional design. *Barofsky v. General Electric Corp.* (1968). But it is clear that both design and utility patents can apply to the same product as long as the design patent protects only nonfunctional aspects of the invention. *Berry Sterling Corp. v. Pescor Plastics, Inc.* (1999).

# CHAPTER 3

# PATENTABILITY—NOVELTY
# AND STATUTORY BAR

## § 3.1 Overview

Three sections of the Patent Act explicitly enumerate the elements of patentability—novelty, utility, and nonobviousness. Section 101 requires that an invention have novelty and utility. Section 102 defines novelty; that section also creates certain "statutory bars" to protection in addition to lack of novelty. Section 103 requires that the invention be a nonobvious development over the prior art.

The novelty provisions in section 102 focus on certain events constituting *anticipation* that may occur *prior to invention* and, if they do, prohibit patentability for lack of novelty. Statutory bar focuses on events that may occur *more than twelve months prior to the inventor's patent application* and which, if they do, prohibit patentability. In other words, the inventor is given a grace period of twelve months from the event within which he may still apply for an invention. But after that grace period, statutory bar occurs and he loses what might be termed his application priority and right to a patent, *even though* the invention still has novelty.

Events of anticipation, defined by the novelty provisions, have no comparable grace period; if an anticipation occurs prior to invention, the inventor has no right to a patent.

Section 102 is somewhat confused by the fact that it does not explicitly distinguish between statutory bar and anticipation. The reader must carefully do this. Also, even though some terms that trigger statutory bar are described in language similar to those relating to novelty, the words do not necessarily share the same meaning. Finally, there is an irregular distinction between those events that may occur domestically and those that may occur in other countries.

Following are the events raising statutory bar, if they occur more than twelve months prior to application:

*Domestic:* Prior patent by anyone, printed publication, public use or sale.

*Foreign:* Prior patent by anyone, printed publication, or prior patent application by the applicant (but only if a patent is granted prior to domestic application).

Following are the anticipation events that defeat a claim of novelty if they occur anytime prior to invention:

*Domestic:* Prior patent by anyone, printed publication, knowledge or unabandoned, unsuppressed, unconcealed invention by others, use by others, or description in another's previously filed and eventually granted application.

*Foreign:* Prior patent by anyone or printed publication.

All of the listed events are limited by the principle of substantial identity. The prior use, knowledge, or other event must be so substantially the same as the invention as to accomplish the disclosure purpose of the patent law. Whether domestic or foreign, anticipation must encompass the invention that is claimed. It is not enough that an invention be suggested by the literature; nor is it sufficient that the literature made the invention inevitable; that bears on the question of nonobviousness. The test, with one major exception, is whether enough of the invention has been disclosed to enable a person skilled in the applicable art to duplicate the product or process.

The major exception is public use, which will foreclose a patent without full disclosure as long as the public use discloses the invention's benefits— *even if it does not disclose the secrets of the invention.* The patent system does not favor granting a patent on an invention whose benefits, at least, already have been made public. Thus, if a senior inventor publicly uses an invention even though without completely revealing its basis, the inventor obviously is barred because of the public use if it occurs more than a year before the application. Less obviously, even a diligent junior inventor also is statutorily barred and cannot obtain a patent despite the lack of truly complete disclosure. See *Dunlop Holdings Ltd. v. Ram Golf Corp.* (1975).

Foreign anticipation can take only two forms: the availability of a documentary description by prior patent or publication. If either of these occurs with respect to the invention at issue, *prior to the time it was claimed to be invented*, the anticipation will bar the issuance of a patent. Domestic anticipation, however, can take five forms: a prior patent, publication, use, knowledge, or invention. Again, if any of these occurs with respect to the invention at issue, *prior to the time it was claimed to be invented*, there is anticipation, a lack of novelty, and a patent will not issue. What constitutes a "printed publication" for documentary anticipation is expanding to include modern information retrieval technologies, such as computers and microfilm. The emphasis is less on whether the information is either "printed" or "published" but on whether it is publicly disseminated or accessible. *In re Wyer* (1981). There is serious doubt, however, whether, absent a change in the statute, the Patent Office will accept computer database information as the equivalent of a printed publication. *In re Epstein* (1994).

The anticipation doctrine can be simplified by noting that foreign anticipation is exclusively documentary and requires that the invention be described; domestic anticipation occurs if the invention is either described or known. Thus, although a United States patent is barred by foreign acts only if they are documentary in nature, mere knowledge or acts evidencing knowledge can constitute anticipation if they occur domestically. On the other hand, although nondocumentary acts—prior knowledge, invention, or use—constitute anticipation domestically, they will not bar the issuance of a United States patent if they occur abroad.

The concept of anticipation underlies interference proceedings based on conflicting claims of two or more inventors to the same product or process. It should be noted that an earlier invention anticipates a later one and has priority for patent protection, but only if it is not abandoned, suppressed, or concealed. 35 U.S.C.A. § 102(g). On the other hand, an inventor need not immediately publicize a discovery to avoid losing out to a junior inventor on grounds of abandonment, suppression, or concealment. However, the inventor must pursue his rights with reasonable diligence. It can readily be seen, then, that the rights of inventors with conflicting claims to patent protection often will depend not only upon who first invented—a principle that furthers the policy of rewarding only those who discovered what was previously truly unknown—but also upon whether the earlier inventor was thereafter diligent—a concept that promotes the policy of disclosure.

## § 3.2 Foreign Anticipation

Foreign anticipation involves only prior patents or publications and it is accurately characterized as documentary anticipation—that is, it takes a printed form. A very limited publication, such as a manuscript deposited in a library, may constitute enough of a printed publication to qualify as anticipation. Oral publication is not enough, although handwritten information may be. Whether something is a printed publication for purposes of the foreign anticipation doctrine is determined by reference to the purposes of the doctrine: whether the document was *published* to an extent that it added to the prior art. The information must be sufficiently *available* or at least potentially so, *to those knowledgeable in the particular art*, to become part of an accessible body of knowledge. Availability often depends, in the case of a library document for instance, on whether the document has been catalogued. *In re Hall* (1986).

## § 3.3   Domestic Anticipation

To the extent that a claim of domestic anticipation is premised upon documentary anticipation, the standards are essentially the same as those for foreign anticipation. Prior use, knowledge, or invention, however, are unique to domestic anticipation. The standards by which they are measured are based on the same factors that require publication as the determinative element of foreign documentary anticipation. Thus, prior use must be of the actual process or product claimed; prior knowledge must be sufficient to encompass the complete product or process claimed. Also, a prior invention cannot be abandoned, suppressed, or concealed. *Ansul Co. v. Uniroyal, Inc.* (1969).

The thrust of the nondocumentary sources of domestic anticipation is that the invention has entered the body of knowledge in the relevant art and is accessible to those versed in that art. Thus, the basis for anticipation, domestic as well as foreign, parallels the purposes of the patent system generally. If the justification for awarding monopoly patent rights is as an exchange for a contribution to the store of knowledge, an anticipation already has so contributed. Since the patent incentive is not needed, protection therefore is not granted.

Judicial construction of each of the three domestic nondocumentary anticipations—prior use, knowledge, or invention—has insured that they fulfill the requirement that the state of the art has been increased. Thus, a prior use must be *active* or *continuous* enough to be accessible to those in the particular art. Because knowledge is not an active concept, it must be *publicly available* in order to bar patentability on novelty grounds. The requirement that a prior invention must not have been abandoned, suppressed, or concealed fulfills the same disclosure function as does the requirement that a prior use or knowledge must be publicly available. For instance, a prior use must consist of an actual reduction to practice so that the invention actually is available. This especially is true when a prior use is not widely disclosed. Equally, prior knowledge that is secret will not qualify as a domestic anticipation, because it is not accessible to the public. *General Tire & Rubber Co. v. Firestone Tire & Rubber Co.* (1972). Although secret knowledge generally is not enough to bar patentability, since atomic energy information may be classified for national security purposes, it is possible, as a matter of law, for information kept so secret to constitute prior knowledge despite the lack of any public disclosure. *In re Borst* (1965).

When an invention is disclosed to the public, the public gains title to it. It follows logically that any kind of public dedication bars a later purported inventor from claiming it.

## § 3.4    References to Prior Publications

Under section 102, a patent is barred for lack of novelty if there is enough in the prior art to enable someone skilled in the area to perform the process or produce the product described in the patent application. The Patent Office will cite prior publications in a "reference." If a reference is held to be an "enabling disclosure," it bars patentability. A reference is considered enabling and the invention is thereby anticipated and unpatentable if the reference discloses information that would enable a person having ordinary skill in the appropriate art to duplicate the invention. The requirement that a disclosure be "enabling" comes not from section 102, but from section 112.

An inventor must fulfill his part of the patent bargain by giving the public sufficient information in his application to allow others to repeat the invention. Section 112 expressly addresses that issue by requiring a specification that will "enable" others to repeat the invention. Since the benefits to the public of the patent bargain would not be jeopardized by prior art if the public is not, by that prior art, thereby "enabled" to duplicate the invention, the requirement in section 112 of "enabling" disclosures has been judicially imported into section 102, which expressly addresses only novelty and anticipation. Therefore, nonenabling prior art is no bar and the importation of section 112 into section 102 effectively furthers the same goal of ensuring that the patent system adds to the fund of public, useful, knowledge.

Sometimes, a reference can be fatal even though, by itself, it is not an independently enabling disclosure, in the sense that every last detail of producing the product or performing the process is to be found in the reference. Since the test of whether a disclosure is enabling is whether the person with ordinary skill in the pertinent art could reproduce the invention on the basis of the reference, there are some things that such practitioners are held to bring with them to the reference. Their skills and expected body of knowledge therefore need not be found in a particular reference in order to make that reference enabling. In other words, other references can be used in order to demonstrate the level of skill in the art. As was said in *In re Wiggins* (1973), a reference concerning a new way of refining petroleum products is still enabling despite the fact that it does not describe how to make the bolts and rivets required for the refinery.

Under that standard, the total combination of prior art and references thereto can make an invention unpatentable if that combination, as a whole, constitutes an enabling disclosure. The combination of references and prior art allows one to "borrow" prior art to understand a reference that by itself (at least to a court or perhaps to a nonskilled practitioner) might not otherwise necessarily constitute an enabling disclosure. In *In re Wiggins,* supra, an earlier publication described a new compound but arguably did not do so sufficiently to anticipate the invention, since the publication named the compound but failed to describe how to make the chemical. But a later patent described a process by which the chemical could have been manufactured. The reference to the earlier article combined with the prior art as revealed in the later patent application to constitute a truly enabling disclosure. A reference, therefore, although it must describe an invention to anticipate need not be wholly independently enabling as long as the reference and perhaps other prior art and references thereto produce what is effectively an enabling disclosure.

Once there has been a prior enabling disclosure, there really is no new invention. However, a reference cannot merely raise a hypothetical possibility. Section 102 says a reference must "describe" the later invention. Thus, although *In re Wiggins* held that prior art could be used to explain a published reference, prior art cannot substitute for the reference itself. The reference must be compared to how much is supplied by the prior art to determine whether the reference is sufficiently complete. If the prior art is the primary source, then there is no anticipation. If the prior art merely fills in some gaps so that the reference clearly describes (in light of the prior art) the invention, then the invention is considered anticipated. As an example, it would not anticipate an invention if a publication merely listed hypothetical or speculative chemical compounds. Such a list is not the required statutory "description" of the compounds but is more akin to a guess. An inventor who successfully describes the new compound has created something novel and unanticipated, despite the reference.

Therefore, whether an invention has been anticipated—whether it is novel—will depend not only on what has been done, practiced, or published before but also on draftsmanship. It will, at least as a preliminary matter, depend upon how the inventor has defined in his claim what the invention actually is. Specifically, whether the invention has been anticipated will depend upon how artfully the inventor or lawyer has drafted the patent application. An astute inventor and his attorney will try to avoid describing the invention in a way that might duplicate all that has gone before. Since the claims define the outer limits of the invention, it sometimes is necessary to draft around prior art.

## § 3.5 Substantial and Realized Anticipation

An anticipating disclosure must be *substantially* identical to the claimed invention to bar it. A rough similarity is not enough. "That which infringes, if later, anticipates, if earlier," goes a patent law aphorism. *Polaroid Corp. v. Eastman Kodak Co.* (1986). Just as it sometimes is doubtful whether a later product or process infringes a patent because the "infringement" does not identically repeat the invention, it sometimes will be argued that a reference does not anticipate because some details are different. A reference need not identify every property of an invention to anticipate it, though; it need only *substantially* do so. *Deep Welding, Inc. v. Sciaky Brothers, Inc.* (1969). The test for anticipation therefore mirrors the substantiality test of infringement. See § 8.1, infra.

On the other hand, not even completely identical anticipations always will bar a later patent. Unconscious or accidental anticipations may be completely ineffective. It is not anticipation when a product or process is developed and the developer is unaware of its existence, as in *Knorr v. Pearson* (1982), in which the senior party claimed to have created a fire resistant I-beam the inventive quality of which was an air passage formed by chance. Priority was awarded, however, to the junior party who realized the necessity of such a passage and consciously designed the product to have it.

When a claim to a mechanical invention includes a structural feature recited as a positive limitation, conception and reduction to practice of that invention require a contemporaneous recognition of that feature. But there is a limit to this. An anticipation need not show, for instance, consciousness of utility or novelty to bar patentability. If an earlier person produced a product and was conscious of its existence but failed to appreciate its utility or novelty, that still constitutes anticipation. In *Standard Oil Co. (Indiana) v. Montedison, S.p.A.* (1981), the court held that the junior inventors were entitled to claim a crystalline form of polypropylene, despite "the inventors' failure to appreciate the product's crystallinity," because crystalline form was inherent to the product and there was realization of the product itself. A chance discovery without realization of its existence is not anticipation; but a valid discovery without realization of its inventive quality is no less anticipation merely because the discoverer was no genius.

Thus, anticipation has to be *realized*; that is, it must be so intentional or noticed that it can be repeated. If the prior knowledge occurred without the conscious realization by anyone of its nature as an identifiable phenomenon, it is thus not anticipatory. Requiring that anticipation be realized provides relative certainty that it has contributed to the known store of knowledge of the useful arts, and therefore that a later grant of a patent for the same phenomenon would contribute nothing. To hold otherwise would mean that purely accidental and unrealized anticipation would bar a later patent on the basis of an event that cannot, by its unrealized nature, contribute to the useful arts. In other words, the anticipation must be appreciated as an identifiable phenomenon, although it need not be understood by the prior observer to be patentable.

## § 3.6  Statutory Bar

The reader must guard against confusing the requirement of novelty with statutory bar, a profoundly different doctrine. Some of the events relating to novelty in section 102 bear a deceptive resemblance to those of statutory bar. However, there are fundamental distinctions. The most basic is that disabling events of novelty relate to the date of invention whereas those of statutory bar are keyed to the date of the application. For instance, the use of an invention by anyone other than the inventor prior to invention is disabling, under the novelty provisions of section 102(a). Under the statutory bar provisions of section 102(b) a use is disabling only if it is *public* and, perhaps more importantly, only if it occurs twelve months prior to the application filing date. Moreover, although a use is disabling under the novelty provisions only if done by another, the statutory bar of public use is disabling despite the fact that it is the inventor who publicly uses the invention. In fact, most of the events described by statutory bar are more likely to be done by the inventor than by another—statutory bar is intended to motivate the inventor to apply for a patent soon after invention but in no case longer than twelve months after any of the enumerated events. On the other hand, examination of the text of section 102(a) reveals that the events determining novelty are by definition events performed by others. Prior knowledge or use is expressly described as applying to others. But the other provisions of novelty are meaningful only if performed by others also. A prior patent or printed publication would be a meaningful novelty event only if it were performed by someone other than the inventor. Obviously, it would be impossible for the inventor himself to describe or patent his invention prior to the true date of invention. (The notion of an inventor attempting to patent that which he already has patented does have relevance to the double patenting bar, however. See Chapter 6, Double Patenting.)

If an inventor is the first to invent but waits more than a year to apply for a patent after someone else *or the inventor* describes, publicly uses, sells, or patents the invention in this country, the invention is unpatentable by the inventor, even though he was truly the one who invented first. This is explained by the patent policy favoring speedy disclosure and the disfavor with which the patent system views inventors who "sit on their rights" (or on their inventions). If the inventor waits, hoping to delay his patent application and thereby effectively extend his patent monopoly beyond its twenty-year limit, while others do any of those acts, he will certainly violate those patent objectives and encounter the statutory bar. Importantly, the "on sale" bar does not mean that the inventor must have actually sold her invention. Any efforts to make a sale, even if unsuccessful, violate the policy of statutory bar against attempts to extend illegitimately the patent monopoly. Even placing an item out to bid constitutes being "on sale." *Envirotech Corp. v. Westech Engineering Inc.* (1990). And, to be on sale the invention need not even be reduced to practice as long as it is conceptually complete. *Pfaff v. Wells Electronics, Inc.* (1998).

Abandonment is the final statutory bar found in section 102. It can occur through literal abandonment—and it often is found that the inventor, in some sense, turned the invention over to the public. But it occurs also when the inventor fails to pursue his patent rights diligently, for instance by commercially exploiting the invention for more than one year prior to application. Note, however, that abandonment only bars the abandoning inventor. Another, later, party is not necessarily barred just because an earlier inventor abandoned the invention. A junior inventor may be entitled to a patent even though an earlier inventor discovered first if that earlier inventor is held to have abandoned, *without divulging the secrets of the invention.* Thus, a senior inventor loses his rights but a later inventor does not necessarily do so also.

## § 3.7   The Policies of Statutory Bar

One effect of statutory bar is to put the inventor on notice that if he does not file within twelve months of invention, he is utterly at risk that some event will occur in the intervening time period that will invalidate the patent and about which he may not even know until twelve months after its occurrence. Unfortunately, this even includes the possibility that someone will pirate the invention. The harshness of this rule is tempered by the clarity of the warning given by the patent statute, which compels the inventor to file either within a year of invention or at least as quickly as possible, and also by the very opportunity to seek and obtain complete government protection through the patent monopoly.

The policies of novelty (which is, in a sense, invention priority) and statutory bar (which is, in the same sense, application priority) are inspired by quite different, although consistently related, principles. Novelty rewards the first person to invent. However, application priority rewards diligence. An inventor faced with the possibility of prior art somehow must deal with the policy of novelty, perhaps by artfully drafting his claims. On the other hand, an inventor contemplating applying for a patent also must deal with the very different but equally important doctrine of statutory bar: even though the inventor was first to invent, he may be barred if he or someone else (even though that someone else may be at best a *later* inventor) publicly uses or sells it or describes or patents it outside the twelve month grace period.

That conflict of policies between rewarding diligence and rewarding invention reaches its height in section 102(g), which determines priority between inventors who may have "invented" at different times. It recognizes that, although one (senior) inventor may have conceived and even reduced to practice a certain invention prior to a later (junior) inventor, nevertheless that junior inventor may be entitled to priority based on his greater diligence. The system of priority created by section 102(g) can become so complicated as to be literally impossible to apply in the rare case involving competing claims to priority by three or more inventors. See § 3.9, infra.

## § 3.8   Publicity and Limited Disclosures

The various kinds of statutory bar involve two central themes, one of which is the policy of barring patents to information that is already in the public domain even as against the otherwise rightful claim of a true inventor. The second, more important theme, is the policy of encouraging diligence and speed in the seeking of monopoly protection and, concomitantly, the discouragement of attempts to extend the effective life of a patent by delaying the beginning of the twenty-year grant. This especially is true of the public use and printed-publication doctrines. Statutory bar, although involving *public* acts, does not base its requirement of publicity solely on the fact that public knowledge is available to others but is concerned primarily with the fact that certain public acts evidence an intent by the inventor to delay unfairly the beginning of the twenty-year grant.

What degree of publicity is required? Generally, only a minimal level, corresponding to the fact that statutory bar does not require publicity sufficient to inform the public but, rather, sufficient to demonstrate unacceptable conduct on the part of the inventor. That is the situation, for instance, with respect to public use. Statutory bar holds that only

minimal public use, even though it does not disclose
the secrets of an invention, should trigger the
twelve-month period in which an inventor must
initiate the patent prosecution process. Since one
function of patent law is to encourage disclosure to
further the advancement of technology, this minimal publicity is enough to bar a later patent. Thus,
for instance, it is not even necessary that the inventor publicly use any more than just one sample of
his product for it to be *publicly* used within the
meaning of statutory bar. Neither is it necessary for
a large number of people to use it for such use to
trigger the public-use doctrine. *Egbert v. Lippmann*
(1881).

However, if the use is limited or restricted *so as
intentionally to prevent disclosure,* as in a *test,* such
"limited" or "restricted" use will not trigger the
statutory bar. *Illinois Tool Works, Inc. v. Continental Can Co.* (1967). When the inventor legitimately
is testing, the law does not impose the penalty
designed for those who are illegitimately delaying
the process. As an example, if an inventor decides to
test limited numbers of his product in a way so that
a limited number of persons are using it and are
pledged to confidentiality, this will not constitute
public use within the meaning of statutory bar.
Experimental use is not only a defense to a claim of
public use but also to the "on sale" bar. When an
inventor attempts to "further refine the device,"
statutory bar is not imposed. In fact, experimental
use is deemed to be so legitimate and desirable that
its continuation will not necessarily prevent an in-

ventor from claiming priority of invention at a time before all testing was completed. *Poole v. Mossinghoff* (1982).

The public-use bar, thus, is subject to this judicially created *experimentation* exception designed to give the inventor a little more time in which to perfect his invention. This exception allows the inventor to engage in a limited public use that does not trigger the bar of section 102(b). A balancing process is employed to determine whether the purpose of the use is truly experimentation or whether it is, instead, simply public use. The degree of public use is balanced against the actual testing that is going on. If the public use is so dominant as to contradict the argument that its purpose is testing, the exception will not be allowed. What otherwise would be public use must be predominantly for experimental or testing purposes. Some attempt to maintain the secrecy usually found in testing normally must be shown. The experimentation exception extends only so far as is necessary and terminates when experimentation is no longer the main purpose of the use. The objectives of an alleged test and its necessity are measured by inquiring into the facts, including such things as the length of time the test continues and the number of times the test is performed. See *Dix-Seal Corp. v. New Haven Trap Rock Co.* (1964).

The tested product is not always identical with that described in the patent application. Thus, among a number of other factual inquiries, the degree of identity between what was publicly used and that sought to be patented becomes important under the principle of substantial identity. However, that inquiry is still based on the function of the public-use doctrine. It must measure whether enough has been disclosed to make the patent surplusage from the standpoint of advancing the art. If the product publicly used is so *substantially* identical to that of the claimed patent, then a patent upon it may be barred under the public-use doctrine. *Dix-Seal Corp. v. New Haven Trap Rock Co.*, supra. Just as only *substantial* identity is required for infringement, 35 U.S.C.A. § 271, only *substantial* identity is required to satisfy the requirement of public use for purposes of statutory bar. If a product or process is used publicly prior to one year before filing of the application, and that product or process is substantially the same as the claimed invention, then that degree of identity is sufficient to satisfy the bar of public use.

Likewise, whether a printed publication will raise statutory bar also depends upon its publicity or accessibility. The key, again, is the *degree* of publicity. It has been held by one court that an uncatalogued masters thesis, for instance, is not so publicly accessible as to raise the bar. *In re Bayer* (1978). But if even a single thesis is cataloged, and thus accessible, the bar may exist. *In re Hall* (1986). Thus, limited access alone does not prevent a publication from raising the bar. There need only be a likelihood that access is sufficient to allow interested parties to find the publication. The probability of sufficient public accessibility was low in *Bayer* only because there was a lack of cataloging. A publication, even if it is difficult to find, may raise the bar if it is available, although only on a limited basis, to some part of the public.

## § 3.9   Competing Claims to Novelty by Two or More Inventors—Priority

When inventions are developed in quick succession, or when the inventive process is prolonged so that the time of "invention" is ambiguous, it becomes highly important, even determinative, to adopt a method of dating events so that the issue of *priority* is consistently decided. Novelty includes the issue of priority since to say something is not novel is also to say that someone or something else has priority. When a reference precludes patentability, one might say that the reference has priority. When two or more inventors claim a patent right, each may be asserting that he, rather than some reference, has priority.

An inventor who does not immediately seek a patent is in jeopardy of a rival claim by a junior inventor who makes the same invention and acts with due diligence. The junior inventor may successfully unseat the senior inventor by proceeding with dispatch. The relative merits of such senior and junior inventors in that situation are mapped out in section 102(g). Priority depends upon three factors: the time of conception, the time of reduction to practice, and the use of due diligence in pursuing both patent protection and perfection of the discovery. By definition, a senior inventor is one who conceives first. The time of conception is defined as that moment when the inventor unambiguously had made mental discovery of the invention. The Federal Circuit has held that the mere formation of the idea, as long as it is definite, permanent, and particular, is enough. The inventor need not know, said the Court, that her idea will work, since that is not conception, but reduction to practice. *Burroughs Wellcome Co. v. Barr Laboratories, Inc.* (1994). In *Burroughs Wellcome*, however, the court also said that the idea, to constitute conception, must be precise enough to allow the skilled practitioner to practice the invention without undue experimentation. It is not completely clear, of course, how an inventor can conceive of an invention without knowing it will work but nevertheless be precise enough so that the invention can be practiced without undue experimentation. Apparently, a "lucky guess" will suffice.

The general rule is as follows, subject to two important modifications discussed below: As between two inventors, *the first to conceive generally has priority* to patent protection. But this is subject to the important rule that the senior inventor must use due diligence from the time of conception—but that diligence is not measured from his conception. The requirement of due diligence is not triggered *until just prior to conception by the junior inventor.* Only thereafter must diligence proceed uninterrupted until reduction to practice is accomplished. Thus, the general rule is first modified as follows: a claim by a senior inventor to priority based on earlier conception, if challenged by a junior inventor, is preserved *only* if accompanied by continuous diligence starting just prior to a junior's conception.

Reduction to practice occurs either at the time when the inventor can prove the product or process was produced or applied successfully or, in any event, no later than the time of filing of the patent application. *Eastman Kodak Co. v. E. I. DuPont de Nemours & Co.* (1969). As a matter of law, the time of application is presumptively the time of reduction to practice unless the inventor can demonstrate an earlier date. Reduction to practice is important because it is the only way a junior inventor can first challenge a senior inventor. Thus, the final modification of the general rule is as follows: A junior inventor can never challenge a senior inventor unless the junior inventor reduces to practice *first*.

The general rule and its two modifications, can be summarized in the following way. A senior inventor, defined as one who conceives first, will have priority over a junior inventor, defined as anyone who conceives later, unless the junior inventor reduced to practice first *and* the senior inventor did not use continuous diligence from a time just prior to the junior inventor's time of conception.

An inventor who first conceives and first reduces to practice will have no problem relative to a junior inventor who conceives last and reduces to practice last. The dispute, thus, will only concern a junior inventor who conceives later but who reduces to practice earlier. A junior inventor's earlier reduction to practice most often will be evidenced by the junior inventor filing his application first. As a practical matter, a first filing often will cause an alleged senior inventor to file his application quickly and claim either (1) earlier conception and due diligence thereafter, or (2) earlier conception and due diligence at least from just prior to the time of conception by the junior inventor, or (3) a factually earlier reduction to practice despite the presumption that the filing date is the date of reduction to practice. Any of those contentions allows the senior inventor to maintain priority over the junior inventor under section 102(g).

Note that the senior inventor need not prove continuous diligence until just prior to the time of conception of the junior inventor. As a result, a potentially insoluble problem can arise with respect to any situation involving more than two competing inventors. Logically and mathematically it can be demonstrated that the scheme of section 102(g) can consistently yield a clear winner only in two-inventor situations. With three or more inventors, *more* than one inventor actually can fulfill the statutory conditions for priority. In that case, a choice must be made upon policy grounds rather than on the basis of the language of the statute. This is because of the ambiguity of the test when applied beyond the two inventor situation. The result is so unpredictable and unexpected that it is termed the "priority paradox." In certain cases involving three or more inventors, it is possible that each inventor will have priority over another but that no one inventor will be prior to *all* of the others. Thus, the paradox gives no clear priority to any one of three inventors. The paradox situation is presented in the illustration that appears below. It can be seen that inventor A is prior to inventor B, that inventor B is prior to inventor C, and that inventor C is prior to inventor A. The chart is more useful for the aid it gives in understanding the priority rules generally than for any serious pragmatic purposes since the actual example is unlikely to occur very often in practice, if at all. Nevertheless, because it is a truly paradoxical situation, it is important to understand what produces the paradoxical result.

**Illustration**

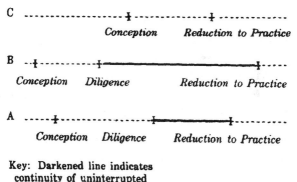

C ------------------- ‡ --------------- ‡ ------------
                    *Conception*      *Reduction to Practice*

B --‡ ----------- ‡————————————————————‡ ----
*Conception*  *Diligence*        *Reduction to Practice*

A -----‡ ----------------- ‡————————‡ ----------
     *Conception*  *Diligence*   *Reduction to Practice*

Key: **Darkened line indicates continuity of uninterrupted diligence.**

[C5870]

The phenomenon can at least partly be accounted for by the explanation that the priority rule does not require any one person to be *most* diligent but only *more* diligent than one other person who conceives later. That comparison only relates one person to another. It leaves undecided the situation, as in the example, in which one person can be more diligent than a second but not more diligent than a third while the second can be more diligent than the third, who is still more diligent than the first. The combination of the relative instead of the absolute requirement of diligence and the variability of the basis of comparison—the date of conception, which varies among the three rather than being one date—produces two variables over three items. That distribution inevitably produces, under strict rules of logic and topology, ambiguity, inconsistency, and paradox.

# CHAPTER 4

# PATENTABILITY—UTILITY

## § 4.1  Qualitative Utility

Patent protection depends not only upon novelty but also upon utility. If novelty is the brain of invention, then one might say utility is its muscle. The utility requirement is derived, first, from the constitutional clause (granting potential patent protection to "*useful* Arts") and, second, from the Patent Act (giving *actual* protection only to "useful" inventions, consistent with the constitutional enabling clause). 35 U.S.C.A. § 101. Even without the language of section 101, an argument could be made for the utility requirement on at least two grounds. The first is the constitutional argument; the second is that the very meaning of "invention" seems to imply something with utility, although this is undermined by the existence of plant and design patents. See § 2.10, supra.

An invention must be of some benefit qualitatively, but no particular quantum of benefit is required. *Anderson v. Natta* (1973). Thus, an invention cannot be patented if it is a mere novelty or curiosity. The quality concept also forbids the grant of a patent on illegal or immoral items. And, by necessary implication, an invention cannot be beneficial if it is solely detrimental. Therefore, dangerous items that have no beneficial use are not patentable.

If the claim of utility is fabricated by the inventor to give his invention market appeal, there may be no intrinsic and therefore legally cognizable benefit. The inventor of an ineffective drug, for instance, may not obtain a patent merely because he convinces gullible patients that it has a nonexistent curative effect. It is not so much that it lacks a minimum *quantum* of benefit (after all, the patients may find it subjectively useful), but it is, instead, that it has an impermissible fraudulent *quality*.

## § 4.2  Presumed Utility

Utility cannot be presumed. It must be disclosed as an integral part of the patent specification. 35 U.S.C.A. § 112. And, in fact, merely proving the utility of a new process may be insufficient if the result it produces is of no demonstrable utility. For instance, that a new chemical produced by an inventive process closely resembles another useful one is insufficient to patent the process or the chemical for it is impermissible to presume that the new chemical would have similarly useful properties.

One of the reasons that utility must be affirmatively demonstrated is that to hold otherwise would be to grant a patent on an unknown range of applications. Because we cannot know whether a process has broad or narrow applications until we are told its exact scope, patenting a process without a description of its utility or that of its products would monopolize something with such broad potential scope as to encompass what essentially is an idea rather than an application.

The bar against presumed utility forces the inventor to limit his claims to the demonstrated usefulness of his product or process. Speculative utility, just like presumptive utility, would allow an inventor to gain a patent on a process or product that eventually might constitute an entire field of knowledge. Therefore, an inventor must identify a *specific* utility. A product must have a demonstrable utility specified in the patent application. A process must demonstrate utility with respect to its product. This is because a process that results in useless products does not increase the fund of useful knowledge nor confer any real benefit.

Of course, a process that results in a useless product might be useful for yet unknown applications. But that states the very argument against speculative or presumptive utility. Open-ended patents are prohibited by the bar against presumptive or speculative utility because, as the courts have described it, such a patent threatens a "monopoly of knowledge." *Brenner v. Manson* (1966).

In *Manson* the chemical process for which patent protection was sought had no demonstrable utility. A strong argument was made, however, relying on the importance of basic research, that chemical process patents need only show a likely utility.

Justice Fortas, writing for the majority, rejected that because such a doctrine, if extended, would have overly broad consequences. If a patent application fails to describe the "specific benefit" of a new process, it threatens to "engross ... a broad field," and is therefore unpatentable. "A patent is not a hunting license." The policy implications of *Manson* are key: the Court clearly wanted to prevent industry attempts to carve out large technical areas—making them immune to research by competitors—with patents that, from the point of utility, are not ripe.

Besides *specific* utility, inventions must have *substantial* utility. Although *Manson* holds that utility for pure research is not enough, drugs that exhibit desirable qualities in standard experimental animals may be patentable even if they ultimately prove ineffective in humans. This is because one need not show proven utility to gain patent protection; it is sufficient to show a reasonable expectation of utility, which such tests presumably demonstrate. *In re Brana* (1995).

# CHAPTER 5

# PATENTABILITY— NONOBVIOUSNESS

## § 5.1 Overview

In a sense, nonobviousness follows on the intellectual heels of novelty; but it is distinctively different. An invention may not have been developed before a certain date. It is, at that point in time, new; it has novelty. However, just because it never *actually* was invented before does not mean it was not hypothetically conceivable. It is possible that someone skilled in the relevant field of technology and familiar with its subject matter could have invented it with comparative ease had he tried; such an "invention" would be novel but obvious to that person.

For most of the entire history of patent law in this country an invention, to be patentable, has had to be nonobvious to those skilled in the art. This was true even prior to the 1952 Patent Act when this requirement, for the first time, was expressly adopted in section 103. A requirement of nonobviousness or something quite similar to it was judicially recognized as a basic requirement of "invention."

71

Nonobviousness is decided in light of the "prior art." Important issues involve how the prior art will be defined. It may consist of many of the same sources and technical literature considered for determining novelty, but, for nonobviousness, there is no need that the invention be "described" in those publications. It need only furnish one skilled in the art with the necessary information that would have made the invention obvious.

Inventions consisting of a combination of well known elements frequently involve nonobviousness issues. The elements may never have been combined before so that the invention itself is novel. But it is sometimes difficult, with all of the elements obvious by themselves prior to the invention, to show that the combination itself is not obvious. It is sometimes said that, for a combination of known elements to be nonobvious, the result must be synergistic—the result somehow must yield a sum greater than its parts. This is no more, of course, than reaching the decision that the result must not be obvious. If the combination of elements yields a result that anyone skilled in the art obviously could predict, the invention fails for lack of nonobviousness. The sum is merely that of the parts. But if a different or unexpected result is obtained by the combination, it frequently is described as synergistic. Of course, that is merely a way of saying no more than an invention has occurred.

In *Sakraida v. Ag Pro, Inc.* (1976), the Court implied that a combination patent of old elements must produce a synergistic result to be protectible.

The Court added that synergism is evidenced by the demonstration of a different function and not simply by the production of "a more striking result than in previous combinations." The Federal Circuit has held, however, that, although synergism is evidence of nonobviousness, a lack of synergism does not necessarily imply obviousness. *Ryko Mfg. Co. v. Nu–Star* (1991).

Another important concept useful in determining nonobviousness is that of "secondary considerations." Secondary considerations are really no more than factual evidence that circumstantially supports a finding of nonobviousness. They assume, however, more than immediately appears on the surface. One secondary consideration is that of commercial success. If a product is immediately successful and sells like wildfire, that is some evidence that the product was nonobvious. The assumption is that an obvious invention would have been developed and marketed sooner. Another secondary consideration is the long-felt-but-unfulfilled-need doctrine. If a need had been felt in a field but had not been satisfied, that is considered some evidence that an invention is not obvious. Again, the assumption is that an obvious invention would have been developed earlier. There are other assumptions beneath this doctrine that are less well articulated, one of them being that sufficient time has passed between the need and the invention to allow for serious attempts at satisfying the need. Still another secondary consideration is copying by others; certainly this indicates the product or process has commercial value but does not necessarily indicate that it is a truly inventive technological advance; it may mean no more than that it is technologically easy to copy or that customers demand it for nontechnological reasons.

Some courts and the PTO have held that two or more prior art references cannot be combined to demonstrate nonobviousness unless there is some "teaching, suggestion, or motivation" in the prior art itself to perform such a combination. There is no statutory support for such a rule, and in *KSR Int'l. v. Teleflex Inc.* (2007), the Court held that no such mechanical rule should apply, that obviousness must take account of the "inferences and creative steps that a person of ordinary skill in the art would employ" including even what is "obvious to try," a standard long rejected by the Federal Circuit.

A final consideration relevant to nonobviousness is the outmoded "flash of creative genius" requirement. In *Cuno Engineering Corp. v. Automatic Devices Corp.* (1941), the Supreme Court held an invention unpatentable because of the absence of this quality. In this context, the "flash of genius" requirement seemed to mean something more than just objectively measured nonobviousness. It implied that an invention must be so nonobvious that no amount of research would solve the problem, absent a sudden experience of insight. Such a subjective standard threatens to impose a very strict and high standard of invention, although the Court has since disavowed any such intention. *Graham v. John Deere Co.* (1966).

During the 1940's the Supreme Court rejected patentability in virtually every case that it decided. The feeling that the Supreme Court was being too strict is a major reason why the 1952 Patent Act adopted an explicit rejection of the "flash of genius" requirement. The Act states: "Patentability shall not be negatived by the manner in which the invention was made." 35 U.S.C.A. § 103. In other words, that an invention was developed through laborious trial and error instead of an insightful "flash of genius" should not determine whether it is nonobvious. The objective standard of looking to the state of the art prior to the time of invention is the sole test of nonobviousness.

## § 5.2  Invention and Nonobviousness

The 1952 Patent Act requires "nonobviousness" in section 103. There was no prior explicit statutory requirement; this new objective formula actually was supposed to decrease the judicial standard of patentability, as developed under earlier statutes. In fact, the addition of the nonobviousness requirement probably has left the earlier standard substantially intact, because some version of nonobviousness was required by courts even without any statutory language. Earlier patent laws only expressly required novelty and utility as tests of patentability, but the additional requirement of nonobviousness was derived from the very notion of invention. This mandated that an invention, to be patentable, had to represent some advance over the prior art so that the ordinary mechanic skilled in that prior art would not have been capable of making the advance. "Invention" required some degree of special subjective ingenuity in the development of the invention. The test was supposed to distinguish between the mere skillful mechanic and the true inventor.

Functionally, the invention requirement was a good way of insuring that the patent monopoly was not awarded when it was not necessary. A skillful mechanic naturally would make advances that were relatively easy and perhaps obvious as a part of his trade. But something was needed to encourage the true inventor. To identify true inventions amidst mere pedestrian advances, the requirement of invention was imposed. Mere skill was distinguished from ingenuity. Thus, the patent monopoly was the motivation offered to the inventor so that he would disclose those advances unavailable to the ordinary mechanic who did not possess the requisite ingenuity. Thus in *Hotchkiss v. Greenwood* (1850), the Court said: "Unless more ingenuity and skill ... were required ... than were possessed by an ordinary mechanic acquainted with the business, there was an absence of that degree of skill and ingenuity which constitute essential elements of every invention." This standard of invention was added to the statutory tests of utility and novelty. This subjective test eventually caused great dissatisfaction.

The subjective standard tended to concentrate on the method by which the invention was developed, and not on how the invention itself related to the useful arts. The "invention" test, in other words, measured the method or process of invention, not its results. In deciding whether "skill or ingenuity" were demonstrated, courts often referred to the prevailing level of skill in the relevant art. But the emphasis was not on whether the invention itself rose above that expected level, but on whether the inventor exhibited the kind of ingenuity that elevated him above the level of the journeyman mechanic. Thus, although prior art became relevant, the emphasis was on the inventor, not his discovery.

Dissatisfaction with the subjective standard grew especially because of the fact that the test of novelty already was satisfied. That alone tended to demonstrate a certain amount of creativity and ingenuity. Thus, by definition, in such cases, when a court rejected a patent solely on the ground of lack of invention, they were rejecting a development that had never been made before. It was sometimes difficult to defend a subjective inquiry in the face of facts that already had demonstrated complete and patentable novelty.

There is little doubt, however, that *some* test of invention is implied by the very existence of the constitutional clause, which grants power to protect "inventions." The disagreement is over its articulation and implementation. Without a statutory definition of invention, the Supreme Court was free to define the invention requirement in a relatively unconfined manner. Historically, the Court changed the test from time to time as it reacted to what appeared to be either too liberal or too strict requirements imposed by the Patent Office or lower federal courts. In response to the perceived inconsistencies produced by such a variable judicial requirement, Congress eventually adopted the section 103 "nonobviousness" requirement.

The judicial standard of invention was an attempt to incorporate into the Patent Act its functional basis—to distinguish between those pedestrian advances that would naturally be disclosed without patent protection because of their easy accessibility to the ordinary mechanic and those true inventions that would be disclosed only in return for patent protection. The new statutory requirement of nonobviousness, and the nonstatutory secondary considerations should be examined with an eye to whether they satisfy the same functional requirements as the old standard of invention.

## § 5.3   Negative Rules of Invention

The somewhat vague standard of invention articulated in *Hotchkiss v. Greenwood* (1850) was applied on a case-by-case basis over the years. Due to the lack of a coherent general definition of invention, *ad hoc* rules arose, derived from individual patent cases. Courts developed "negative rules of invention" by using very general terms to explain specific cases. For instance, the substitution of a different material in an existing device was held, as a matter of law, to be no more than what a skilled mechanic would do. Other negative rules forbade protection for mere automation of formerly manual steps, mere change of form, degree, or proportions of elements of more complex machines, making lighter, more compact, or more portable formerly stationary, heavy, or bulky things, and mere omission, substitution, reversal, relocation, division or multiplication of already existing elements. See *Merck & Co. v. Chase Chem. Co.* (1967).

But "negative rules" tend towards both overinclusiveness and uncertainty. Simple changes indeed usually are obvious and not the mark of invention. Most of these changes are merely the result of the journeyman mechanic. But an absolute prohibition in the form of a negative rule does not allow for the truly nonobvious, novel, ingenious development that by happenstance coincides with a negative rule. In addition, the gradually increasing collection of negative rules simply did not address the need for a general doctrine which could embrace the concept of invention in all cases. The broad reliance on *ad hoc* instead of general rules created uncertainty over whether a new case not addressed by already existing negative rules would be barred by a newly formulated rule. A general conceptual standard clearly was needed.

Part of the dispute concerning the "negative rules" was caused by the persistence of what seemed to be a subjective, instead of objective, test of invention. The freewheeling judicial standard created by *Hotchkiss* inevitably spawned negative rules of invention which, though couched in the appearance of accuracy and certainty (in fact, they are sometimes referred to as the "objective tests"), suffer from the twin defects of overbreadth (because some inventions were not truly obvious despite the fact that they violated one of the negative rules) and uncertainty (because there was no general standard that applied across the board and that prevented the sudden announcement of new rules). The flexible judicial standard of "invention" inevitably led to the requirement in *Cuno Engineering Corp. v. Automatic Devices Corp.* (1941) for a "flash of creative genius," a standard now rejected by the last sentence of section 103.

The negative rules of invention still are viable, however. The Supreme Court held, in *Graham v. John Deere Co.* (1966), that, although the Patent Act codified the concept of invention in section 103 under the rubric of nonobviousness, the "general level of patentable invention" remained the same as before. The Court stated that all codification accomplished was to specify the requirements of nonobviousness. This perpetuated the old negative rules of invention because, if section 103 merely codified rather than changed the previous requirements for invention, then those negative rules still are valid. The emphasis, however, under section 103, is no longer on the manner in which the invention is made. To the extent that there must be something ingenious or creative about an invention, it is the invention itself that must demonstrate the genius and not the inventor. Thus, at least, those negative rules still existing should have a new objective gloss.

But the persistence of any of the negative rules threatens to undermine the generality of section 103. An old result produced by "equivalent substitutions," for instance, might be flatly barred by traditional rules, because the Court has held that mere substitutions producing the same result do not qualify as nonobvious inventions, under the rubric of "synergism." *Sakraida v. Ag Pro, Inc.* (1976). It is possible that as the Court moves toward more objective indicia, it will recognize that the test of nonobviousness rarely can be articulated in a black-letter fashion. Although the Court has rejected the view that the standard of invention was lowered by section 103, there seems to be less reliance now on negative rules.

The Federal Circuit's dislike of negative rules is well-illustrated in its acceptance of synergism as evidence of nonobviousness, while at the same time insisting that a lack of synergism does not mean an invention is unpatentable for obviousness.

The tension, however, between the rigidity but appealing nature of clearly knowable, easily-applied rules of patentability and the flexibility of more general rules is best illustrated in a relatively recent amendment to section 103 reversing a Federal Circuit decision. *In re Durden* (1985) held that obvious biotech processes are not rendered suddenly patentable merely because they employ patentable starting materials. Congress, responding to complaints that this handicapped the foreign prospects of our biotech industry, and over the objections of many patent professionals, added language to section

103(c) which mandates as a matter of law that certain biotech processes are nonobvious if they use or result in a novel, nonobvious product. Thus, despite the fact that history seems to show the defects of rigid rules, their appeal is strong.

## § 5.4   The Statutory Test

The standard of nonobviousness is applied in three steps—(1) a survey of the scope and content of the prior art, (2) an examination of the differences between the invention and the prior art, and (3) a determination of the level of ordinary skill in the art. In the light of that three-stage process, one can decide whether the differences revealed in the second stage are nonobvious. *Graham v. John Deere Co.* (1966). The Federal Circuit has held that the so-called "secondary considerations" constitute a fourth stage. *Vandenberg v. Dairy Equip. Co.* (1984). See § 5.6, infra.

Procedurally, prior art is demonstrated in two ways. First, the duty of candor, see § 7.8, infra, requires that applicants themselves specifically identify the relevant prior art. Thus, the application itself will include various citations to prior art and a statement of how the invention is a significant advance over the prior art. Also, the Patent Office, during the examining process, cites "references" that it maintains are relevant prior art.

The first step is to survey the scope and content of the prior art, defining which prior art is both applicable and relevant. The relevant, applicable, prior art must be that which is either *pertinent* to the invention or *analogous* to that which is clearly pertinent. Therefore, the definition of the prior art is not always or even often limited to one narrow area. The pertinent art always is defined in functional rather than commercial terms. For example, if the invention concerns a way of sealing a room, the prior art will not be limited to the art known by those in the particular commercial area ordinarily involved, which means that known by carpenters or contractors. Instead of the commercial definition of the art, patent law prefers the functional, conceptual, or generic definition. The art would not be that of doors but of closures generally. It is the general, not the specific—the genus, not the species—that defines the prior art. Therefore, the prior art is usually defined as the basic mechanical or scientific field applicable to the claims even though the people in that *technical* field ordinarily might not work in the relevant *commercial* area. In addition to the relevant applicable art and all others "reasonably pertinent" thereto, the relevant applicable art includes "analogous" areas. Analogous areas are those arts to which a person skilled in the directly pertinent art reasonably would refer in order to solve the problem.

Step two, an examination of the differences between the invention and the prior art, requires reconstructing the prior art. Reconstructing the prior art always is done from the perspective of hindsight. Reconstruction involves the application of a hypothetical standard—what the reasonable person skilled in the art would have known—as of an objective time in the past. Of course, it always will be problematical to make the claim through hindsight that a reasonable person would have known of certain prior art. Hindsight reconstruction very often courts the danger of reading the invention itself into the prior art, because with knowledge of the invention, it is easy to believe that certain prior art or knowledge makes the invention obvious. The claim that prior publications or knowledge in arguably analogous areas would have been known or reasonably accessible to a skilled practitioner in the directly pertinent art always is tenuous. When reconstructing the prior art, one must not read into it the very teachings of the invention at issue. *Graham v. John Deere Co.,* supra.

The third step involves not only assessing the level of skill but applying it to the invention itself. This inquiry is neither mechanical nor structural but *functional,* applying to the invention as a whole. Even though it may be obvious that a certain object can be constructed in a certain way, its utility and novelty may lie in its functional use, not its construction. Therefore, the prior art must be used to determine whether the invention's new and useful function, not necessarily its construction, is nonobvious. For instance, a chemical is not obvious just because its structure is the logical and obvious development of already existing prior art if the inventive *function* of the chemical is not its obvious structure but its nonobvious effect on other chemicals or things. Nonobviousness is *not* to be measured by the *degree* of change over the prior art but "by reference to the purpose sought." *Carter–Wallace, Inc. v. Otte* (1972).

The test of nonobviousness thus always must be directed toward the inventive new properties of the discovery, and not other features that may or may not themselves be nonobvious. In fact, the very obviousness of an invention's structure may make its unexpected function nonobvious. A chemical easily may be described theoretically as an obvious derivative of other known chemicals. Similarity of related chemical formulas may make nonobvious an otherwise obvious derivative if the actual substance described by the compound has surprising, nonobvious qualities. A yet unanswered issue in this context is whether the invention covers only the nonobvious uses of a chemical or whether the entire chemical might receive protection.

Nonobviousness does not mean a complete break from the prior art; likewise, obviousness need not mean that the invention was imminent. A development need not be the very next logical step in order to be obvious, nor need it be even within two or three steps of the first logical one. On the other hand, invention involves at least as much patient logical experimentation as it does ingenuity and patent law rewards perspiration as well as inspiration. Since nothing can be completely nonobvious in the sense of a clear break with the past, it therefore is just a matter of degree between what is obvious and what is nonobvious.

Similarly, the obvious is not just that which is guaranteed to work. An invention may be obvious even if it was not certain to work. Likewise, obviousness is not contradicted merely because nobody tried it. The failure of others to try something is only a "secondary consideration" that is seldom determinative. The failure of others is persuasive, if at all, only in a well established field, since it can be explained by a lack of demand as well as by nonobviousness.

The nonobviousness of any invention must be unambiguously revealed in the application itself. A patent cannot rely on undisclosed properties, uses, or qualities for nonobviousness. The general rule is pungently restated in Justice Fortas' aphorism that the patenting process does not confer a hunting license. *Brenner v. Manson* (1966). However, a minor line of cases does suggest that later discoveries of nonobvious qualities may support patentability but this seems to be limited to features which, though unrealized or misunderstood at the time of application, were nevertheless inherent to what was disclosed in the patent application *Westmoreland Specialty v. Hogan* (1909). It is doubtful, however, that without some previously disclosed nonobvious inventive step, a later-discovered advance can support patentability on its own.

## § 5.5  Nonobviousness and Novelty

Nonobviousness and novelty intersect because of the similarity of some of the factual questions involved in both inquiries. Novelty requires that the invention has not been anticipated. This necessarily involves an investigation of the prior art; that is, what people actually knew, published, and did at earlier times. Likewise, the standard of nonobviousness requires an investigation of the prior art; that is, in light of the prior art, the invention must not have been obvious. Note, however, that there is no hypothetical inquiry in the test for novelty: actual anticipation is the standard. "Secondary evidence," such as commercial success and unexpected results, is admissible to show that an invention was not obvious to those skilled in the prior art. But under section 102, that evidence is not relevant to the question of novelty.

Even though both novelty and nonobviousness involve a survey of the prior art, novelty only considers prior art with respect to substantial identity; nonobviousness, however, considers the prior art with respect to what the next obvious step in the inventive process would have been. The novelty inquiry is into the *entire* prior art, whether or not applicable, pertinent, or analogous. All that matters is that *somewhere* in the prior art the invention may be substantially identically disclosed. Thus the search is quite wide but the test is quite narrow— the entire area is covered, but it must reveal substantial identity between the prior art and the invention. On the other hand, with respect to nonobviousness, it is quite possible that if all technological knowledge were considered almost every invention would be found obvious. Since only the prior art that is pertinent or analogous is surveyed, such a conclusion is far less probable. The search is relatively narrow—limited to only the pertinent and analogous art—but the test is much broader. Instead of testing for substantial identity, section 103 asks only whether the invention is obvious.

## § 5.6   The Secondary Considerations

Secondary considerations, the "subtests" or the "objective tests," of nonobviousness, are highly relevant, and, according to the Federal Circuit, constitute a fourth step in the *John Deere* nonobviousness analysis, assuming a "nexus" to the inventive characteristic is first established. *Vandenberg v. Dairy Equip. Co.* (1984). The secondary considerations include commercial success, long felt but unsolved needs, failure of others, copying by others, the very existence of a well-established prior art, the fact that experts express disbelief at a discovery's announcement, and later improvements upon that discovery. See *Graham v. John Deere Co.* (1966). (There are also subtests of *obviousness,* for instance the existence of simultaneous and independent inventions by others in the field. This involves the "history of the art" discussed below.) But courts have been reluctant to treat these tests as direct indicia of nonobviousness. Secondary standards can be "manipulated" by the marketplace. The standard then will not necessarily reflect inventiveness so much as economic happenstance. In any event, secondary considerations were, prior to the Federal

Circuit's decision in *Vandenberg*, used only when there was some real doubt over the question of nonobviousness. It is often stated that secondary considerations never can be determinative, but all this seems to mean is that in a clear case those considerations cannot change the result. Except in a clear case, or when it is certain that the secondary considerations exist for entirely irrelevant reasons (those related to the market rather than to technology), they normally are highly persuasive.

A combination of old elements frequently raises issues of nonobviousness and of the secondary consideration of the "well-established" prior art. The discovery of wholly new elements in fact may be a much rarer phenomenon than the discovery of a new result. Whether a result is really "new," of course, will depend upon what the prior art indicated was possible. In fact, it may be only in an area of well-established prior art that it might really be nonobvious to try a new combination of old elements when no new results are or should be expected.

The "history of the art" sometimes can demonstrate that an invention is nonobvious. The history involves such factors as how long the art tolerated an unmet need, how long work was devoted to the problem, how many researchers investigated the need, whether more than one inventor concurrently solved the problem, and how much the invention has replaced prior art. As is true of secondary considerations generally, these facts obviously are subject to both abuse and misinterpretation, because they assume certain things about the economics of research and development. However, they can be treated as simply descriptions of the state of the prior art itself—of what skilled practitioners were capable—and in that sense they can be useful objective indicia of nonobviousness. The history of the art is thus relevant to both the first and third questions of nonobviousness. But the patent system is not supposed to reward commercial success. Since our economic system rewards development for other reasons than simple technical achievement, the history of the art may not always be directly related to the legitimate purposes of patentability.

Some courts have held that it is relevant if the prior art makes the invention *less,* rather than *more* likely. In other words, prior art that "teaches away" from the invention, makes the inventor's discovery even more nonobvious. *General Battery Corp. v. Gould, Inc.* (1982). Other courts have gone even farther with this same line of reasoning to reach an opposite result, seemingly injecting an impermissible element of subjectivity into the nonobviousness inquiry, by holding that when an inventor ignorantly proceeds in the face of prior art that teaches against the invention, to grant a patent would reward "ignorance and naivete—presumably not qualities ... patent ... is designed to reward." *Brunswick Corp. v. Champion Spark Plug Co.* (1982).

The secondary tests are highly useful because they call upon judges to undertake tasks similar to those that courts traditionally perform. Courts are used to examining the forces of the marketplace. Secondary considerations are economic and motivation issues and closely resemble the inquiries routinely made, for instance, in tort and contract law. Additionally, they are objective and prevent the court from wandering too far from established facts. For instance, it is difficult for a court to declare an invention obvious when the invention has met with instant success in an industry characterized by high levels of research and development. Thus, any attempt to apply a subjective "hindsight" test tends to be countered by an examination of secondary considerations.

Nevertheless, courts have been unwilling to adopt these secondary considerations as *the* standard of patentability because they overemphasize the influence of market conditions. For instance, they could reward a *lack* of inventiveness in the case of either infant or dying industries that might involve technological advances obvious to anyone carefully scrutinizing the prior art. An invention so patented would be protected merely because, in a poorly funded industry, others were not assiduous in scrutinizing the prior art. This, of course, assumes a certain lack of competition, for surely in a competitive environment the prior art would be the first thing consulted by those seeking a competitive edge.

Normally, then, the secondary considerations should have great significance. A court that declares obvious an "invention" that achieves great commercial success in a field in which significant research is conducted may be very unrealistic. Rejecting the

secondary consideration of commercial success in
such a case probably is due to an impermissible
hindsight assessment of nonobviousness by the
court.

When abused, however, the secondary considerations can obscure the requirements for patentability. It is not always clear whether a commercially
successful venture is due to a nonobvious *idea* or
something technological. An idea might indeed be
novel and nonobvious and might well support many
commercial ventures. But since ideas per se are
unpatentable, a successful commercial venture
alone is insufficient and what must be nonobvious
is not the idea or the venture but a technological
application. To avoid abuse of its addition of a
fourth analytical step to the three set forth in *John
Deere*, the Federal Circuit requires that a "nexus"
to the inventive characteristic be established before
the secondary consideration is utilized. *Vandenberg
v. Dairy Equip. Co.*, supra. This addition of a nexus
requirement means that this so-called fourth step is
not quite the same as the three required by *John
Deere* although any difference was diminished when
the Federal Circuit held that a nexus is presumed
when the very invention described in the patent
application enjoys commercial success. *Ryko Mfg.
Co. v. Nu–Star, Inc.* (1991).

## § 5.7  The Importation of Section 102 Prior Art into Section 103

There are two typical sources of prior art: (1)
printed publications, such as books and articles, and

(2) testimony and statements of skilled practitioners and experts. The most common sources, however, are publications; this includes prior patents. A patent *application,* however, is statutorily confidential and is deemed nonpublic until a patent is granted. As a result, unless it is cited in some other publicly available patent application or office proceeding, if a patent application is abandoned or even if it is rejected, it never becomes public and the Patent Office does not search these records as prior art for nonobviousness because it is and always remains legally unavailable. However, if an application becomes public through eventual approval by the Patent Office, it then can serve as a source of prior art.

Clearly, with respect to the issue of *novelty* (which simply asks whether the invention ever "existed" before), an earlier patent application, even if unavailable, is a valid source of prior art that may anticipate a later invention. But, for *nonobviousness* purposes (which asks if a hypothetical practitioner would have thought the invention obvious relying on actually available sources), the use of unavailable prior art is questionable since the hypothetical skilled practitioner could never refer to it. Nevertheless, much, if not all, section 102 prior art is imported into the section 103 nonobviousness inquiry.

Under section 102(e) novelty, a patent can be barred by an earlier patent application if that application, as prior art, anticipated it. Perhaps surprisingly, that prior art also is available to make the later invention obvious even if the patent application, which is confidential until protection is granted, was factually unavailable to the second inventor at the relevant time. Section 103 does not contain such a direction; nevertheless, courts feel that the policies of the Patent Act would be frustrated if these items were treated as prior art under section 102 but not under section 103. As Justice Holmes has said: "The delays of the patent office ought not to cut down the effect of what has been done." *Alexander Milburn Co. v. Davis–Bournonville Co.* (1926). Similarly, section 102(f) secret prior art— which would be relevant to the issue of novelty between two inventors, perhaps, but never would be the kind of public knowledge that would inform the "ordinary skill" of a practitioner of the art—is nevertheless accepted as section 103 prior art. *Oddzon Products, Inc. v. Just Toys, Inc.* (1997). That this principle applies equally to nonobviousness as well as novelty is better explained by reasons of symmetry than logic.

Section 102(g) specifically identifies some prior art for *novelty* purposes—those inventions that have not been abandoned, suppressed, or concealed— which may not be publicly available. A junior inventor will be barred *on novelty grounds* if a senior inventor has priority even if that senior inventor has not publicly disclosed his invention as long as the nonpublic nature of the senior inventor's conduct does not reach the level of abandonment, suppression, or concealment. *Dunlop Holdings, Ltd. v. Ram Golf Corp.* (1975). Section 102(g) applies on its face only to novelty questions but it appears that it may define prior art for the nonobviousness inquiry as well. *Kimberly-Clark v. Johnson & Johnson* (1984). But see *MCV, Inc. v. King–Seeley Thermos Co.* (1989). Thus, it is possible that an inventor may be (nonpublicly) developing an invention, not having suppressed, abandoned, or concealed and that under section 102(g), his acts will prevent, on priority grounds, a later inventor from claiming it as his own novel discovery. Also, however, nonpublic prior art may bar a quite different later invention on nonobviousness grounds despite the fact that as undisclosed prior art, it really is not the kind the hypothetical skilled practitioner ever could have known about. But a patent application cannot be used as section 102(g) prior art to bar patentability of another application when the two applications are owned by, or assignable to, a common owner. 17 U.S.C.A. § 103(b)(1)(B).

The effect of automatically recognizing as prior art for nonobviousness purposes the kind of prior art that is used for determining novelty is the creation of a doctrine of constructive prior art. Constructive anticipation for novelty purposes is a result of statutory command under section 102(d) and (e). The importation of constructive prior art, however, for nonobviousness purposes under section 103 is strictly a matter of judicial fiat. *Hazeltine Research, Inc. v. Brenner* (1965). Because a patent may be granted long after its application date, it suddenly may become available as constructive prior art with respect to an already issued patent since that issued patent may have been filed *after* the constructively and retroactively available application was filed. Obviously, this can happen because patents are not granted in the order in which their applications are filed. With respect to abandoned and rejected applications, which are kept confidential, prior art only arises upon an actual publication and so this problem of retroactive obviousness does not occur unless such applications are cited in other, publicly available, applications or Patent and Trademark Office ("PTO") proceedings.

# CHAPTER 6

# DOUBLE–PATENTING

## § 6.1 Attempts to Extend the Patent Monopoly

Having developed a useful, nonobvious, and new invention, the inventor may claim a patent. The inventor is only entitled to one patent for any one invention, however. *Laskowitz v. Marie Designer, Inc.* (1954). This may seem obvious, but there is a natural temptation for inventors to try to extend patent protection as far as possible—sometimes beyond the statutory period. One way of attempting an impermissible extension is by breaking up one invention and trying to secure a series of patents. In spite of both the strict bar against double patenting and what seems an obvious rule, inventors sometimes claim only certain features of their inventions, saving others for later patenting as the earlier patent expires, thereby obtaining greater protection than the statute is intended to furnish.

The rule against double patenting relies on the same principle as do the anticipation and nonobviousness doctrines. Nobody, including the inventor himself, may duplicate a prior invention and obtain a patent for it. Thus, if an inventor is to obtain a patent on an invention related in any way to an earlier one, it must be clear that the second invention is distinct and substantially different from the first. Not surprisingly, the later invention must satisfy all the requirements of patentability. On the other hand, an inventor may be able to gain different patents for inventions that, although intimately related, are definable as either different categories of subject matter or distinct entities.

It therefore is possible to obtain a patent on a machine and a patent on a composition of matter that is produced by the machine, if both the composition and machine are independently patentable entities. However, if it would be impossible to produce one without inevitably producing the other—if the machine were the only possible way that the composition could be produced—then the two inventions are the same and the double-patenting bar would prevent the grant of two separate patents. *James v. Campbell* (1882). A closely related issue is that of the "best-mode" disclosure requirement, see § 7.5, infra. Obviously, these two doctrines tend to interact. Likewise, the duty of candor, see § 7.8, infra, is involved in any type of illegitimate attempt to expand the patent monopoly and brings with it the issue of patent misuse, see § 8.7, infra. Of course, there are a few legitimate, although limited, statutory ways by which the patent term may be extended. See § 1.2, supra. And, in fact, special bills, of less questionable constitutionality in light of *Eldred v. Ashcroft* (2003), are often enacted by

Congress extending the terms of patents that are about to expire.

The double-patenting bar also involves the requirement of nonobviousness by forbidding the issuance of a second patent that is obvious in light of the first or for an obvious modification of an earlier patent. *In re Zickendraht* (1963). If the modification naturally would follow the development of the earlier patent, the inventor cannot claim a second patent for the later modification without running afoul of both the double-patenting rule and the nonobviousness or anticipation doctrines. Of course, a patentable "improvement" (under section 101) of an earlier invention will not be barred by the double-patenting doctrine. This is true even though technically the earlier patent "dominates" the improvement, that is, even though, until the expiration of the first, the second, "narrower or more specific claim" will by definition infringe the earlier, broader claim. *In re Kaplan* (1986).

## § 6.2   Terminal Disclaimer

The terminal disclaimer allows inventors to incorporate later developments into their original patents without violating the double-patenting bar. 35 U.S.C.A. § 253. Since the purpose of the double-patenting bar is to prevent extensions past the statutory period for any one invention, it does not contravene that purpose if an inventor agrees, in his later patent application, to allow the second patent to expire simultaneously with the first. This is called terminal disclaimer, since the inventor agrees to disclaim any right to have the patent terminate later than the earlier patent. The concept is best understood by realizing that the terminal portion of the later patent is disclaimed by the inventor. Since they both terminate at the same time, the inventor who agrees to a terminal disclaimer can obtain his second patent without violating the policy of the double-patenting rule.

# CHAPTER 7

# THE PATENTING PROCESS

## § 7.1 Overview

Patent Office procedures would amount to little more than mechanical techniques were it not for the fact that various rights can be gained or lost at each procedural stage of the patenting process. Patent rights themselves are defined in terms of many of the procedural steps that take place along the way, for instance in terms of the claims made by the inventor in his patent application. In addition, patent rights may be limited or eliminated at various stages of the process, for instance by acceding to the requests of the patent examiners that certain claims be redefined in a more restrictive manner or even eliminated. Many other rights can be challenged and defeated at other points, for instance by interference proceedings between inventors claiming rights to identical or similar inventions. Therefore, the procedure of obtaining a patent intersects with the substantive rights themselves and to a significant extent helps define those rights.

The application process is crucial. Since the art of claim drafting, for instance, is so highly developed and even stylized, there is a particular significance

to its language and form. The language of the
application itself may have far more effects than
will the language of a complaint, answer, or many
other legal documents. Because of the unique ex
parte nature of the patent prosecution process, with
only the partial "opposition" of the Patent Office
itself, there is a unique duty imposed on the applicant to exercise far more diligence and candor than
normally is expected of an attorney or his client in
relation to a judicial or other legal body. 35 U.S.C.A.
§ 115. Also due to the ex parte nature of the
proceeding, there is a greater tendency to construe
language and interpret actions *against* the inventor,
just as contract interpretation tends to construe
ambiguous language against the party who drafted
it. (The drafting party, it is felt, could have avoided
or changed the language entirely had it so wished.)
Finally, a large body of regulations has been developed by the Patent Office with which the practitioner must be familiar.

## § 7.11   Provisional Patent Applications

A provisional application is an abbreviated application composed only of the specification and whatever drawings that may be necessary to understand
the invention, and it is viable for only twelve
months. The importance of the provisional application, which is not examined, is that a later, nonprovisional application based on the same specification
can use the provisional filing date for domestic
priority purposes and yet the patent term is meas-

ured from the filing date of the nonprovisional. An important disadvantage, however, is that, since the specification cannot be altered, all subsequent claims must come within its express language.The advantage to the inventor is that she can claim an earlier priority date—avoiding, for instance, the danger of statutory bar—without the necessity of committing herself to particular claims until twelve months later and yet have the twenty-year patent term measured from that later date. 35 U.S.C.A. § 111(b). The extra time allows the inventor to engage in acts (like public use or sale) that might otherwise be impermissible, and allows the inventor to garner resources and funds for a full-scale application, as well as information necessary to draft optimum claims.

## § 7.2   The Patentee

The Patent Act is quite specific about who may claim patent rights. Although an invention otherwise may be patentable, if the wrong person claims the patent, all may be lost. The person claiming the patent must be the original and authentic inventor. 35 U.S.C.A. § 111. He cannot be assigned the right to pursue the patent in his own name and neither can he have obtained the patent idea from others. Thus, this doctrine does more than merely prohibit the "stealing" of another's patents. It also prohibits even a permissive use for purposes of obtaining patent protection. If an inventor wishes to give his idea to a friend, employer, or relative, that inventor

must obtain the patent himself and then assign it—
or at least assign the right to obtain the patent *in
his own name.* He cannot delegate the patent to
another, although he can delegate the patenting
process to another. Likewise, if a person finds an
invention developed by someone else for which a
patent has not been sought, he cannot pursue that
patent on his own behalf, even if the real inventor
has no objection. If the patentee is not the real
inventor, he simply is barred from the patent system until the rights are first procured either *by* the
true inventor, or *in the name of* the true inventor.
35 U.S.C.A. §§ 102(f), 111, 116.

It is not uncommon, of course, for parties to be
assigned the rights to the invention by mutual
agreement. Assignees, usually the employers of the
inventor, must have the real inventor file the patent
application; however, if, by the exercise of due diligence, they cannot find the inventor or, alternatively, cannot compel him to comply with their agreement, the statute allows the patent to be granted in
the assignee's name. 35 U.S.C.A. § 118.

## § 7.3 Joint Invention

Joint patent relationships raise problems related
to the inventorship doctrine. The decision about
who actually invented a product or process is critical in a patent system that requires original and
true inventorship by the patentee. If the wrong
party claims inventorship, or if an application includes wrong as well as right parties, the patent
may fail.

The patent system is not so rigid as to bar good-faith applicants who mistakenly include incorrect parties as well as correct parties. Even some bad faith errors can be cured. The 1982 amendment to sections 116 and 256 codified *A.F. Stoddard & Co. v. Dann* (1977) to allow the correction of names in most instances of mistake—for example, nonjoinder (excluding the right parties) when the unnamed inventor acted in good faith, and misjoinder (including the wrong parties) without regard to good faith. But in the latter case, illustrating the limits of agency discretion, see § 7.6, infra, the Patent Office—unlike a reviewing court—cannot correct a bad faith misjoinder. See *Stark v. Advanced Magnetics, Inc.* (1997).

But joint inventorship itself is ambiguous. It is a rare case when two or more individuals start together with the purpose of developing a new product and finish together with a patentable invention. What usually happens is that different parties contribute different things at different times to the process. Some contributions may be more important than others. Some contributions may be noninventive—that is, they may not bear on utility, novelty, or nonobviousness, or they merely may be obvious technical developments or improvements. Still other parties may make general suggestions that do not rise to the level of actually contributing to the inventive process. Finally, one party may contribute to one phase of an invention—the discovery of a new but apparently nonuseful compound—and another party may contribute a remaining, but essential, part of the inventive process—for instance, the new use to which the new compound can be put. In the case of a chemist who discovers a new compound and an engineer who discovers that the compound does something useful, if the entire discovery taken as a whole is not obvious, both the chemist and the engineer may have jointly invented the product.

Whether each individual contributed to the inventive process is as much a legal as a factual determination due to the requirement of inventorship. The test is that each person claiming to be an inventor, must work on the subject matter and make some original contribution to the inventive thought and to the final result of at least one claim. 35 U.S.C.A. § 116. There obviously can be more than one person doing that, but each person must independently qualify under that standard. Mere cooperation in a project will not qualify all parties as inventors. But aggregate effort can result in a joint invention if the test is satisfied. A party cannot claim coinventorship if it does not participate in the conception of at least some phase of the invention. This participation has to involve more than mere testing or refinement. *Burroughs Wellcome Co. v. Barr Laboratories Inc.* (1992).

Apparently, equitable estoppel or laches can bar a claim of coinventorship. A very singular case holds that equitable concerns for the economic well-being of a patent owner can override even the most basic constitutional principles of patent law. *MCV, Inc. v. King–Seeley Thermos Co.* (1989). *MCV* held that laches and estoppel can bar a claim of coinventor-ship, which might have led to invalidity of the patent. The Court said that, *inter alia,* to allow a claimant who inequitably sat on his rights for four years to then claim patent rights tardily could inval-idate the patent or, at least, upset the marketing plans of the patent holder. This case seems to subordinate the public interest and some of the very requirements of patentability, which are rooted in constitutional principles, in favor of private econom-ic concerns. The precedential strength of such an apparently fragile doctrine is uncertain.

## § 7.4 Prosecuting a Patent Application

After a nonprovisional patent application is filed, and an initial examination is made, an application may receive an initial office action of allowance or, more commonly, complete or partial rejection. If rejected, the claims then can be amended and even the specification can be modified, although new matter may not be introduced that would have the effect of increasing the scope of what was originally disclosed by the application. In response to any rejections, the inventor either will contest the rejec-tion by presenting evidence in reply to the sub-stance of the examiner's rejection, or the applicant may add to or modify his claims. Once claims have been twice-rejected, the applicant can appeal to the Patent Office's Board of Appeals. If the applicant is dissatisfied with the Board's decision, he then has the option of either pursuing his appeal to the

United States Court of Appeals for the Federal Circuit or to the United States District Court for the District of Columbia (in which case he preserves his rights to review by the Court of Appeals and, eventually, the Supreme Court).

During the Patent Office's examination a number of informal communications and even interviews may occur between the primary examiner and the applicant. The examiner may provide the applicant with various references unearthed during the examiner's search of the prior art; the examiner also might raise various objections to other facets of the application that the examiner might find deficient. As claims are rejected, the examiner must cite the best references he can find. As the process continues, a record gradually is created, often including statements by both the examiner and the applicant, usually concerning objections raised by the examiner and replies made by the applicant.

The applicant must demonstrate with *particularity* his reasons for differing with the examiner's decision. Whenever he responds to a rejection, if he is amending the application, the applicant must explain exactly how the amendments avoid the problems or clarify difficulties that the examiner has raised. If the examiner has cited references, the applicant must show how any amendments made in response thereto avoid those references. Although after the second rejection there are certain restrictions upon the general scope of further amendments, and the applicant may thus be required to refile (continue) the application, in practice the process of examination, rejection, amendment, and further continued applications can go on for many cycles until eventual acceptance or a stated final rejection. Any time after a second examination on the merits, the Patent Office may declare it final and the applicant has the option of either appealing or refiling still another continuation before the effective date of the final rejection.

Continuations have become controversial. In a substantial number of patent prosecutions, the applicant intentionally engages in continuation practice in order to preserve the ability effectively to expand the scope of the patent over the course of the patent prosecution. Section 120 of the patent Act allows the filing of a continuation patent any time before a patent is actually issued or before an application is abandoned. After a final rejection—or in some cases, even after an allowance—the applicant will file a continuation application, and abandon the original application. This allows the applicant to keep the original priority filing date but file additional or different claims. A continuation normally repeats the original specification but also may include new matter (which will not benefit from the original filing date) in which case it is called a continuation-in-part. In theory, and often in practice, this can go on for the entire life of the patent, where a continuation "child" of the original patent "parent" is always alive, allowing the applicant to file more and more claims that match the developing market for the invention. Patent reform proposals have included limiting the ability to file more than one continuation as of right to avoid these abuses.

During the application process, the Patent Office reaches important and final conclusions regarding novelty, nonobviousness, utility, and satisfaction of the formal statutory requirements, normally without ever hearing from anyone except the applicant himself. Because of (1) the practical expense of litigation and (2) the deference given to agency action (in the case of the Patent Office, the presumption of patent validity, 35 U.S.C.A. § 282), there is great danger that the applicant may gain an unfair advantage over third parties who are not privy to the process. Moreover, although an examiner's *rejection* is reviewed administratively by the Board of Appeals, *allowance* of a claim is not similarly reviewed. It is unlikely that an applicant will ever, even implicitly, challenge an allowance. The Patent Office itself has no power to reverse an allowance of a claim; its only power is to remand a dubious allowance. An examiner's allowance, even though not reviewed administratively, emerges from the Patent Office with the legal strength of the presumption of validity and the practical strength of being able to be fully upset only through litigation. Therefore, it is perhaps the most notable characteristic of the patenting process that the individual patentee is able to gain extraordinarily powerful legal rights through ex parte means. Furthermore, it has been held that rebutting the presumption of validity under 35 U.S.C.A. § 282 only can be accomplished "by proving facts with clear and convincing evidence." *Perkin-Elmer Corp. v. Computervision Corp.* (1984).

## § 7.5 The Specifications and Claims

The two distinctive parts of a patent application are the specification and the claims. The specification is essentially a description of the invention. It might be thought of as instructions on how to perform the invention. The Patent Act requires that the patent application sufficiently disclose the invention *in its best mode* to enable a person skilled in the applicable art to repeat the invention. 35 U.S.C.A. § 112. The specification illustrates the novelty that distinguishes the invention from the prior art, shows how the invention is actually useful, and, at least by implication, shows what it is about the invention that would not have been obvious to one skilled in the prior art. Thus, the specification is not just a convenient way of describing the invention, nor is it merely a nice introductory preamble to the body of the application. Instead, it fulfills an important statutory requirement.

The Act further requires that the specification be an *enabling disclosure*. It cannot be *indefinite*. It must be specific enough to enable a skilled practitioner to accomplish the invention in its best mode. A vague specification, one that requires the skilled practitioner to do the invention by trial and error, is not an enabling disclosure and thus is invalid. In addition, the specification must give a description that is "clear, concise and exact." 35 U.S.C.A.

§ 112. A broad specification, one that is not clear, concise, or exact, is invalid because it would include too much even though the claim primarily defines the scope of the monopoly. An inventor cannot defend overbreadth by arguing that the patent is not susceptible to a particular definition—for instance, by saying a broad interpretation would include nonpatentable subject matter. A broad specification would impermissibly state a general idea or concept, which lies outside the legitimate scope of the Patent Act.

The specification cannot be so inexact as to require a practitioner to experiment until success is reached. It must employ terms that are workable. As long as the specification is workable, experimentation may be necessary to adapt it to a specific and narrow application. A workable specification that requires experimentation for special adaptation, rather than workability, is permissible.

The "best-mode" requirement similarly is flexible. The specification need not give the best mode that is theoretically possible. However, it must be the best mode of which the inventor is aware *at the time of filing the application*. It is therefore a subjective doctrine.

An almost identical requirement to the best-mode doctrine is the "how-to-use" doctrine. The how-to-use requirement, in a sense, is a gloss added to the best-mode requirement; it insures that a disclosure will be truly enabling. The how-to-use requirement typically is fulfilled by specifying times, dosages, or other details with respect to a product. It has been held that, as is true of "best mode," the test of "how-to-use" is a subjective one, requiring only that the applicant reveal what he knows about the invention's utility. *In re Bundy* (1981). The "best-mode" and "how-to-use" tests may be combined to yield the requirement that an applicant must state how-best-to-use the invention.

The claims fulfill the basic functions of the patent laws, protecting the inventor by preventing exploitation while requiring that patentability be clear while the specification demonstrates patentability. The claims define the inventor's rights, and, in light of the specification, illustrate how the invention fulfills the requirements of novelty, utility, and nonobviousness. The claims thus describe the perimeter of the invention, much in the way a claim to a mine lays out the boundaries of what is the miner's and what is either unexplored or already unearthed. Since, under that analogy, the miner's claim both defines what is his *and* serves to prevent trespassing, it should be apparent that the patent application claim serves that same dual purpose: it demonstrates patentability (identifying novelty, utility, and nonobviousness) as well as defining that which would constitute infringement.

The language of the claims should be descriptive and not functional. Functional language describes the invention's effect on other things but fails to describe the invention itself. For instance, to claim a novel element, the claim must specify something about the invention that does not appear in the prior art. But if a claim simply states a new function or property, there is nothing new being claimed; it may well be a thing that is already in the prior art. If all that is claimed is a new function or property of something already in the prior art, such a claim would be barred by the rule prohibiting patents on newly discovered properties of old elements.

Thus patentability will rise or fall upon the claims. Proof of infringement, likewise, will depend upon the claims since the claims define the limits of the invention. Typically, claims are written in multiple format so that they become progressively narrower. Although the applicant optimistically hopes to have the broadest claim accepted by the Patent Office, by including narrower claims as well, he can increase the chances of having, at some point, one or more claims accepted.

## § 7.6   The Limits of Agency Discretion

The Patent Office is an administrative agency; patent practice is essentially part of administrative law. Thus, because of the constitutional and statutory sources of patent law, and the fact that the law is applied in the first instance within the confines of administrative practice, the statute and regulations set fairly literal limits on the exercise of agency discretion. There is a real constraint on how far administrative *or* judicial construction can stretch the plain meaning of statutory language.

For instance, until recently, the rule that only the actual inventor can sign a patent application was relatively fixed. Patent rights have been denied even in cases involving innocent error when the wrong party signed the application. In one case involving a good faith error, the true inventor had attempted diligently to correct the application but the Patent Office initially barred the inventor's application anyway. Even the court that reversed the Patent Office recognized that the office had no choice but to reject the erroneous application, saying the Office, "cannot be expected" to do otherwise. *A.F. Stoddard & Co. v. Dann* (1977). *Stoddard* has since been codified by an amendment to section 116 that also now authorizes the correction of innocently erroneous attributions of inventorship. But, as discussed earlier, see § 7.3, supra, the statute still limits the PTO's discretion—but not that of a reviewing court—to good faith misattributions.

Nevertheless, *Stoddard* reaffirms the general doctrine that normally an inventor is at the mercy of the statutory language. At least until an applicant reaches the judicial arena, the statute will be construed strictly—and it should be, holds *Stoddard*. In addition to renewed support for strict statutory construction, *Stoddard* also demonstrates the importance of patent law's constitutional status. With the Constitution's goal of protecting the rights of inventors as its guiding principle, the court claimed it could reverse a rejection that might appear to bar a rightful inventor from patent protection. It is unlikely, however, that a potentially limitless attack on the plain wording of the Act will be successful often enough to enlarge significantly the narrow confines in which the Patent Office operates.

## § 7.7  Claims Drafting

Claims drafting is a technical art partly due to the rather severe consequences the language of the claims can have. Claim interpretation (and thus drafting) decides the inventor's rights and the infringer's liability.

The artful drafting of claims must accomplish two conflicting goals. The language of the claims must be definite and precise so that it adequately describes the perimeters of the invention. The claims also must be narrow enough so that they do not extend beyond the scope of the specification. They must not be so broad as to violate the statutory command to describe with specificity. They should not be so narrow, however, that they give up what is legitimately the property of the inventor. Since the language of the claim is drafted by the inventor, or by her agents, she is bound by the language chosen. Thus, the claims and their language are strictly construed. The specification is the dictionary to which the courts refer when the language of the claim is questioned. The claim is thus read in light of the specification so that the same word is given the same meaning throughout the application.

As the claims or elements in any one or more claims increase, the narrower the patent effectively becomes, since all of those elements or claims must be satisfied in order to prove infringement. Therefore, as the claims or elements increase, in effect, the less the inventor is defining as his discovery. "[I]n a patent claim, more means less." *Jamesbury Corp. v. Litton Industrial Products, Inc.* (1978).

There are three basic parts of the typical claim—the *preamble,* the *transition,* and the *body.* The preamble generically defines the invention (such as a door or closing device or some other such basic definition). It defines in generic terms either an essential limiting element (a wheel, a door, a plug, or something else that states, essentially, how far the patent goes) or an intended use or the function or environment of the patent (a device to seal airtight, to restrict access, to create a series of compartments, or something comparable). The transition defines how the preamble and body relate to one another. It typically uses the words "comprising" (an "open" transition since it does not limit the preamble merely to what follows) or "consisting" (a "closed" transition since the preamble is then limited to exactly what follows and no more) or similar language. The last part is the body, which states how the invention is limited to certain elements or characteristics. An example of the simplest type of claim might be: "A flat plate [the preamble] consisting of [a closed transition] a wooden surface with a knob attached [the body]."

Claims may be either independent or dependent. If dependent, each claim becomes progressively narrower than the preceding one. Independent claims, of course, stand on their own. Thus, the first claim might state that the invention is a closing device comprised of a flat surface and a mechanism for maintaining constant position. The second claim might, if dependent, limit that further, stating that the invention is what was stated in claim 1, but identifying that the closing device is a latch. The next dependent claim might further limit claim 1 by identifying that the flat surface extends past the contours of the container to be enclosed. This narrowing process prevents the invention from "reading on," or infringing upon the elements of prior art. This process can go on and on, each time limiting the claims further, and thus giving up a broader claim to invention and, of course, to future claims for infringement, but likewise, perhaps, being more patentable and thus more acceptable to the Patent Office.

Although claims must be definite, so-called means-plus-function claims are allowed. This permits an inventor to state the function of a particular element generally, without specifying it further, instead using the general term "means." An inventor of an aeronautical device might use in her claim, therefore, the language "means generating thrust" so that her claim would cover all aircraft engine systems whether using propellers, turbines, or other means of propulsion. The danger of following this practice is that the claim becomes unbounded by any particular application and potentially approaches the dimensions of an idea which is, of course, forbidden in patent law. The statute therefore requires that such a means-plus-function claim be limited to the "corresponding structure, materi-al, or acts described in the specification and equiva-lents thereto." 35 U.S.C.A. § 112, ¶ 6.

## § 7.8   The Duty of Candor

The patent process is relatively unique because it involves the grant of a monopoly by an administra-tive agency to a typically unopposed party at a time prior to that at which other parties who might wish to contest the grant have the opportunity to be heard. This would be less significant if other parties could freely thereafter contest the issuance of the patent. But for two reasons this is not the case. First, there are the practical difficulties of expensive complex patent litigation; to tell a party that a patent can be contested judicially is far more easily said than done. Second, it is a general principle of administrative law that deference is given to agency decisions. To review all agency actions in a plenary fashion would make the agency useless; therefore, some level of deference is appropriate. In patent law, that deference takes the form of the presump-tion of patent validity. 35 U.S.C.A. § 282. See § 7.4, supra. The Supreme Court has held that reviewing courts, specifically the Federal Circuit, are to give PTO decisions the greater deference to which agen-cies are entitled compared to the lesser deference a district court decision merits. *Dickinson v. Zurko* (1999). See § 7.10, infra.

In response to these two factors, which recognize the practical influence that the initial Patent Office decision has in finally determining most patent issues both before and even after judicial review, and concomitantly, the unique position an applicant has to influence or affect the initial decision, a duty of candor is imposed upon the applicant. Since the patent process is ex parte and because that process will inure to the benefit of the applicant, this duty of candor is meant to balance the unfairness that otherwise would occur if the applicant were to have the benefits of an ex parte process without any corresponding accountability.

A breach of the duty can result in the striking of an application or in the invalidation of a patent; it can defeat an otherwise valid claim of infringement; it even can result in a patent being issued to a rival party in an interference proceeding despite priority or other merit lying in the party who violated the duty. The duty of candor is thus enforced with the threat of invalidity. In addition, if the positive duty of candor is breached to the extent of an actual fraud, attorney's fees may be awarded against the defaulting party in a later lawsuit. Attorney's fees always are available in patent litigation if it involves an "exceptional" case. 35 U.S.C.A. § 285. And it has been held that, among other things, an exceptional case may be one involving a breach of the duty of candor. *Pickering v. Holman* (1972).

Substantively, the duty of candor requires that the applicant inform the Patent Office of all material information of which the inventor *actually* is aware. Although something more than simple negligence therefore is needed, something less than conscious fraud is required to constitute a breach of the duty of candor. Gross negligence may be enough. *Jaskiewicz v. Mossinghoff* (1987). The duty of candor is violated when the applicant, or someone whose conduct is chargeable to the applicant, intentionally, or perhaps only with gross negligence, fails to disclose material prior art knowing of, or perhaps only being grossly negligent about, its materiality. *Hoffman-La Roche, Inc. v. Lemmon Co.* (1990).

A person is subject to the duty of candor only to the extent of his actual participation in the patenting process. The duty thus varies according to the person's role. A different duty might be imposed upon a person who is relatively passive during the process with respect to a prior art reference, for example, than upon his attorney who may be consciously aware of some pertinent information unearthed during the patent prosecution process. However, it is not unusual for the sins of the attorney to be visited upon the client. The misconduct of foreign attorneys, in fact, has been visited upon an applicant's domestic attorneys despite the fact that the domestic attorneys were not aware of the fraud. *Gemveto Jewelry Co. v. Lambert Brothers, Inc.* (1982).

An applicant and his agents thus have the affirmative duty to disclose *material* information; it is not enough to avoid actively misleading the Patent Office. Information is material if "there is a substantial likelihood that a reasonable examiner would consider it important." *Digital Equip. Corp. v. Diamond* (1981), citing 37 C.F.R. § 1.56 (PTO

Rule 56). Thus, an applicant who knows of information (or who perhaps only, through calculated recklessness, is ignorant of such information) bearing upon patentability that is quite likely to be considered *important* by an examiner, *even if it is not determinative,* has the duty of disclosing the information. This objective standard with respect to materiality, in contrast to the relatively subjective standard of state of mind, potentially is quite harsh. Because the applicant may be held in breach merely for the failure to so disclose and because the material information need only be important, the potential impact of the duty of candor is sizeable.

## § 7.81   Publication of Patent Applications

In an effort to harmonize United States patent law with international practice, Congress enacted provisions which call for publication of a patent application eighteen months after filing, even before any patent is granted. 35 U.S.C.A. § 122. Although on the face of it this appears to alter radically traditional patent principles (under which an inventor always had the ability to keep her invention confidential if the application was either rejected or withdrawn), it actually has limited import. The publication requirement is only binding on those applications that are filed in other countries or under treaties that also impose publication after eighteen months. Thus, an inventor can avoid this domestic publication, if he wishes, by refraining from filing elsewhere. And, of course, an inventor who chooses to file elsewhere under such circumstances has already accepted the inevitability of publication.

## § 7.9 Reissue and Reexamination

Reissue patents are available to cure defects caused by various errors in the original patent. 35 U.S.C.A. § 251. For instance, the Patent Act requires that all joint inventors be named in the application. Thus it is error to omit any inventor. Likewise, it is error to include as a joint inventor one who was not. In such cases, an application for reissue is available to cure the defects in the original patent documents. The reissued patent will date back to the original patent and therefore, with one exception, the reissued patent must be identical to the original except for the correction of errors. The exception applies to those reissues requested within two years of the original, in which event a reissued patent may be broader with respect to its claims.

The possibility of a reissue is an attractive opportunity to a patentee, suddenly aware, perhaps through an infringement suit or perhaps before anyone even challenges the patent, of prior art references or other facts previously not revealed or other shortcomings in the patent. The attraction of a reissued patent is that it preserves the statutory presumption of validity of section 282. Ordinarily, if a challenger can point to serious defects in a patent, the challenger may defeat the presumption and attack the patent frontally. A reissued patent, however, comes rearmed with the presumption because it has been reexamined in light of the newly discovered information. The reissued patent is treated as if the new information had been present at the original examination so long as the original defect was not a product of intentionally deceptive conduct. The exception for intentionally deceptive conduct is very important because it prevents patentees from attempting to "sandbag" the Patent Office by breaching the duty of candor and then awaiting future developments, relying on the availability of reissue to immunize them from their inequitable conduct. Reissue is not available to cure such breaches. *Digital Equip. Corp. v. Diamond* (1981).

Under a corollary to the exhaustion of remedies doctrine of administrative law, courts may stay an infringement suit while a reissue is processed. *Fas–Line Sales & Rentals, Inc. v. E–Z Lay Pipe Corp.* (1979). Some courts, however, have held that it would be fruitless to wait for a reissue, especially when the court is about to consider the same facts being presented to the Patent Office. Considering the time already invested, a stay for reissue may serve no purpose when a court effectively can examine the patent in the same or even less time as the Office. See *Starlight Assocs. v. Berkey–Colortran, Inc.* (1978).

Reexamination is a process by which any third-party can request that the PTO conduct another, although limited, examination of a subsisting patent. 35 U.S.C.A. §§ 301 *et seq.* Although the statute does not command that the process be *ex parte,* the Office regulations create an essentially ex parte procedure, despite the fact that the process is initiated by a third party.

The scope of a reexamination is limited to only prior patents and publications. Thus, the PTO does not conduct a full-scale prior art search as it does in the initial patent examination process. Matters of fraud or breach of the duty of candor that could totally invalidate a patent are not addressed by a reexamination proceeding. A patentee who wishes these matters to be considered so as to protect the patent from later attack on those grounds still must resort to a reissue proceeding to gain protection.

## § 7.10   Judicial Review

The creation of the United States Court of Appeals for the Federal Circuit has significantly changed judicial review of litigation involving issues of patent law. The Federal Circuit also has assumed the appellate jurisdiction of the Court of Customs and Patent Appeals, which was abolished by the 1982 legislation establishing the Federal Circuit.

The existence of the Federal Circuit has the following two major effects. It substantially changes the appellate litigation of any lawsuits involving issues of patent law. It also changes the mechanics of review of decisions of the Patent Office Board of Appeals. First, any appeals of district court decisions in which jurisdiction is based upon patent law now automatically go to the Federal Circuit instead of, as was the case prior to October 1, 1982, to the various courts of appeal that ordinarily would hear appeals from the district courts within their respective circuits. Second, with the demise of the Court of Customs and Patent Appeals, an appeal from the Board of Appeals of the Patent Office now goes to the Federal Circuit instead of to the Court of Customs and Patent Appeals, although provisions still exist to proceed by way of original civil suit in district courts. The scope of review exercised by the Federal Circuit over PTO findings of fact is the more deferential administrative agency standard mandated by the Administrative Procedure Act. It allows reversal when there is a lack of "substantial evidence" (including findings that are "arbitrary, capricious, [or] an abuse of discretion") rather than the stricter "clearly erroneous" standard mandated by Federal Rule 52(a) applicable to district court findings. *Dickinson v. Zurko* (1999).

This does not mean, however, that every case that may involve patent issues will be appealable to the Federal Circuit, because the Act speaks in terms of cases in which "the jurisdiction of that court was *based,* in whole or in part," on the Patent Act. 28 U.S.C.A. § 1295(a)(1) (emphasis supplied). Thus, cases in which patent issues may be only collaterally raised and in which jurisdiction is based wholly upon other statutes still may be appealable to the other circuit courts.

What centralizing review in the Federal Circuit is designed to achieve, however, is more consistency and coherence in patent law. Instead of having each

different court of appeals applying its own construction of the patent laws, as well as an additional view
emanating from a specialty court, the former Court
of Customs and Patent Appeals, we now have only
one. In addition, the Supreme Court no longer is
faced with the same kind of pressures to decide
issues formerly raised by intercircuit differences on
patent matters.

Instead of appealing a Patent Office Board of
Appeals' decision, applicants still have the option of
going to the District Court for the District of Columbia to seek an order requiring the Patent Office
to issue a patent that has been denied. Likewise,
parties to an interference also may still choose
between the option of appealing to the Federal
Circuit, formerly to the Court of Customs and Patent Appeals, or of litigating the issues substantially
*de novo* in any district court in which venue is
proper, the Patent Office not being a necessary
party. The major change is that appeals from all of
those district court decisions now proceed to the
Federal Circuit instead of, as was formerly the case,
to the otherwise appropriate circuit courts.

Thus, all patent cases arising in the district
courts, in which jurisdiction is founded upon the
Patent Act, whether they are, for instance, infringe-
ment cases between private parties or, instead,
cases arising out of proceedings in the Patent Office
Board of Appeals, now go on appeal to the Federal
Circuit. Similarly, all true appeals from the Patent
Office Board of Appeals go to the Federal Circuit.

# CHAPTER 8

# INFRINGEMENT

## § 8.1 Overview

A determination of patent infringement involves a two-step process. First, the claims are analyzed by studying all of the relevant patent documents, to find what are the claims' patentable advances over the prior art. Second, the claims must be "read on" the accused device or process. This merely means that the device or process is examined to see if it is substantially described by the claims; in other words, the claims are tested to see whether they describe the accused infringement. With respect to a combination patent, since it is only the combination of elements that constitutes the patent, a claim of infringement can succeed only if each element is substantially duplicated. The critical test in any infringement suit, applying the doctrine of equivalents, is whether the allegedly infringing device performs substantially the same function in substantially the same way to obtain substantially the same result as the patented product or process. *Warner-Jenkinson Co. v. Hilton Davis Chem. Co.* (1997).

## § 8.2  File Wrapper, or Prosecution History, Estoppel

Because of the ex parte nature of the patenting process and also because of the fact that the inventor drafts the specifications and claims himself, the inventor is bound by the decisions made during the prosecution of the patent application. The file wrapper is very simply the entire history of the inventor's prosecution of the application before the Patent Office, complete with any amendments, statements, or replies. This becomes critical when an inventor agrees to certain changes recommended by the examiner during the patenting process. The examiner may cite a reference to prior art and propose to reject a claim on that basis. The inventor may reply by a statement narrowing the claim to avoid that prior art or the obviousness which that reference may demonstrate. The correspondence with the applicant narrowing the claim to avoid the examiner's objection becomes part of the file wrapper. Later, in an infringement action, the inventor will not be allowed to state that the claim was meant to be broader than that which the narrowing process produced.

The inventor cannot later complain that the examiner's objections were wrong. The inventor is the captain of the patent ship, so to speak. Since the inventor is the draftsman of the claim and is in charge of the prosecution of the application, he will be bound by any statements made to the Patent Office, even if he agreed to changes about which the examiner was wrong. Since the proper course for an aggrieved applicant who disputes an examiner's position is to appeal the rejection, a later complaint that an agreement to narrow a claim was because of an erroneous rejection by the examiner will not be allowed. The inventor is estopped by the file wrapper, whether right or wrong. There is an essential inconsistency between the doctrine of file wrapper estoppel, and the doctrine of equivalents, an inconsistency that has been addressed, and partially resolved, by the Supreme Court in *Festo Corp. v. Shoketsu Kinzoku Kogyo KabuShiki Co.* (2002). See § 8.3, infra.

## § 8.3 Claim Interpretation—Differentiation, Literality, and Equivalence

The inventor is subject to rules of claim interpretation that are similar to principles of statutory construction. The doctrine of *claim differentiation,* for instance, assumes that different claims apply to different devices or processes. Claim interpretations that tend to make one or more claims surplusage and merely repetitive of other claims are avoided. On the other hand, the rule of claim differentiation is really a guide or presumption, not a hard-and-fast rule, and the plain language of a claim that effectively duplicates another claim will not be contorted to read differently than it does. Claim construction is a matter of law, and it is up to the judge to determine the meaning of each and every word in the claims; this is so even though the Seventh Amendment guarantees a jury trial for patent infringement actions. *Markman v. Westview Instruments, Inc.* (1996). In construing the meaning of words in a claim, when there is a choice, the narrower meaning of a word in a claim controls. *Athletic Alternatives, Inc. v. Prince Mfg., Inc.* (1996).

Two further doctrines, that of *literal overlap* and that of *equivalents,* respectively narrow and broaden patent claims and thereby (but inversely) the possibilities of infringement. First, literal overlap of a claim over an accused structure requires that, for infringement, each and every element of the claim be found in the alleged infringement. The requirement of literal overlap presumes that each and every element of a claim is material and essential.

The doctrine of *equivalents* basically performs the opposite function of the literal-overlap doctrine. The doctrine of equivalents dispenses with any requirement of literality (that the claim must "literally" read on the accused devise or process) and holds that each element of an invention need not be identically present in the accused infringement. Instead of absolute identity, all that is required is a substantial equivalent. Something is substantially equivalent if the skilled practitioner would know of the *practical interchangeability* of the accused infringement's elements with those specifically identified in the patent specification. The doctrine of equivalents is limited, however, by the doctrine of file wrapper estoppel. To the extent that an inventor has limited his invention in a particular way in the proceedings before the Patent Office, he will not be allowed later to broaden the claims through the doctrine of equivalents if that broadening will have the effect of nullifying the limitations to which the inventor agreed before the examiner. In fact, the Supreme Court has held that any kind of narrowing amendment related to patentability, and not just those made to overcome prior art, will presumptively bar the doctrine of equivalents. The patentee, however, can avoid this bar by showing that an amendment did not really cede claim to the particular equivalent because, for example, it was unforeseeable at the time of the amendment. *Festo*.

The doctrine of equivalents is meant to discount the presence of minor changes and substitutions in the accused infringement. It prevents the elevation of form over substance that otherwise might allow a canny infringer to avoid the exact duplication of an invention while still capitalizing upon the work of the inventor. But the Supreme Court has cautioned that the doctrine is to be confined to finding that each and every element of a claim, or its equivalent, is found in the alleged infringement. It is error to apply the doctrine to the invention as a whole (that is, finding that the invention as a whole performs substantially the same function, in substantially the same way, to achieve substantially the same result). In addition, this is not the same as the slightly different doctrine of equivalents used to interpret the scope of a means-plus-function claim. In means-plus-function claims, what the Supreme Court has characterized as a "limiting" doctrine of equivalents prevents those claims from having unlimited scope (that is, limiting means-plus-function claims to only equivalents of what appears in the specification). *Warner-Jenkinson Co. v. Hilton Davis Chem. Co.* (1997). See § 7.7, *supra*.

It should be noted that the doctrine of equivalents will have varying breadth depending upon the patent. A pioneer patent will have greater breadth than a much later improvement because of the very nature of the policies underlying patent law. The essence of a pioneer invention is that it discovers a very large field for which the inventor is fairly rewarded with a relatively broad patent. However, the inventor of a much later and perhaps less important improvement has not discovered a large field at all and to a great extent her discovery really sits on the shoulders of earlier pioneer inventors. She therefore is rewarded with a commensurately smaller field to monopolize and the range of equivalents thus shrinks.

## § 8.4   The Patent Rights

A patentee has the *exclusive* right to *make, use, offer to sell*, or *sell* the invention. 35 U.S.C.A. § 154. But see § 1.2, supra. The right includes the right to *refrain* from making, using, offering to sell, or selling the invention. In many foreign countries, the inventor is obliged to "work" the patent and if he does not do so, he can be required to grant a compulsory license to others who wish to exploit the invention. But an American patentee is under no such duty, although there are antitrust implications involved in the failure to work a patent. The owner of a patent has no duty to exploit the invention and has the right to exclude all others from using, making, offering to sell, or selling it, although the Supreme Court has recently made this right somewhat less apparently absolute. See supra, § 1.2.

The term of a United States patent is twenty years from the application filing date and is nonrenewable. 35 U.S.C.A. § 154. At the expiration of the term, the invention automatically is dedicated to the public and everyone then has the right to make, use, offer to sell, or sell the invention. An important result of this is that, because of the strong policy in favor of strict observation of the twenty-year period, amendments of patents, reissues, and other modifications of patent applications are retroactively limited so as to date back to the original patent. The monopoly period does not begin to run until the actual issuance of the patent. Therefore, competitors are free to use, make, offer to sell, or sell an invention for which a patent application has been filed, until the actual grant. The words "patent pending" on an article give no protection at all during the period prior to the grant. On the other hand, some courts have rather jealously guarded the interests of the inventor in the last portion of an expiring patent's term, holding that even gearing up for production may infringe the imminently expiring patent if what is done amounts to testing the completed though unassembled patented device. *Paper Converting Machine Co. v. Magna–Graphics Corp.* (1984). And Congress, similarly, has defined infringement to include even the filing of certain FDA applications for drugs still under patent. 35 U.S.C.A. § 271(e)(2).

## § 8.5   Direct, Indirect, and Contributory Infringement

Anyone who, without permission, makes, uses, or offers to sell, or sells the patented invention is a *direct* infringer of the patent. If a person actively encourages another to make, use, offer to sell, or sell the invention without permission, the person who induces is liable for *indirect* infringement. Finally, *contributory* infringement can be committed by knowingly offering for sale, selling or supplying a nonstaple item for which the only or predominant use is in connection with a patented invention.

Direct infringement can be committed innocently. The direct infringer need have no knowledge of the patent. The exclusive right granted to the patent owner does not allow for any defense based on good faith or ignorance. On the other hand, a patent owner is required to mark a product invention with notice of the patent or give actual notice to an infringer, if the owner is to recover money damages. However, that requirement is subject to the exception that a patent owner is not prejudiced by the fact that *another* infringer has produced the item without notice of the patent even though a later, second infringer otherwise could legitimately claim that he copied an unmarked product. A patent owner is not expected to have infringing items marked with notice and thus is not required to forego monetary relief in a situation in which a second infringer proceeds to replicate the first unmarked infringement. *Wine Railway Appliance Co. v. Enterprise Railway Equip. Co.* (1936).

Even if a seller does not commit direct infringement, if he asks or induces another to do so, or if he sells a product with advertising or instructions about an infringing use, and intends to cause the buyer to make, use, offer to sell, or sell a patented invention, he may be liable for inducing another to infringe as an indirect infringer. *Fromberg, Inc. v. Thornhill* (1963).

Contributory infringement can occur only in connection with a *sale* of a component knowing it to be specially made or adapted for use in a patented device or process and the component is not a staple article suitable for some substantial noninfringing use. Thus, a contributory infringer can be liable for infringement even though what he has sold is completely in the public domain and has no patent protection itself. It has the practical effect of extending the patent to items that are not patented and presents the possibility of a sanctioned monopoly over the unpatentable. Contributory infringement effectively allows the patent system to extend to ineligible subject matter. Of course, this presents serious constitutional questions.

Although good faith or ignorance is no defense for direct infringement, that is not the case with contributory infringement. Thus, it is a defense for an accused contributory infringer to show that he had no knowledge that the goods were substantially suitable only for infringement. Contributory infringement, however, is founded upon the sale of items for which there is no other substantial use other than in the patented invention. It therefore is unlikely that, at least with respect to anything but the simplest of inventions, a seller could market such items without knowledge that there was an infringement occurring. The statute redundantly, in fact in three ways, states the requirement that there be no substantial noninfringing uses for the suspect items by requiring that the article be "especially made or adapted," "not a staple or commodity," and not "suitable for substantial noninfringing use." 35 U.S.C.A. § 271(c). This overemphasis on the statutory requirement that contributory infringement must involve the sale of material the virtually sole use for which is in the patented invention, makes it unlikely that anyone but an indirect infringer will be brought within its reach. In fact, contributory infringement is little more than an evidentiary device to dispose of evidence of "active inducement," in proving indirect infringement.

However, it still is possible for an accused contributory infringer to plead lack of knowledge successfully. This would occur in a claim of contributory infringement through an ultimate direct but innocent infringer. In *Aro Mfg. Co. v. Convertible Top Replacement Co.* (1964), buyers of Ford autos did not know that Ford had not entered into an effective license agreement with the patent holder on its convertible tops. Thus, each buyer of those

Ford autos was a direct, *though innocent,* infringer.
Sale of later convertible tops to the Ford owners
arguably caused the Ford owners to continue the
direct infringement. But since the manufacturers of
the replacement tops did not *know* of the lack of a
license and of the resulting direct innocent infringement, they did not know of the infringement. Since
the statute requires that contributory infringement
be "knowing," 35 U.S.C.A. § 271(c), they were
therefore not liable. Once a seller is notified of
infringing uses, however, as happened later in *Aro,*
the patent owner then can successfully sue the
seller for all *later* contributory infringements. *Aro*
distinguished, however, between the knowledge requirement for a *contributory* infringer and the absence of any knowledge requirement for a *direct*
infringer. *Aro* also held that if the contributory
infringer knows of the infringement, it does not
matter if the direct infringer to whom the materials
are sold has no knowledge of the infringement.

Infringement only occurs if one of the patentee's
four exclusive rights is exercised—using, making,
offering to sell, or selling—and it is only the patented device or process that can be infringed, not a
smaller unpatented part of it. For instance, with
respect to a combination patent, making only one
part of the invention, or even many parts short of
completion, does not constitute direct infringement.
But an accused infringer may manufacture a number of elements of a patent, selling them with the
expectation that the buyer will then infringe by
supplying the last element. The seller thereby may
become an indirect or contributory infringer.

An effort to avoid the reach of the patent laws by
duplicating only some of a combination patent

sometimes may be successful, however. When the potential infringer manufactures all but the last element, that probably constitutes indirect infringement, since it is done with the intent that the buyer will infringe and in fact does induce infringement. If the indirect infringement claim fails, contributory infringement may be found, depending on the characteristics of the various elements. If the elements are staple items with substantial noninfringing uses, such as rivets, bearings, nuts, bolts, and the like, there may be no contributory infringement. Staples with substantial noninfringing uses specifically are excepted from the statute. But, staple or not, if such a person intentionally does encourage and know of the intended use, that person might be actively inducing infringement.

Recent statutory revisions have seriously undermined the previously accepted hornbook law that the Patent Act has no extraterritorial effect. *Deepsouth Packing Co. v. Laitram Corp.* (1972), which held that there is no infringement even if all the parts of a combination patent are manufactured domestically if the final construction occurs abroad, has been statutorily rejected. Now, under 35 U.S.C.A. § 271(f)(1), one who supplies the components of a combination patent that are combined abroad is an infringer, even though the actual foreign acts may not themselves be infringing. In *Microsoft v. AT&T Corp.* (2007), the Court held that a master copy of software that is then later copied and installed into computers abroad does not constitute the "component" contemplated by

§ 271(f). The Court reaffirmed the general principle that patent law has no extraterritorial reach absent express legislative exception, saying it would not expansively interpret the statute absent such an express exception to the general principle. Furthermore, the importation of an unpatented product that was fabricated abroad through a process patented here, even though the process may not be patented abroad, is an infringement under section 271(g). Nevertheless, the Federal Circuit has reaffirmed the essential vitality of *Deepsouth* by holding that a method or use patent can be infringed only if every step of the method occurs within the United States. On the other hand, a product patent can be infringed even if one part of the product is located abroad, as long as the product or system "as a whole" is used here. *NTP, Inc. v. Research in Motion, Ltd.* (2005).

## § 8.6  Repair and Reconstruction

Although the patent owner possesses the exclusive right to use, make, offer to sell, or sell the patented invention, that right terminates immediately upon sale of the invention. Thus, once a patented item is sold, the buyer has complete freedom to resell the device or to use it as extensively as he wishes. In other words, the first sale "exhausts" the patent rights. But the right that is exhausted only relates to the particular article sold. In time, all things wear out, and a difficult issue arises with respect to the buyer's efforts to restore a worn invention.

The distinction is between permissible *repair* and forbidden *reconstruction*. The question is whether the buyer has the right to restore the invention or whether the efforts constitute a new "making" of the item and not just the legitimate use of a sold item to which he has title. Repair rights inhere in the purchase of a patented invention. However, reconstruction—the making of a new device—is forbidden because it constitutes infringement of the exclusive right to make the invention anew. *Cinema Patents Co. v. Craft Film Laboratories, Inc.* (1932).

The right to use, however, which clearly accompanies the purchase of a patented product, carries with it the right to repair. A number of factual issues commonly determine the question as to what is permissible repair. Among these are the fractional cost of the replaced item compared to the whole device and the qualitative character of the item, including whether it is so perishable as to imply that it is meant to be replaced as a normal item of repair. From that perspective, the repair-reconstruction dichotomy involves what only can be termed consumer expectations. But the repair-reconstruction dichotomy is also one of law. It has been held as a matter of law that the replacement of a worn out part that is an essential element is permissible repair. This is true, at least, when one part of a patented combination has a shorter life than the whole. It has been said that repair of the whole by replacement of the part is merely an attempt to give appropriate life to a premature death. The test is not, however, whether an owner would think repair was minor or major. Instead, the test is whether the owner actually is reconstructing the device as to "in fact make a new article." *Aro Mfg. Co. v. Convertible Top Replacement Co.* (1961), quoting *United States v. Aluminum Co. of America* (1945).

Thus, it is erroneous to frame the issue in terms of the "essentialness," "keyness" or "spentness" of any one element. It may be true that one element of a patented invention is more distinctive, characteristic, or even factually essential. But the theory of a combination patent is that no single element deserves protection. Considering the combination as a whole, the test is this: the repair of any one element cannot infringe unless in fact the invention has been *rebuilt* or *made anew*. Although there is no right to *rebuild* an invention, there is always, as a matter of law, the right to *repair* it. *Dana Corp. v. American Precision Co.* (1987).

## § 8.7  Infringement  Defenses—Misuse  and Experimental Use

"Misuse" means that the patent owner has overreached and tried to do more than legitimately is authorized by the patent monopoly. This can involve more than just patent law, for the abuse of a legal monopoly easily can become a forbidden monopoly prohibited by the antitrust laws. But somewhere between legitimate use and antitrust violation lies a wide range of acts that, although not so gross as to constitute antitrust violations, are nevertheless abuses of the patent right for which the penalty is the temporary loss of the patent privilege.

Until a patentee "purges" himself of the misuse, he cannot enforce the patent. Misuse assumes infringement but immunizes it. It bars relief because of the patentee's culpable conduct.

The misuse doctrine intersects with contributory infringement. Misuse commonly concerns the attempt by the owner of a patent to prevent the sale by others of an unpatented item whose sole substantial use is in his invention. The owner seeks to dominate the sale of the nonstaple by claiming rival sellers are contributory infringers. The defendants then claim that plaintiff's attempt to sell the nonstaple exclusively is a misuse of the patent monopoly. They claim the attempt is effectively one to extend a patent over the unpatented item, which at first seems untenable and, perhaps, a misuse. However, if the contributory infringement section is to be given any effect, if the owner is to have any protection against contributory infringements, it is difficult to avoid this result. Contributory infringement, as a result of its statutory definition, inevitably carries with it the guarantee of collision with the misuse doctrine.

Misuse is the "attempt to 'extend the patent' and thus monopolize the market for the unpatented component." *Rohm & Haas Co. v. Dawson Chem. Co.* (1979). Under the doctrine of *Mercoid Corp. v. Mid–Continent Investment Co.* (1944), the very possibility of a legitimate extension of a patent over unpatented elements was doubtful. A broad reading of *Mercoid* would disallow even a contributory infringement suit for the sale of nonstaple items whose *only* use was in the patented invention. That broad reading of *Mercoid* then would prohibit as misuse any attempt to "tie" the sale of nonpatented items with the patent itself. *Mercoid* thus effectively destroyed most contributory infringement claims.

Because of the perceived harshness of the *Mercoid* doctrine, Congress enacted section 271, which states that an infringer cannot plead the defense of misuse if all that the patentee has done is that which, if done by someone else, would constitute contributory infringement. Thus, although under *Mercoid* it might have been misuse to tie the sale of a patent to a nonstaple element whose only or substantially only use was with the patent, that is now not so because that act (the sale of the nonstaple), if done by someone else, would constitute contributory infringement. A patent owner is now free to do that which would be contributory infringement by another. Under section 271 it is not misuse. *Rohm & Haas Co. v. Dawson Chem. Co.,* supra.

Under *Rohm & Haas,* a patent owner is now free, given section 271, to tie sales to nonstaples. The defendant in *Rohm & Haas* argued that section 271 only codified the result of *Mercoid.* Under the defendant's view, contributory infringement had all but been abolished by *Mercoid* and, therefore the defense of section 271, keyed in as it was to contributory infringement, was very limited indeed. However, the court held that section 271 rejected the *Mercoid* doctrine. The court also held, however, that misuse was still a possible defense, but only if a patent owner tied the sale of *staples* to his patent. Of course, by definition, the sale of staples never can qualify as contributory infringement if done by another and therefore is not immunized by section 271. Thus, for instance, if the plaintiff had refused to sell its unpatented chemical, which was useful *only* in connection with its patented process, unless buyers also purchased, besides the process, various other unpatented chemicals which had many different uses unconnected with the process, that would have constituted misuse. Tying the sale of the process to the chemical wasn't misuse, because, having no noninfringing use, it was not a staple. But tying the sale to other, staple, chemicals, is prohibited misuse.

Therefore, a patent owner legitimately can sue for contributory infringement if a seller is vending a nonstaple item whose only substantial use is in connection with the patented device. The patent owner will be liable for misuse in this context only if he refuses to license the patented process except upon agreement to purchase items which have other uses, in other words, staple items.

The experimental use exception, to the extent that it exists, allows an accused to avoid liability by showing that he was using or making the invention only for purely experimental reasons. However, the defense is so extremely limited that it is not clear that it applies to any meaningful activity: any commercial use and, in fact, any use within the business of the accused, even if not commercial or profitable in nature, cannot qualify as experimental. A use is experimental only if it is, besides being solely noncommercial and not business-related, "solely for amusement, to satisfy idle curiosity, or for strictly philosophical inquiry." *Madey v. Duke University* (2002). On the other hand, there is a statutory experimental use exception, although of a very limited sort, in section 271(e)(1) which allows what would otherwise be infringing genetic engineering research if performed to obtain information for certain drug development purposes. *Merck KGaA v. Integra Lifesciences I, Ltd.* (2005) held that such research comes within section 271(e)(1) even if it turns out not to be useful for such informational purposes as long as there was a reasonable basis to believe it would, thus allowing for the inevitable mistakes and failures in the scientific method.

## § 8.8   Prior User Defense

Partly because of the growing allowance of patents claiming business methods and partly because of a general trend toward harmonization of United States patent laws with international norms, Congress has enacted "prior user" rights. These allow a person who has been utilizing a business method prior to its patenting by another person, to continue to use the method under limited circumstances. 35 U.S.C.A. § 273. The prior user must have actually practiced the method one year prior to the earliest filing date of the patent application and he must have used the method commercially sometime prior to that date.

## § 8.9　Licensee Estoppel

A patent holder cannot rely on the terms of a license that bars its licensee from contesting the validity of a patent. Because the integrity of the patent system is so important, and because a licensee is frequently the best-informed and best-situated person to contest a patent, a licensee can seek to have a patent declared invalid despite contractual terms that may forbid such a challenge. The interest in policing the patent system and ridding it of invalid patents is simply more important than the interests of contract law in that context. *Lear v. Adkins* (1969). Furthermore, such a licensee need not even disclaim the licensee before challenging the patent, and may continue paying royalties, remain a licensee in good standing and, at the same time, sue for a declaration of invalidity. *MedImmune, Inc. v. Genentech, Inc.* (2007).

# CHAPTER 9

# REMEDIES

## § 9.1 Overview

The remedies for infringement under the Patent Act consist of: (1) injunctive relief, 35 U.S.C.A. § 283, (2) damages, adequate to compensate the plaintiff but in no case less than what would constitute a reasonable royalty, which damages can be trebled when appropriate, 35 U.S.C.A. § 284, (3) attorneys' fees in exceptional cases, 35 U.S.C.A. § 285, and (4) costs, 35 U.S.C.A. § 284.

Unlike the Lanham Act, which governs trademarks, the Patent Act does not define damages in terms of profits, see § 18.3, infra. Since the prior Patent Act did include profits, there is reason to believe that the deletion of the term is meant to distinguish between damages and profits. *Georgia–Pacific Corp. v. United States Plywood Corp.* (1965). Yet if the patentee sustains the high burden of proving that "but for" the infringement, it would have received the infringer's sales, it can recover those lost profits as damages. *Milgo Electronics v. United Bus. Communications* (1980).

## § 9.2　Injunctive Relief

The general principles of equity apply to injunctions under the Patent Act, including the standard equity defenses. However, there is a reluctance to grant preliminary injunctive relief since courts consider that to grant relief based on patents granted through ex parte proceedings held before overworked examiners is to carry the presumption of patent validity beyond its intended purpose. *Carter-Wallace, Inc. v. Davis–Edwards Pharmacal Corp.* (1971). In fact, the standard of "likelihood of success on the merits," usually applicable to preliminary injunctions is radically altered in patent cases. Traditionally, a plaintiff had to demonstrate "beyond question that the patent is valid and infringed." The Federal Circuit, however, has rejected the "beyond question" rule replacing it with a requirement of a "clear showing" that is still, of course, something beyond the traditional burden of "likelihood of success on the merits." Once validity and infringement clearly are established, immediate irreparable harm is normally presumed for purposes of preliminary injunctive relief. *Atlas Powder Co. v. Ireco Chems.* (1985). The tendency of courts to almost automatically grant permanent injunctive relief upon proof of infringement has been radically altered by *eBay, Inc. v. MercExchange* (2006), which held that the traditional equitable principles (irreparable injury, inadequate remedy at law, balance of hardships, and the public interest) must be applied.

## § 9.3　Damages

The Patent Act authorizes damages "in no event less than a reasonable royalty for the use made of the invention by the infringer together with interest." Even prejudgment interest normally is to be awarded without satisfying the standard common law requirements of liquidation and exceptional circumstances. *General Motors Corp. v. Devex Corp.* (1983); 35 U.S.C.A. § 284. When there is an established royalty, there is little problem in setting a minimum amount. *Tektronix, Inc. v. United States* (1975). Sometimes, however, royalty rates may be depressed because of the infringement itself or other factors. The court has the power to treble damages whenever it is shown that the plaintiff was damaged to a greater extent than the demonstrated royalty rate or other proffered evidence.

## § 9.4　Attorneys' Fees

The traditional American rule that each party bear its own attorneys' fees is varied by statute in patent law. In an "exceptional case," the prevailing party may be granted such fees. Thus, either the plaintiff or defendant may recover them when the case is deemed exceptional. An exceptional case is one involving knowing infringement by a defendant, *Sarkes Tarzian, Inc. v. Philco Corp.* (1965), or "when the plaintiff has acquired his patent by fraud or brings an infringement suit with no good faith belief that his patent is valid and infringed." *Arbrook, Inc. v. American Hospital Supply Corp.*

(1981). See also *Hughes v. Novi American, Inc.* (1984).

## § 9.5 Eleventh Amendment Immunity

States are protected from suit for patent infringement by Eleventh Amendment sovereign immunity as they are from trademark and copyright suits. See §§ 17.8, 26.6, infra. This is so even if Congress expressly attempts to abrogate such state immunity, which it has done in the patent statute. 35 U.S.C. §§ 271(h), 296. Although patents are property under the Fourteenth Amendment and thus are protected against state deprivation without due process, absent a "pattern of patent infringement," states enjoy immunity against patent suits.

# CHAPTER 10

# PATENT LAW AND THE INTER-SECTION OF STATE AND FEDERAL REGULATION

## § 10.1 Overview

Inventors have state remedies in addition to federal patent protection. The relationship between federal and state protection is governed by the doctrine of federal preemption. Whether a state doctrine can coexist with federal patent protection depends upon whether the state doctrine is inconsistent or incompatible with federal protection. To the extent that the state remedy interferes with federal regulation, the state doctrine is preempted under the Supremacy Clause of the Constitution. "States may not offer patent-like protection to intellectual creations which would otherwise remain unprotected as a matter of federal law." *Bonito Boats, Inc. v. Thunder Craft Boats, Inc.* (1989).

For instance, state unfair competition laws prevent acts characterized by deceptive or other unfair conduct. In *Sears Roebuck & Co. v. Stiffel Co.* (1964), the Supreme Court held that state unfair competition laws could not be used to prohibit a company from marketing an unpatented pole lamp even though it confusingly resembled that manufactured by the plaintiff. According to the Court, to do so would give the plaintiff the equivalent of a patent monopoly. In *Compco Corp. v. Day–Brite Lighting, Inc.* (1964), the Court similarly held that state unfair competition laws could not prohibit a defendant from manufacturing an unpatented item, although a state could impose requirements to prohibit confusion as to the identity of the manufacturer. In other words, state doctrine can protect against undesirable conduct in the manufacture and marketing of certain products, but it cannot protect against the manufacture itself, which is regulated exclusively by the federal patent laws. See *Bonito Boats, Inc. v. Thunder Craft Boats, Inc.*, supra.

On the other hand, not all state doctrine regulating intellectual property impermissibly "clashes" with federal protection. In *Kewanee Oil Co. v. Bicron Corp.* (1974), the Supreme Court held that state trade secret law could prohibit the disclosure of industrial technology developed by the plaintiff even though that technology was unpatented. Trade secret law does not necessarily interfere with federal policies—it provides far weaker protection, it addresses different, noninventive subject matter, and focusses on conduct instead of technology. Since, at least within those limits, trade secret law and patent law can coexist, the doctrine of preemption does not apply. The doctrine of preemption applies to copyright law as well as to patent law, see § 26.1, infra. Similarly, state claims, such as unfair competition or interference with prospective advantage that allege misconduct by the patentee in obtaining or enforcing the patent address not the patent, but the activities of the patentee and are thus not preempted. *Dow Chem. Co. v. Exxon Corp.* (1998).

The exact dimensions of the federal preemption doctrine are uncertain. In *Bonito Boats*, supra, for instance, the Court held that a state attempt to prevent copying of boat hull designs was preempted by the patent laws. Because the designs were functional, they did not clearly qualify for design patents. Furthermore, because they were functional, they would certainly have to qualify under the requirements of novelty, nonobviousness, and utility in order to gain utility patents. The Court made it fairly clear that the state provisions were preempted because they intruded upon an area that could be protected only by federal patent law and, if that protection had not been granted, the hull designs must belong to the public domain. Nevertheless, Congress attempted to reverse the effects of *Bonito Boats* by enacting specific legislation, the Vessel Hull Design Protection Act, intended to protect boat hull designs, despite their functionality. If that legislation is constitutional it means that preemption based on a presumed constitutional purpose to maintain the public domain may be in question. 17 U.S.C.A. §§ 1301 et seq.

Finally, another area at the intersection of state and federal regulation is state immunity from patent suits, under the Eleventh Amendment. See

§ 9.5, supra. Congress tried to abrogate that immunity by defining "whoever" in section 271 to include states and their instrumentalities. The Supreme Court has held that the Constitution's grant of immunity to the states cannot be abrogated by Congress under the Patent Clause nor, of course, the Patent Act itself. Furthermore, the immunity cannot be abrogated under the Fourteenth Amendment unless it is shown that the states have engaged in a pattern of patent infringement. *College Savs. Bank v. Florida Prepaid Postsecondary Educ. Expense Bd.* (1999). The same is true of trademark and copyright infringement. See §§ 17.8, 26.6, infra.

# PART II

# TRADEMARKS

## CHAPTER 11

## THE FOUNDATIONS OF TRADEMARK PROTECTION

### § 11.1 Origins and Development of Trademark Law

Some of the most important and disputed issues in contemporary trademark law can be traced back to its historical development. For instance, the current disagreement over the objectives of trademark protection has its parallel in the history of conflicting claims for trademark protection from different interest groups centuries ago. A useful place to start the exploration of today's controversy over the objectives of trademark law is to look at the original purpose of guild members during the medieval period who affixed the mark of their guild to the goods they sold. The mark was meant to identify the good as the product of a particular craftsman or group of craftsmen. The original function of trademark, therefore, was simply to indicate the origin of goods, by identifying the craftsmen who produced them. But those producers also saw in trademark the opportunity to gain a competitive edge over others. This partially explains the development of the philosophy underlying the current trademark statute, the Lanham Act, 15 U.S.C.A. §§ 1051 et seq., which provides the owner of a federally registered mark with protection against use of similar marks if any confusion might result—confusion impliedly *not* limited to that merely over the origin of the goods. Reflecting back upon trademark's historical development highlights the dual function this source of protection serves—as a mechanism for providing identification as well as a technique for providing a marketing advantage.

Thus trademarks originated as devices to identify in the marketplace the craftspeople responsible for producing goods for sale. There are indications that long before medieval days, the practice of affixing producers' marks existed in the Mid and Far East, where archeologists have found such symbols on unearthed artifacts. The medieval European practice of inscribing the name or mark of the manufacturer is the direct antecedent of our modern federal trademark law. Statutes dating back as early as the thirteenth century show that this technique was eventually recognized as having social consequence and economic importance. It seems that these statutes were meant to protect the public by preventing the sale of unidentified goods whose quality could not be ascertained. But it was not just the public nor the individual manufacturer who valued trademarks. Within the medieval guilds, it became an important way the members of the guilds could control the quality of their coworkers. Naturally, however, the immediate effect of these early trademark statutes was to offer the manufacturer a valuable method of marketing his goods.

In its infancy, the Anglo–American common law of trademark clearly was meant only to prevent "palming off," that is, passing off goods of one producer as those of another. The legal protection meant that a producer could prevent others from producing goods and selling them as those of the original producer; it protected, in other words, against a junior producer trading on the good will of a senior producer. Today, trademark law allows the buyer to assert a preference in his or her purchasing, allows the manufacturer to promote its product, and (perhaps only incidentally, at least in most cases) serves to assure a certain level of quality.

The growth of an increasingly complex and sophisticated body of state trademark common law was accompanied by attempts to federalize it, despite the lack of an express constitutional grant of power to do so. The first trademark laws were enacted by Congress in 1870 and 1876. Those statutes were declared unconstitutional in 1879 by the Supreme Court. *United States v. Steffens* (1879) (The Trademark Cases). The Court held that Congress had no power to regulate purely state matters such as trademark rights. In response to those cases, Congress passed statutes in 1881 and 1905 solely addressing the interstate use of trademarks. In 1946 Congress passed the most recent substantial revision of federal trademark legislation, the Lanham Act.

Thus, to an important extent, federal laws do not expressly create new rights nor do they even codify the common law of trademark; instead, they merely provide a structure within which the common law of trademark can be enforced at the federal level. This is because unlike the Patent Clause, there is nothing specifically applicable to trademark law in the Constitution. The only relevant constitutional grant is the Interstate Commerce Clause, which allows Congress to regulate interstate commerce and to enact necessary and proper legislation to achieve that regulation.

## § 11.2   Common Law Trademark

The manner in which a businessperson acquires a trademark is different from that in which other intellectual property, such as copyright or patent, may be legally protected. A trademark cannot be appropriated *in gross* (by itself) because its nature is incapable of such existence. A trademark is something that only exists with respect to some other commercial activity; this principle is at least in part due to the history of trademark law. Since it developed as a device to identify a businessperson's goods, the trademark, absent the sale of goods, had no function, and therefore no existence as a trademark. A device meant to identify the origin of goods, which identifies neither origin nor goods, is simply not a trademark. Thus, a trademark is always *appurtenant to* (in connection with) commercial activity. It is because of this central characteristic that trademark law differs from that relating to other intellectual property. Accordingly, it is said that trademark rights cannot be obtained by mere adoption. They must be appropriated through use and thus rights to trademark are acquired solely through priority of use. *United States v. Steffens* (1879).

The common law always has recognized that one goal of trademark law is to prevent mistake, deception, and confusion with regard to the origin of goods. *Time, Inc. v. Motor Publications, Inc.* (1955). Protection of the public is thus one central feature of common law trademark. An immediate byproduct of prevention of confusion and protection of the public, however, is that businesspeople who have adopted trademarks acquire a means of protecting their good will. Thus, trademark law tends to protect both sellers and purchasers.

The expanded function of trademarks can be attributed in part to the fact that the modern market is not susceptible to or even dependent upon knowledge of the identity of different sellers. Trademark does serve to indicate origin, as one court has said, "though the identity of that source may in fact be unknown to the public," *Scott Paper Co. v. Scott's Liquid Gold, Inc.* (1977). The functions of the modern trademark thus have expanded, as the modern market has evolved, to include (1) an indication of origin, (2) a guarantee of quality, and (3) a marketing and advertising device. *Reddy Communications*

*v. Environmental Action Foundation* (1979). Therefore, the legal protection of a trademark serves both
to protect the public from confusion as well as to
protect the trademark owner from losing his market. In fact, it is the express purpose of the Lanham
Act to protect the owner's rights as well as those of
the public. 15 U.S.C.A. § 1127. Although the purposes of trademark have thus expanded, the Lanham Act did *not* change the common law doctrine
that a trademark must be in use before it can be
protected. Thus, the in gross/appurtenant dichotomy is at least partially still viable.

Trademark law traditionally has been considered
a part of the law of unfair competition. At the most
basic level, it is unfair competition for a competitor
to "palm off" his goods as those of another. The
essence of the tort of unfair competition also explains why trademarks can be acquired only by use.
At least at common law, trademark has no purpose
absent competition. Therefore, only when there is
the prospect of competition (within the same geographical area or between the same or similar products) does trademark law, as a category of unfair
competition, have a legitimate place.

Because, logically, trademarks at common law
could be acquired only through commercial use, not
through mere adoption, trademarks could be enforced only within the geographic area in which the
commercial activity of the owner was conducted and
only between products that were similar enough to
be competitive. *Hanover Star Milling Co. v. Metcalf*
(1916). Although the test of trademark ownership

became priority of use, it is not surprising that priority had to occur within the geographical or product limits that characterized the owner's use. Therefore, it was possible at common law that owner A's use might precede owner B's use in time, but that B would have superior rights if B used the mark first within a geographic area or in connection with a particular product line over which the dispute centered.

Because the common law of unfair competition focussed as much on fairness as on competition, intent became important. Trademark law frequently turned on the good faith of the parties. A good faith user who had no knowledge of a prior user frequently could defeat a claim of unfair competition. A user rarely could prove lack of knowledge, however, unless geographic or product restrictions were involved. A user usually could maintain credibility and succeed with a good faith defense only if he were using the mark at some distance from the first user, or in connection with a line of products so different from those of the earlier user that the latecomer would not be expected to be aware of the earlier use.

## § 11.3   Federal Registration

Because of the *Trademark Cases,* see § 11.1, supra, only interstate trademark activity could be subject to federal regulation; a national system of trademark registration was the eventual result. Instead of creating a system of federal rights, the federal trademark statutes essentially became a register of state trademark rights, dependent in large part on state common law for their genesis, with certain modifications to regulate their use on an interstate basis.

A national system of trademark registration has numerous advantages over state common law trademark rights. First, the acquisition of federal registration allows the registrant to overcome any claims by later users of good faith. Federal registration upon the Principal Register, see § 12.6, infra, gives *constructive notice* to all later users. 15 U.S.C.A. § 1072. As a practical matter, this constructive notice changes the substance as well as the procedure of trademark rights, because it effectively abrogates the doctrine of geographical limits. Constructive notice affords the registrant nationwide trademark enforcement. Thus, despite the traditional doctrine that trademarks are rights appurtenant to commercial activity and are not rights in gross, they in fact become rights in gross in all geographically distant areas in which the registrant is not using the mark.

Second, federal registration affords the registrant the opportunity to use the federal courts without any other basis of federal subject matter jurisdiction, such as diversity of citizenship or other federal questions. Third, federal registration, although expressly only offering a registration procedure and a federal forum, is accompanied by certain statutory rights aside from the above-mentioned constructive notice, most notably *incontestability,* 15 U.S.C.A. § 1065, which arguably gives a registrant trademark rights to which he would not have been entitled at common law. The federal trademark laws, then, are more than a system of federal registration of marks.

Nonetheless, the basic scheme of the Lanham Act is still that of a national registration system. It explicitly expands common law rights by allowing service marks, 15 U.S.C.A. § 1053, as well as trademarks, and creates the new categories of collective and certification marks as well, 15 U.S.C.A. §§ 1054, 1127. One section of the Lanham Act, section 43, 15 U.S.C.A. § 1125, significantly expands common law rights and creates a new federal cause of action. These rights go beyond the protection of marks meant to indicate origin. Section 43 of the statute is the federal counterpart of certain state unfair competition and antidilution rights. It prohibits the deceptive marketing of goods and services that causes injury to other competitors. This prohibition is not limited to the use of a competitor's trademark, and it has no geographic or product scope limitations, either. In effect, the provision sometimes protects the owner of a mark from its use by any other person in any way at all. Section 43 thereby incorporates into the trademark law a nontrademark remedy. It also includes provisions against "cyberpiracy."

The addition of an "intent-to-use" provision to the Lanham Act was accompanied by what is referred to as the "deadwood" provisions. The intent-to-use provision allows applicants to register marks that are not yet used, avoiding the previous, controversial, and arguably illegal, practice of maintaining a "stable" of marks that essentially were held in reserve, under the subterfuge that they were actually, although minimally used. To rid the system of those controversial marks more quickly, the "deadwood" provisions shorten the term of federal registration and the time for periodic renewal thereafter, from twenty to ten years, thereby increasing the likelihood that the registrations of essentially unused marks will be allowed to expire. 15 U.S.C.A. §§ 1058, 1059.

# CHAPTER 12

# DISTINCTIVENESS

## § 12.1 Overview

The requirement of distinctiveness is an articulated policy of federal registration. The Act states: "No trademark *by which the goods of the applicant may be distinguished* from the goods of others shall be refused registration...." 15 U.S.C.A. § 1052 (emphasis added).

The distinctiveness requirement is roughly analogous to the requirement of novelty for patent rights and to the requirement of originality for copyright. Without distinctiveness, either based on the inherent nature of the mark or developed by the owner through marketing, trademark rights fail.

Naturally, a trademark must be distinctive if it is to serve the function of identifying the origin of goods and thereby avoid confusion, deception, or mistake. If a trademark is to protect purchasers from confusion over what they are purchasing, then the trademark somehow must be recognizable, identifiable, and different from other marks.

The most distinctive marks, of course, are coined or fanciful ones. Distinctive and original devices, it has been held, not only serve to identify very effectively the origin of goods but they also assist in calling attention to the goods; they serve, in a sense, a marketing function on their own. *Ex parte Galter* (1953). Even though distinctiveness is thus profitable to the owner, it is nevertheless a prerequisite to the owner's freedom to appropriate a mark. Nondistinctive marks are not available for appropriation by an owner, at least not until they become distinctive.

The distinctiveness requirement has two themes. It allows a first user to object to a later user on the basis that the later user's mark is not distinctive if it too closely resembles that of the first user. The second theme is a policy opposing the domination of the common or descriptive terms of the marketplace, similar to the policy against ownership of trademarks in gross. A mark must be distinctive to prevent the preemption of these terms and their withdrawal from the public domain, especially since all competitors may need access to these words, terms, symbols, or other devices, to identify their goods.

## § 12.2 Different Markets

The general rule, both at common law and within the federal registration system, is that conflicting claims to trademark ownership are resolved according to priority of appropriation. *Modular Cinemas of America, Inc. v. Mini Cinemas Corp.* (1972). A rule favoring the first user obviously protects what is assumed to be an established identification by buyers of the product with the trademark owner. Although this normally will be true, it is quite possible that the first user will have established an identification between himself and the product only within a limited geographical area.

A second user therefore may establish a strong consumer identification in an area geographically removed from that of the first user. In a sense, then, the second user is really the first user within its geographical market. Thus, the rule of priority of appropriation frequently is modified to favor the second user, provided the second use was established in a distant geographical area. However, the second user will obtain rights only if that use was in *good faith*.

There are at least two rationales for this exception. The first user, by neglecting to expand its business geographically, assumes the risk that a second user may legitimately, innocently, and in good faith use the same mark in a distant area. The other rationale is one of equity. An injustice would be worked on the second user who, with no notice of the earlier use, invested time and resources into developing what he had no reason to believe was anything but his own mark. Therefore, as between that innocent second user and the first user who has no complaint except the appropriation of the mark in a distant market that he was not exploiting, the second user will prevail.

The claim of the prior user to rights in an area in which it has no established use is very much the same as a *non*user who wishes to appropriate a mark merely by adopting it. In the undeveloped territory, the prior user (elsewhere) and the non-user are functionally on an equal footing. Neither has established any use *in that area* but wishes to have rights merely based upon adoption. That is a claim in gross; it is not appurtenant to any commercial activity.

Under federal registration, however, the rule of priority is quite different. The change is due to the doctrine of *constructive notice.* Upon federal registration, the owner of the registered trademark can claim nationwide constructive notice. 15 U.S.C.A. § 1072. A junior user cannot claim lack of notice because everyone is conclusively presumed to have the notice that federal registration legally provides. Thus, there can be no good faith user after federal registration, despite the fact that factually a second user may proceed innocently and in good faith.

## § 12.3　Prior Use

The federal bar against registration of a mark resembling that of a prior user is primarily a codification of the common law. An applicant cannot obtain rights in a mark that another person has not abandoned if use of that mark by the applicant would be *likely* to cause confusion, mistake, or deceit. Thus, the prior-use bar for federal registration involves the following factors:

(a) the possibility that the prior use has been abandoned,

(b) the *likelihood* (not necessarily the actuality) of

(c) confusion, mistake, or deceit

(d) as applied to the market for applicant's goods, not in the abstract.

15 U.S.C.A. § 1052(d).

A mark is deemed abandoned only if acts of abandonment as well as an actual intent to abandon are present. Even if an owner has failed completely to use its mark, the abandonment exception will not apply unless the owner has no intent to use the mark anymore. In other words, nonuse does not constitute abandonment by itself. *Beech–Nut Packing Co. v. P. Lorillard Co.* (1927). However, three consecutive years of nonuse raise a presumption of abandonment. The doctrine of excusable nonuse mitigates even that long a period of nonuse if the prior user can demonstrate that the nonuse was only a temporary withdrawal from the market that was caused by external forces. Upon a showing of three years' abandonment, the burden to rebut the presumption is on the prior user who must demonstrate an intent to resume use.

Assuming the prior user has not abandoned the mark, an applicant cannot gain registration if the mark so closely resembles that of the prior user that it is likely to be confusing, deceitful, or cause mistake. Since a likelihood of confusion is enough to bar the registration, evidence of actual confusion never is required, although it clearly can be highly persuasive. Likelihood of confusion traditionally is determined on the basis of seven elements. These are (1) similarity of marks, (2) similarity of products, (3) physical area and manner of concurrent use, (4) degree of care likely to be exercised by consumers, (5) strength of the mark, (6) actual confusion, and (7) wrongful intent. None of these factors is dispositive by itself. *Int'l. Kennel Club v. Mighty Star, Inc.* (1988).

Whether a mark is likely to cause confusion will depend in part upon the similarity of the marks. Clearly, identical marks will be very likely to confuse. The more dissimilar the marks are, the less likely is confusion. The more similar the products are, the more likely a mark will be confusing, assuming some similarity between the marks. Not surprisingly, a sliding scale has been developed by which similarity of both product and mark are measured. When the products are identical, only an approximate similarity of mark need be demonstrated, since a consumer is likely to be confused when similar marks are found on identical goods. In the same vein, a consumer is likely to be confused when identical marks are used even if the goods are not at all the same, although some connection is required between the goods in terms of consumer expectations.

The conditions of the marketplace dictate the result. The more common it is for the product to emanate from the same marketer, the more likely consumers might presume a common source and thus confusion is more probable. The characteristics of the market therefore must be considered in measuring the likelihood of confusion as applied to the applicant's goods. A court must note the characteristics of the consumers who will rely upon the mark. Thus, purchasers of aircraft probably are highly sophisticated. They are unlikely to confuse one manufacturer with another even though they use similar marks. In the same vein, buyers of very expensive merchandise presumably will take great care in choosing their goods and it is unlikely that even with similar marks a buyer will make a mistake as to the source. People in a market characterized by low priced massive sales, however, especially if it is characterized by impulse buying, may be very prone to confuse even different marks if there is any similarity at all. An unsophisticated market such as one composed of children, is also likely to be deceived by marks that are only roughly similar.

Under the Lanham Act the prior use does not have to be as a trademark. The language of the Act simply states that a previously used "mark" cannot be appropriated by an applicant. Thus, it has been held that a mark used by an organization, but not in a trademark sense, is still the kind of mark that would bar later appropriation by another for use in trade. In *Sterling Drug Inc. v. Sebring* (1975), the prior user was a science research institute that did not market goods under a trademark at all, but did conduct scientific research in connection with the mark in question. This prior use of a mark, despite the lack of trademark use, was sufficient to bar later use in a confusingly similar environment by the applicant.

## § 12.4  Secondary Meaning and Descriptiveness

The bar against descriptive marks simply reflects the requirement of distinctiveness. 15 U.S.C.A. § 1052(e)(1). It often is said that a mark should not be analyzed in a piecemeal fashion. Instead, the mark as a whole must be tested for descriptiveness or secondary meaning. A mark that merely describes a product cannot possibly distinguish one producer from another. As an obvious example, "apple" would be a descriptive (in fact, generic) name for that fruit, and, as a mark, would serve only to confuse the consumer, for it would tell nothing about the different origins of a selection of apples produced by different producers. Moreover, to allow an owner to preempt the term "apple" would afford the owner a monopoly of something that is necessary to describe the goods for sale. Naturally, "Apple" is descriptive only as to the fruit but not, for example, as to a computer.

Of course, it is possible that a descriptive term could indicate origin. However, at common law, the fact that a descriptive mark also was distinctive was irrelevant. All descriptive marks, no matter what degree of distinctiveness they also acquired, were ineligible as trademarks. This is not so under the Lanham Act.

A mark that is deceptively *misdescriptive* also is ineligible. 15 U.S.C.A. § 1052(e)(1). The bar against misdescriptiveness is aimed at marks that are descriptive of something other than the product or service to which they are attached and that, left unexplained, somehow would deceive a consumer. As an example, the term "fresh" is descriptive of a particular quality of fruits and if applied to apples would be descriptive and therefore ineligible. Additionally, "fresh" would be deceptively misdescriptive if the apples were dried or frozen. The bar against misdescriptive words sometimes serves as a way of preventing an owner from asserting that a challenged mark is not descriptive because its goods or services are inferior to the mark's connotation.

A descriptive term is ineligible for trademark protection unless it acquires secondary meaning. *Park'N Fly, Inc. v. Dollar Park & Fly, Inc.* (1985). In a sense, this says nothing more than that a descriptive word may be appropriated once it becomes nondescriptive, because the acquisition of secondary meaning shows that a formerly descriptive mark has developed a significance that distinguishes the goods of the producer from the goods of others. For instance, the mark "red" would be descriptive of apples and thus ineligible for trademark appropriation. However, if a producer effectively markets his apples with the term "Red" so that after a while consumers immediately associate the mark "Red" with only one producer of apples, that consumer identification is a sign of secondary meaning. A "Red" apple, under the example, connotes a certain producer, and not color at all. The acquisition of secondary meaning is equivalent to the loss of descriptiveness.

Secondary meaning does not indicate, of course, that the meaning somehow is inferior or unimportant. In fact, the acquisition of secondary meaning is of basic and primary importance in determining whether rights exist. Secondary meaning is effectively the primary meaning and, within the particular trade and market, secondary meaning is the *natural* meaning of the mark. Secondary meaning is acquired rather than inherent and is developed in the marketplace through use that makes the mark distinctive of the owner's goods or services. *Coca-Cola Co. v. Seven–Up Co.* (1974). It essentially implies that an otherwise descriptive mark has been used so long that it has come to be synonymous with the goods or services with which it is connected, at least with respect to the content of the particular trade and with respect to the consumers within that market. Proof of secondary meaning is aided by a prima facie presumption afforded by five years of continuous use in commerce. 15 U.S.C.A. § 1052(f). A user who comes to the Patent and Trademark Office (the "PTO") with a mark he has used for five continuous years may benefit from the presumption despite the fact that the mark is facially descriptive or nondistinctive in some other way. A frequent practice is for a rejected applicant to accept registration on the supplemental register, see § 12.6, infra, and, after five years of continuous use, reapply for registration on the primary register. Under the Lanham Act, it is not important that a mark may be descriptive as well as distinctive. The only requirement is that a mark be *primarily* distinctive rather than *primarily* descriptive.

To establish secondary meaning, the trademark owner must demonstrate an established association between the mark and a single source for a significant portion of the consuming market. Establishment of secondary meaning depends upon a number of well-defined factors. The amount of advertising, the number of sales, the character of the market (including the nature of competitors and the conditions under which the product is purchased), and evidence of consumer identification and response, are all relevant. *In re Soccer Sport Supply Co.* (1975). However, some of these factors are more persuasive than others. Since secondary meaning really is directed at consumer response, evidence indicating consumer attitudes is highly probative. Thus, the number of sales or the amount of advertising is admissible, but if these expenditures were not successful in changing consumer attitudes, the evidence almost always proves to be irrelevant.

The dynamics of the descriptiveness/secondary-meaning structure have been well charted in an opinion by Judge Friendly, *Abercrombie & Fitch Co. v. Hunting World, Inc.* (1976), in which he distinguished four categories of marks. They are:

    (a) generic

    (b) descriptive

    (c) suggestive

    (d) arbitrary or fanciful.

Under this scheme, absent secondary meaning, generic and descriptive marks are ineligible for trademark registration since they both are essentially descriptive. Likewise, suggestive and arbitrary or fanciful marks serve to distinguish the goods or services of the owner and thus are eligible for registration.

According to Judge Friendly, a generic term refers to the genus of which the product or service is a species. Although both a generic term and a descriptive term can come to have a secondary meaning, only descriptive terms can become eligible for trademark registration through the acquisition of secondary meaning. A generic term, no matter how distinctive of the owner's goods or services it becomes, never is eligible for trademark protection. Thus, the word "spoon" is generic and ineligible. Courts are unwilling to foreclose a market to competitors who need the word to indicate the identity or character of their product.

On the other hand, a descriptive term can become distinctive and thereby eligible for registration. "Lightweight" could not be registered as a mark for a spoon absent secondary meaning because it is descriptive of a characteristic of the spoon—its weight. (If the spoon is, in fact, quite heavy, it would run counter to the "deceptively misdescriptive" bar and thus it still would be ineligible despite any contention by the owner that it did not describe the product.) A generic term actually *defines* the product or service. A descriptive term merely identifies a significant characteristic of the goods or services.

A suggestive mark is one that may be partly descriptive but is primarily distinctive. If a mark conveys the nature of the product only through the exercise of imagination, thought, and perception, it is suggestive. On the other hand, if a mark immediately conveys the nature of the product, it is descriptive. The category of suggestive marks was necessary only because under prior versions of the federal trademark law, a mark that was in any way descriptive was ineligible for registration. Thus, a category of suggestive marks was developed by the courts to allow registration of marks having some, even though minimal, descriptive qualities. Under present law, if a mark is suggestive, there is no need for proof of secondary meaning as long as it is not primarily descriptive.

Arbitrary or fanciful marks convey nothing about the nature of the product except through knowledge of the market. For instance, the word Kodak conveys nothing about photographic equipment except to those knowledgeable about that trade. Of course, this presumes that knowledge has not become so widespread and the association has not become so strong that the word has lost the ability to distinguish one line of products from others. When a mark, even a fanciful, arbitrary, suggestive, or descriptive one that initially acquired secondary meaning becomes generic, it loses eligibility for trademark protection.

Since only suggestive and arbitrary or fanciful terms are registrable without proof of secondary meaning (note that generic terms are ineligible even with that proof), registration affords a presumption that the mark is suggestive, arbitrary, or fanciful.

The various categories in the descriptive/distinctive continuum are applicable only within specific markets and relate to specific products. Thus, a mark may be generic with respect to some products or within some markets and even arbitrary or fanciful with respect to others. For instance, the word Kodak might become generic with respect to cameras, but not with respect to photographic film. It certainly would not become generic with respect to apples. More specifically, the word Xerox might become generic with respect to photocopiers but might only be descriptive with respect to the actual copies made—a "Xerox" copy. It might be suggestive with respect to a work of art composed of electrostatic prints and it might be fanciful or arbitrary with respect to fruits and vegetables.

It is not unusual that a legitimate trademark, even an originally fanciful one, may lose its status by becoming descriptive or even generic. In *Bayer Co. v. United Drug Co.* (1921), the term "aspirin" was found to have lost its distinctive meaning identifying the Bayer company's particular product but, instead, came to be a generic description of the underlying drug. Similarly, in *DuPont Cellophane Co. v. Waxed Products Co.* (1936), it was found that the public had come to identify all plastic material of a certain type by the term "cellophane," a term that clearly was suggestive if not fanciful when first coined by DuPont.

The centrality of the marketplace in determining whether a term is truly distinctive is best illustrated by the phenomenon of "recapture" in the Singer cases. In *Singer Mfg. Co. v. June Mfg. Co.* (1896), the Court found that the symbol "Singer" had lost its distinctiveness as the public came to identify all sewing machines as Singers. However, the company continued to use its name on all its products and after more than a half-century, it succeeded in regaining exclusive rights to the term. *Singer Mfg. Co. v. Briley* (1953). Although recapture is rare, its principle (that trademark rights turn exclusively upon consumer and marketplace perceptions) is determinative and fundamental to all distinctiveness cases. See *Miller Brewing Co. v. Falstaff Brewing Corp.* (1980).

Because of the specific bars aimed at immoral or scandalous marks, national symbols, or names of living figures, 15 U.S.C.A. § 1052(a)-(d), (f), acquisition of actual secondary meaning will not legitimize such a mark. These statutorily prohibited marks are specific exceptions to the secondary-meaning doctrine in section 1052(f). On the other hand, even though a surname ordinarily is not accepted for trademark protection, the acquisition of secondary meaning of a surname will avoid the bar since it is not one of the specifically enumerated exceptions to the secondary-meaning doctrine in section 1052(f). *Ex parte Rivera Watch Co.* (1955).

Finally, the Supreme Court has formulated a distinction between trade dress product-packaging, which can be protected under section 43(a) without secondary meaning, *Two Pesos, Inc. v. Taco Cabana, Inc.* (1992) and trade dress product-design, which demands the acquisition of secondary meaning to be protected. *Wal-Mart Stores v. Samara Brothers* (2000). Importantly, the Court has specified that when it is difficult to determine whether trade dress is design or packaging, it is better to err on the side of design and require secondary meaning.

## § 12.5   The Bars Against Surnames, Geographic Marks, and Immoral Marks

Federal registration is unavailable to marks that are *primarily merely* surnames. 15 U.S.C.A. § 1052(e). If the mark's character as a surname predominates in terms of its "primary significance to the purchasing public," then it is prohibited. But if the mark is not *primarily* a surname, registration is proper. *In re Hutchinson Technology, Inc.* (1988).

Whether a mark is primarily a surname may be affected by its use as a trademark. The acquisition of secondary meaning may not only raise but affect the issue of whether a mark is primarily a surname. Obviously, the more a surname (used as a mark) becomes associated with a particular product, the more its significance and importance to the relevant public becomes associated with the product and the less it becomes associated with its significance as a surname. Whether a mark should be eligible for registration depends upon its impact on the relevant market and not on the public as a whole. Therefore, a user of a mark that was initially primarily a surname may by advertising and marketing actually affect the eventual status of a mark in terms of whether it will lose its primary significance as a surname by acquisition of secondary meaning, and instead acquire primary significance as a mark for a particular product.

The primary significance of a mark in terms of surname status must be measured with direct reference to the product and not in the abstract. Merely because a surname is very common does not mean that it is primarily a surname. As applied to a certain product, its association in the mind of the consumer is of controlling significance. Even a common name such as Jones, when applied to a particular product market, may evoke associations with the product. As long as the purchasing public associates the name with the product and not *primarily* with its surname status, it is eligible for registration. Thus, acquisition of secondary meaning is central. Likewise, if a name is very famous, that, too, is not controlling. If a name such as Mozart is primarily perceived as a surname, a user could not register it until and only if the user succeeded in investing the mark with secondary meaning. But "Mozart" for apples would be registrable upon gaining secondary meaning even though non-apple-purchasers still would just recognize the composer. Furthermore, under the traditional doctrine that trademarks are to be examined in their entirety, and not dissected, simple inclusion in a mark of a mere surname by itself may not disqualify a mark if as a whole it is something other than primarily merely a surname. *In re Hutchinson Technology, Inc.* (1988).

The rule against surnames applies even to a user whose surname is the same as the mark. Courts, however, are reluctant to bar categorically the use of one's own surname. But the only specific exception that affords a user any absolute right to his own surname is simply that a user may identify himself in connection with a product provided the name is not used as a trademark. 15 U.S.C.A. § 1115(b)(4). For instance, a Mr. Campbell would not be allowed to use his name as a trademark to market soups. However, he would not be flatly barred from indicating somewhere on the product that he is the owner of the business so long as he does not attempt to market the goods under that name.

The use of one's own surname as a trademark inevitably involves principles of equity as well as of statutory law. First, courts are reluctant to prohibit use of one's own natural surname because of the perceived unfairness in barring someone from a seemingly justifiable act. This equity will be destroyed if there is evidence that the user was attempting to deceive the public or if it is clear that he was only using his name to benefit from the efforts of a first user. Second, assuming the second user has sincerely attempted to use her own surname with no intent to deceive or unjustly benefit from another's efforts, courts often will fashion a remedy tailored to the individual case, requiring some type of disclaimer or explanation to accompany the mark so as to avoid confusion with a prior mark while, at the same time, allowing the second user to exploit what is perceived as, in a sense, a natural right. *Taylor Wine Co. v. Bully Hill Vineyards, Inc.* (1978).

The prohibition against both geographically descriptive and geographically misdescriptive marks is similar to that against surnames. First, the prohibition is subject to the secondary-meaning exception so that continued use may make a geographic mark eventually eligible. Second, the bar is against marks that are "primarily" geographically descriptive or misdescriptive. Thus, the acquisition of secondary meaning need not utterly destroy the geographic sense of the mark; it need only counter the geographic meaning in the minds of persons in the particular market.

With respect to geographically descriptive marks, the bar is meant to prohibit the preemption by one party of a term that should be in the public domain. On the other hand, the bar against deceptively misdescriptive geographic marks is based upon the prevention of mistake, confusion, or deception. Its protection is aimed at the public whereas the bar against geographically descriptive terms is meant to protect competitors.

At common law, geographic terms and descriptive marks of all kinds were ineligible for trademark protection. The predecessor statute to the Lanham Act barred virtually any mark that had geographic implications. The Lanham Act changed that by barring only those marks that were "primarily" geographic. 15 U.S.C.A. § 1052(e). The dramatic difference in emphasis made geographic terms eligible unless the geographic significance outweighed all other meanings. The bar against geographic marks is merely a variation of the bar against descriptive marks. Its treatment with respect to secondary meaning is undoubtedly the same as for descriptive marks generally. For a geographic mark to be registrable, it must be established that consumers associate the mark with a single source for particular products. *Prestwick, Inc. v. Don Kelly Building Co.* (1969). The acquisition of secondary meaning essentially means, at least in that particular market with respect to that particular product, that the geographic mark is not really a geographic term at all. Its secondary meaning has come to predominate if the mark is not *primarily* geographic.

Primarily geographical significance is measured with respect to the market and the goods of the applicant. Thus, a mark is prohibited only if the term is primarily geographically significant with respect to the particular product in the market in which it is sold. Within that market the test of primarily geographical significance is whether the term conveys an immediate geographical sense to the consumer *with respect to the particular product.*

The test must consider whether "the public would make a goods/place association, i.e., believe that the goods ... originate in that place." *In re Societe Generale Des Eaux Minerales De Vittel* (1987). If an otherwise geographical term conveys something other than geographical significance, it fundamentally is arbitrary, because its relationship to the product is not natural but contrived and unrelated to any inherent meaning in the mark.

Whether a mark is primarily geographical is not determined by majority vote. It does not matter that not all consumers associate the mark with a particular geographical area. Merely having some geographic significance will not bar the mark, but proof that some or even many consumers do not associate the term with a geographic area will not save it. The test is whether the term has primarily geographic significance to some recognizable portion of the consuming market. *In re Charles S. Loeb Pipes, Inc.* (1975). The thrust of "primarily" does not require that the mark as a whole primarily connote a geographical area. Instead, it is a limitation measured with respect to any significant portion of consumers to whom a primary association with geography is fatal to the mark. It does not mean a primary portion of the market makes the association; rather, that the association is primary to a cognizable portion of the market.

In summary, it does not matter whether a geographic mark is termed primarily descriptive or misdescriptive because (1) the mark is barred if it is primarily descriptive and (2) a defense that the mark was not descriptive would make it primarily misdescriptive. In other words, there need be no inquiry into whether the goods actually come from the geographic area in question since the central question is whether the term has primarily geographic significance. Once a mark is found to be primarily geographically significant, the mark is ineligible whether or not it accurately describes the product. It is barred for being descriptive if it accurately describes the product, and barred for being misdescriptive if it does not. Once a mark is found to be geographically descriptive, only a finding of secondary meaning will save it, and that will not be possible if it is materially deceptive. *In re California Innovations, Inc.* (2003)

The words of the trademark statute forbid registration of:

> immoral, deceptive, or scandalous matter; or matter which may disparage or falsely suggest a connection with persons, living or dead, institutions, beliefs, or national symbols, or bring them into contempt, or disrepute.

15 U.S.C.A. § 1052(a). Unlike the bar against surnames and geographical terms, the bar against immoral, scandalous, and similarly offensive marks cannot be cured by acquisition of secondary meaning—at least not so long as the mark remains offensive. Until an offensive mark obtains so much secondary meaning as to abolish the offensiveness, it still will be barred, unlike surname status, for example, which need only be diminished to some-

thing less than "primary" significance. Since the only kind of use that could make an offensive mark registrable is the type that would completely alter the significance of the mark, there is little likelihood that an offensive mark ever can gain registrability.

Marks such as "Bubby Trap" for brassieres, *In re Riverbank Canning Co.* (1938), "MESSIAS" for wines, *In re Sociedade Agricola E. Comerical Dos Vinhos Messias, S.A.R.L.* (1968), "Only a breast in the mouth is better than a leg in the hand" for a chicken restaurant, *Bromberg v. Carmel Self Service, Inc.* (1978), "Cocaine" for an energy drink, and "Redskins" for a football team, *Pro-Football, Inc. v. Harjo* (2003), have been deemed offensive.

In addition to considerable ambiguity as to how far the statutory prohibition extends, there is some uncertainty over standing to raise an objection to registration. It has been held that, since the statute specifically contemplates a wide range of individuals as well as classes who may find a mark offensive, these persons, even though without commercial or competitive standing, are the logical and therefore appropriate parties to raise the issue. *Ritchie v. Simpson* (1999).

## § 12.6  The Supplemental Register

The Lanham Act provides that a nondistinctive mark cannot be placed on the principal register of trademarks. And, if a mark is not on the principal register, it has no real protection under the federal trademark statute. Many marks that are ineligible for protection within the United States however, may be eligible in other countries because of differences in trademark statutes. To have protection in many other countries, treaties often provide that a foreign mark must be registered in its home country. Therefore, the Lanham Act provides for registration of marks that are *capable* of distinctiveness, even though they are not, at the time, actually distinctive in the United States.

Thus, even if a mark is rejected by the PTO for nondistinctiveness, a user may request registration on the supplemental register to have a basis for seeking protection in places outside the United States. 15 U.S.C.A. § 1091. This does not bar the user from later registration in the United States upon acquisition of secondary meaning because the statute specifically provides that registration on the supplemental register shall not bar later registration on the principal register. In addition, registration on the supplemental register allows the registrant use of a federal forum, even absent diversity of citizenship or other federal question jurisdiction, and provides the protection of section 1052(d), which prohibits registration of marks similar to those already registered on either the principal or supplemental register.

# CHAPTER 13

# DILUTION AND THE EXPANSION OF TRADEMARK DOCTRINE

## § 13.1 Overview

At common law, a trademark was intended primarily to distinguish between different sources so that the consumer would not be confused between similar products. In a market that has evolved to the point at which the consumer probably neither knows nor cares exactly who the producer is, the trademark serves a substantially different function. In a market composed of anonymous sources, trademarks are treated not so much as identifying the particular source, but rather as indicating a common (though anonymous) source of ownership such as a product line. The trademark tends to trade on consumer loyalty instead of producer identity. It attributes to the product the image upon which the trademark is based. The reaction of the consumer is central. The consumer may prefer a certain product not because the trademark has identified a source whom the consumer values, but because the trademark itself has a certain value.

Once the trademark itself has acquired independent value, legal protection will not simply depend upon the likelihood of confusion as to the source of origin. The value of the trademark to the owner is no longer solely to tell the consumer which goods are the owner's and which are not. The trademark itself is sought to be protected when it has value of its own. It is, in other words, protected against *dilution*. When the value of the trademark goes beyond its utility in avoiding confusion, then it is clear that the factor of confusion does not cover the whole field. Other factors become equally or more important. *Allied Maintenance Corp. v. Allied Mechanical Trades, Inc.* (1977).

## § 13.2   Trademarks and Goodwill

In a market in which the trademark functions not to distinguish on the basis of origin but on the basis of attributing to the product qualities of consumer preference based on advertising, its value to the owner is essentially good will. By investing resources in the mark itself as opposed to the product, the owner is developing a symbol of its reputation.

As the function of trademarks changes from distinction between different origins to an embodiment of the owner's reputation and goodwill, the standard of infringement also will change. For instance, if a mark is limited solely to the common law function of distinguishing between origins, there can be no infringement unless the element of distinction somehow is impaired. In other words, confusion is the only relevant factor for infringement purposes if the mark is used solely to distinguish origin. If consumers are not confused as to origin of the owner's goods, there should be no legitimate complaint about someone else's use of the mark. Any complaint about infringement in the absence of confusion must be aimed at a function of the mark other than distinctiveness, since the result meant to be protected against (confusion) is not present. In the absence of confusion an infringement charge usually is based on the modern expansion of trademark beyond the function of distinguishing between origins.

The adoption of some elements of common law unfair competition into federal trademark law was marked by the deletion from the Lanham Act of any requirement of actual confusion by purchasers as to source. In 1961, the Act was amended to prohibit any use of a mark that is likely to cause confusion, apparently in any way at all, not just confusion by purchasers as to the source of a particular product. 15 U.S.C.A. § 1114(1). This shift in trademark law is based in large part on the unfairness perceived in allowing competitors to profit from the reputation of others.

The development of a property right in the good will embodied in a trademark is the basis of modern expanded trademark rights and antidilution concepts. The rights in a trademark at common law were only those meant to prohibit confusion with respect to the origin of products. Therefore, those rights were very limited and were highly evanescent, since they could exist only with respect to the sale of particular products. The bar against ownership of trademark rights *in gross* illustrated that trademark rights were not owned, as is typical of all other property rights, without respect to actual use.

Thus, as courts sanctioned good will as a protectible feature of trademarks, the property interest in a trademark expanded. As that interest expanded, the bar against ownership *in gross* was eroded.

If a product unrelated to anything the owner is marketing is sold with the owner's mark on it, there may be no traditional trademark confusion at all. Yet, under the goodwill theory of trademark, an owner might succeed in enjoining the use of its mark on an unrelated product even though consumers are not confused about the owner's actual products, because of a fear that consumers may think less of the owner if the goods are inferior. Thus, market scope becomes significantly expanded. On the other hand, if an infringer is marketing unrelated products far superior to those of the owner, at least theoretically the owner is not injured with regard to reputation.

Nevertheless, there are cases stating that inferiority of the infringing product is not relevant. *Mobil Oil Corp. v. Pegasus Petroleum Corp.* (1987). This is based on the belief that the owner of a mark should not have to determine whether its reputation is being hindered or benefitted. In this view, a mark is like someone's face and nobody has a right to appropriate the use of a mark any more than they have the right to use that person's likeness without permission. The rationale behind these cases is quite ambiguous. One prophylactic theory is that all uses should be prohibited that might be detrimental. Another is that it is difficult to prove inferiority or superiority, and it should not be the owner's task to establish quality. Thus, the scope of trademark protection has exceeded the common law limits of simple source confusion and, much like rights in one's likeness, provide protection under a theory of misappropriation, thereby converting trademarks into property rights *in gross*.

## § 13.3   Likelihood of Expansion

Frequently, courts examine the use of a mark by a second company on dissimilar goods by weighing the likelihood that the owner might expand into the dissimilar market in the future. This inquiry is justified upon the basis that protection of trademark, although only appurtenant to a specific use, nevertheless extends to products that the consuming public naturally would associate with those already marketed by the owner. *Scarves by Vera, Inc. v. Todo Imports, Ltd.* (1976). The potential for confusion is considered a harm against which trademark legitimately offers protection. Note, however, that the confusion against which there is legal protection under the likelihood-of-expansion doctrine is not confusion between competing products. For instance, if the owner markets "SweetTest" apples against various apple competitors, the confusion against which the common law protects—without regard to the expansion doctrine—is the confusion between the owner's apples and apples marketed by competitors. Trademark at common law would forbid another apple marketer from attempting to confuse the public about which apples were marketed by the "SweetTest" owner and those marketed by imitators. However, under the likelihood-of-expansion doctrine, the owner also would have protection against a marketer of "SweetTest" oranges, even though the owner does not market oranges. The potential for confusion does exist, but not with respect to any present use of the mark by the owner.

Thus, the expansion doctrine provides an owner with protection over uses that, at best, are hypothetical. Through this doctrine, the owner can extend protection to any field that the public naturally might associate with the present commercial activity of the owner. This amounts to a right at least partially *in gross*—it is tantamount to the claim of an owner that he has the right to a trademark simply by adoption, rather than by use. At common law a person could not simply adopt a mark and forbid others from its use on the claim that there was a future intention to enter a market. A right could be developed only after use. Under the expansion doctrine, however, modern trademark law allows an owner to prohibit use of the mark in commercial areas that are not presently used by the owner.

Consumer expectations help limit this doctrine. If consumers reasonably would expect the owner to be involved in other commercial areas, then those are included in the expanded market. Consumer expectations are based in part on relationships between the product marketed and those in the expanded area. For instance, apples and oranges might be related in use—they are both fruits. Likewise, razor blades and shaving cream might be considered related in use. These types of related areas might be reserved to the prior user even though he did not actually enter the related market.

Another limitation is market reality. Closely allied with the consumer-expectation test, this factor recognizes that confusion is likely to occur if certain products commonly are marketed by the same source even though they are not related in use. A chemical company might market synthetic fibers and also cookware liners. Even though they are not related uses, they are related in terms of market realities. See *Scarves by Vera, Inc. v. Todo Imports, Ltd.*, supra.

Another test of the limits of expanded markets is the similarity of consumers. If two products commonly are marketed to the same group of consumers, courts are likely to enjoin the infringing marks. Thus, in one case a car wash with the name "Allstate" was found to infringe the right of the owner of "Allstate" who used the mark in connection with automobile equipment, automobile insurance, and similar products. Despite the fact that the owner did not run a car wash, the consumers as a class were so identical as to threaten the possibility of confusion, or at least dilution, between the owner and the infringer. *Allstate Insurance Co. v. Allstate, Inc.* (1969).

One factor in the protection of a mark in activities foreign to the owner's actual use is the implicit expectation that the owner might expand into these related areas. However, it is clear that the owner need not prove any such intention. The burden is on the defendant to prove that its use is so foreign to anything expected of the owner that consumers would not identify its product with the owner.

The possibility of confusion is in many cases simply a legal conclusion drawn from the factors already discussed. Once it appears that products are closely related in use, especially to the point that consumers would associate the two together, and once it becomes clear that the same body of consumers might purchase the dissimilar goods, and after it is demonstrated that the goods are commonly produced by the same sources, courts often presume that confusion is likely. Since there is no need to prove actual confusion, that presumption is difficult to rebut. Even evidence of a lack of confusion frequently is rejected on the somewhat circular basis that actual confusion, or the lack of it, does not prove the case.

The interest of the owner in having access to related markets thus is difficult to defeat. Once the relatedness of the markets is demonstrated, an infringing use can be enjoined on the basis of (likely) confusion that follows as a legal implication. The same facts that indicate a likelihood of expansion—relatedness of product, market, and consumer expectations—also compel the conclusion of likelihood of confusion. As a matter of practical litigation, therefore, it is unlikely that proof of confusion or its absence ever will be decisive.

## § 13.4  The Interests Protected

Courts have identified three interests that are protected by modern trademark law's incorporation of the dilution doctrine. These are the right of the prior user to enter a related field, the right to protect its reputation from association with inferior goods, and the right of the public in being free from confusion and mistake. *Scarves by Vera, Inc. v. Todo Imports, Ltd.* (1976).

When determining whether a later user can use the mark of an earlier user in a market not yet entered by the earlier user, courts consider a number of factors. One of these is the intent of the later user, because an actual intent to profit by someone else's mark or, worse, to deceive the public, easily will persuade a court to enjoin use of the mark. *A.T. Cross Co. v. Jonathan Bradley Pens, Inc.* (1972). Another factor is the nature of the consuming public. *Ortho Pharmaceutical Corp. v. American Cyanamid Co.* (1973). A market of consumers that buys on impulse is more likely to reach inappropriate conclusions based on similar marks than is a market populated by sophisticated consumers.

Despite the fact that inferiority of the goods is not decisive in determining the question of dilution, the relative quality of the products is one of many factors that courts consider. Thus, it is somewhat relevant that a second user may attempt to vend cheap products by trading on the marketing power of a high-quality mark. One case has defined the interests protected in dilution cases as including that of the owner "in protecting the good reputation associated with his mark from the possibility of being tarnished by inferior merchandise of the junior user." *Scarves by Vera, Inc. v. Todo Imports, Ltd.,* supra. On the other hand, it is not so clear that a later user will be successful very often by showing that its products are superior to those of the first user, although logically that would follow.

The possibility, rather than the actuality, of confusion is considered the relevant factor in modern trademark decisions incorporating the dilution doctrine. The cases place the burden of proof on the defendant and imply that once the possibility of confusion is demonstrated, it is irrelevant that no confusion has yet occurred. The virtual impossibility of proving a negative is heightened in these cases by the equal difficulty of disproving a hypothetical—the possibility that consumers *might* be confused. Moreover, an owner need not prove that all or even most consumers will be misled. Instead, it is necessary only to prove that a recognizable number of consumers may be misled. Some cases effectively have held that when the trademark itself is the basis of the sale, rather than any consumer identification of the source, then confusion is completely irrelevant. *Boston Professional Hockey Ass'n. v. Dallas Cap & Emblem Mfg., Inc.* (1975).

Since it has been recognized that confusion is unnecessary to prosecute a dilution case, courts have identified the distinctiveness of plaintiff's mark as the interest being protected. Even absent competition and any confusion, the use by another tends to dissipate the strength of the mark. Thus, dilution cases sometimes will turn on the strength of the mark prior to the alleged infringement. Note, for instance, that the federal antidilution statute applies only to "famous" marks. See § 13.6, infra. Strong marks will benefit much more than will weak marks from the dilution doctrine. The greater the distinctiveness or strength of the mark, the greater the possible injury and, therefore, the greater the likelihood that the law will protect the mark from dilution.

For instance, if consumers purchase shirts with alligators on them merely to have the alligator, it does not matter if a competitor markets an alligator shirt with a conspicuous disclaimer that they are only imitations. In this case, the owner has acquired a right in the mark itself, because the prohibition of the infringement does not prevent confusion so much as it prevents the marketing of similar marks. Confusion, if any, goes only to the mark and not to the product. In a sense, then, the requirement of confusion becomes collapsed into the element of similarity of mark. Such an expanded trademark theory elevates the trademark to a property interest. See *Boston Professional Hockey Ass'n. v. Dallas Cap & Emblem Mfg., Inc.,* supra. Once the marks are confusingly similar and the mark is the basis of commerce, relief is awarded under this doctrine to prevent dilution but not confusion.

## § 13.5    State Antidilution Statutes

Although the Lanham Act has been amended so that the confusion necessary for infringement is not limited merely to that between competing goods, but is extended to confusion generally so as to include some dilution doctrine, that development has occurred only recently. In addition, federal courts have been somewhat reluctant to embrace the dilution doctrine wholeheartedly and therefore have construed the "confusion" requirement with varying degrees of strictness. In fact, it is possible that with the adoption of an explicitly federal antidilution statute limited to "famous" marks, see § 13.6, infra, courts will be more reluctant to expand the Lanham Act to embrace dilution concepts in other ways. Finally, even with federal acceptance of the dilution doctrine, many marks that are either not registered or otherwise ineligible for registration are protected solely by state law. But state law until recently has consisted entirely of common law and there has been judicial resistance to the dilution doctrine at the state level. To overcome this attitude, a dilution theory has been created by statute in a great number of states.

State antidilution statutes typically disregard the requirement of competition and confusion between goods. See, for example, West's Fla.Stat.Ann. § 495.151; N.Y.—McKinney's General Business Law § 368–d. The statutes forbid any practices that confuse consumers with regard not to goods but to sources. By dismissing the requirement of competition, the statutes allow owners to enforce their marks with respect to a wide range of products and markets, in none of which the owner needs to be active in order to restrain the forbidden practices.

## § 13.6   The Federal Antidilution Statute

Probably because dilution is inconsistent, and perhaps even incompatible, with traditional trademark law, there was no such federal cause of action under the original Lanham Act. An antidilution provision was added by Congress, however, in 1996. 15 U.S.C.A. § 1125(c). The Trademark Dilution Revision Act of 2006 significantly expanded its reach, requiring only a likelihood of dilution, instead of economic injury or actual dilution, thus statutorily rejecting *Moseley v. V Secret Catalogue, Inc.* (2003). The amendments also defined dilution to include specifically tarnishment and blurring.

Unlike state antidilution statutes, the federal statute applies only to "famous" marks, and, except for willful or bad faith dilution, affords only injunctive relief. A mark's status as "famous" is determined by measuring distinctiveness, use, advertising and publicity, geographic and trade channel penetration, sales, recognition of both parties in their respective areas of trade, use by other, third parties, and federal registration status.

# CHAPTER 14

# LOSS OF TRADEMARK PRO-TECTION AND PARTIAL PROTECTION

## § 14.1 Partial Rights

Because trademark rights never were considered to be property rights at common law except insofar as they actually were used in a particular commercial activity, the resolution of conflicting rights to the same trademark were and are determined, under common law, on the basis of both priority and market. The first user normally has priority but priority is measured and awarded only with respect to the market in which the first user conducted commercial activity. Since it was possible or even probable that a first user limited its commercial activity to only one area, it was not unusual for a second user to acquire rights in another area. With respect to that second area, the second user was, of course, actually the first user.

Even with the advent of federal trademark legislation, it still is possible for the common law to operate in the traditional manner described above with respect to unregistered marks and marks that for some reason will be decided on the basis of common law without regard to federal legislation. For instance, despite registration, disputes concerning products or services outside those for which the mark was registered may be determined on the basis of traditional common law rules. *Natural Footwear Limited v. Hart, Schaffner & Marx* (1985). With federal registration, of course, the doctrine of regional priority has been eroded by the doctrine of constructive notice.

Under the Lanham Act, a second user cannot gain an equitable claim to use of the same mark if it adopted the mark after the first user registered because of the Act's constructive notice effect. 15 U.S.C.A. § 1115(a). Since a second user never gains rights if it uses a mark knowing of a prior user, the Lanham Act, through constructive knowledge, effectively cuts off all claims of second users *after registration*. There remain at least two sources of potential conflict.

First, constructive notice does not affect *preexisting* rights between two users. Thus, just as in the common law example described above, it is possible that a registrant may have acquired rights in a mark while another user may have acquired rights in a remote area. The first user—or, in fact, a later user—may apply for registration based on the common-law rights it has even though the other user also has common-law rights. The resolution of these conflicting rights within the Lanham Act is difficult.

Second, between application and publication (which is when constructive notice occurs), it is

possible for a second user to adopt the mark innocently without notice, constructive or otherwise.
Resolution of those rights also is somewhat problematical.

Thus, the possible positions of the registrant and
other users can be categorized as follows:

(a) An earlier user may apply for registration
even though a later user has acquired certain
rights in other areas.

(b) A later user may apply for registration even
though an earlier user also has acquired rights in
other areas.

(c) An earlier user may apply for registration
even though a later user may acquire rights in
the interim between application and publication.

Even though the situations in (a) and (b) are
fairly indistinguishable, they present problems because of the Lanham Act's language. At common
law, in different markets, it did not matter so much
who was the earlier user so long as each party used
the mark without knowledge of the other. Alternatively, at common law one could say that each
person was the earlier within its own particular
area (since the common law does not have the
doctrine of constructive notice). This is not the case,
however, under the Lanham Act. Under 15 U.S.C.A.
§ 1051, an applicant must certify that nobody else
has rights to the mark. But the Lanham Act provides for the possibility of *concurrent use* irrespective of who was the first user. 15 U.S.C.A. § 1052.
The rights to concurrent registration (somewhat

different than the right to concurrent use), however, expressly are limited to those parties who acquired rights prior to the *application* of another. Thus, the later party in situation (c) would not be entitled to a concurrent registration. 15 U.S.C.A. § 1052(d).

Under section 1052, no applicant can be refused registration unless the mark was used *previously* by another, thus making the distinction usually not made at common law between an innocent first user and an innocent second user. Thus, the applicants in situation (a), under a literal interpretation of the statute, should not be refused registration whereas in situation (b) the PTO has the power to refuse registration to the later user even though that user has undeniable rights that cannot be cut off even if the earlier user were to apply (because of the provision for concurrent use). However, the later user in situation (b), if refused initial registration, may oppose the registration of another, may obtain a concurrent registration, or, perhaps like the later user in situation (c) who innocently used during the interim period, simply may maintain the right to use the mark within the area already developed despite the registration of the applicant.

A claim based on first use generally will be rewarded with registration. A claim based on first application, despite it being the second use of the mark, occasionally is rewarded with registration in order to encourage use of the federal registration system. The merits commonly are determined in an inter partes as opposed to the more normal ex parte proceeding.

## § 14.2  The Rights of a Senior Registrant Against a Preregistration User

The courts uniformly have held that federal registration does not affect those rights already established by good faith junior users. *Thrifty Rent–A–Car System v. Thrift Cars, Inc.* (1987). A junior user has the right to continue the use within the limited area in which it has been established despite registration. Established use is a defense to an infringement claim even if the federal registration has become incontestable. Section 1115(b)(5) provides that continuous use from before registration or publication is a defense to an infringement action even as to incontestable registrants. The defense, however, is limited "only for the area in which such continuous prior use is proved. . . . "

Likewise, a federal registrant cannot even enter the geographical market of a junior user who established its rights prior to registration or publication. *Mister Donut of America, Inc. v. Mr. Donut, Inc.* (1969); *Thrifty Rent–A–Car System v. Thrift Cars, Inc.*, supra. Thus, although the senior user has federal registration and has the right to federal protection, he cannot enjoin the junior user from its established market nor can he enter that market himself.

However, the senior registrant has the benefit of constructive notice on a national scale upon everyone except for the junior user who established rights prior to registration. But even with respect to the junior user, the senior registrant is entitled to prohibit the junior user from expanding beyond the limits of the established market. The sole issue in these cases often is defining the limits of the market that the junior user has established.

There are some cases indicating that so long as the junior user is expanding into an area in which the senior registrant has no intention of entering, there are no grounds upon which to enjoin the junior user from so using the mark. In such a case, there is no likelihood of confusion and since confusion is the basis for infringement, there can be no injunction based upon infringement. *Dawn Donut Co. v. Hart's Food Stores, Inc.* (1959); *Fairway Foods, Inc. v. Fairway Markets, Inc.* (1955). However, these cases are rare and even they note that an injunction would be appropriate once the senior registrant shows an intent to enter the market. One of these cases, *Dawn Donut,* involved a junior user *after* registration—in other words, an *unauthorized* user—but this case is complicated by the fact of substantially concurrent use of a similar mark, although in different commercial activities, for a long period of time.

## § 14.3  The Rights of a Junior Registrant Against a Preregistration User

A junior user faces serious problems when applying for federal registration if a senior user exists who has established rights in certain limited areas. Those problems will vary depending upon whether the junior user knows about the senior user's activities at the time of application and also will change depending upon whether, through time, the junior user's registration becomes incontestable.

A junior user who knows about a senior user has the duty to disclose that in the federal application and then seek a concurrent rather than exclusive registration. In such a situation, an inter partes proceeding most likely will result in registration being awarded on a concurrent and limited basis.

A junior user who does not know about a senior user legitimately can receive a registration provided that it is true that "to the best of his knowledge and belief," 15 U.S.C.A. § 1052(a)(1), he has the right to the mark. Such an applicant nevertheless may fail because of the provision in section 1052(d) providing for the refusal of registration or, at the very least, the grant of concurrent registration when it appears that another person has "previously used" the mark. However, if the senior user's existence is not discovered before registration is granted, the registration will be valid and after five years has passed from the date of registration, the mark will become incontestable. 15 U.S.C.A. § 1065.

There is a statutory distinction between a junior and senior user in federal registration even when both parties clearly have developed protectible interests in different geographical areas. Section

1052(d) prohibits registration as a matter of right to a user of a mark that was "previously used" by another. Thus, junior users face a barrier that senior users do not. A senior user legitimately can claim that nobody else has used the mark previously, despite the fact that junior users may have unquestionable rights in separate geographical areas. A junior user, however, with an equal and perhaps even greater geographical right, faces the barrier of previous use and thus must avoid the barrier by complying with the remainder of section 1052(d), which provides for concurrent registration only if the obstacles of confusion, mistake, or deception can be avoided. A senior user who seeks concurrent registration under the provisions of section 1051(a)(1)—these provide for concurrent registration but raise no barrier similar to section 1052(d)—theoretically faces no such obstacles. That senior user is, according to section 1052, entitled to registration as of right since nobody previously used the mark.

## § 14.4   Concurrent Registration

Concurrent registration is available when more than one person is entitled to use a mark because of actual use prior to any application for the mark, provided that confusion, mistake, or deception is unlikely. 15 U.S.C.A. § 1052(d). However, there seems to be a general presumption in favor of prior users, which means that if the applicant is the first to use the mark, nationwide registration presumptively belongs to it. In theory, however, there does not seem to be a firm legal basis for this presumption except for the provision in section 1052(d), which affords an absolute right to a prior user and arguably something less than that to a later user dependent upon the absence of confusion, mistake, or deception.

The first user is very likely also to be the first applicant. If he is successful in gaining registration, he obtains incontestability for the mark after five years. In that event, the most another user could gain is the right to continue use in areas where that user has established rights. What might appear to be a presumption in favor of the prior user is merely a result of the following pragmatics of trademark litigation. Even if a second user contests the registration, it has no absolute right to oppose it, since it cannot claim that the use was a "previous" one. The most that it can claim is that the use of the mark made it nondistinctive as applied to the registrant, as in *Giant Food Inc. v. Malone & Hyde, Inc.* (1975). Obviously, that kind of a claim raises a question subject to far more dispute than the simple factual inquiry involved in a senior user's opposition based on a "previous" use.

The Court of Customs and Patent Appeals has stated that a senior user is entitled to a presumption of nationwide registration with a limited registration restricted to areas of actual use going to the junior user. However, it also stated that when the junior user is the first to apply for registration, there is reason to award that party nationwide registration. The junior registration restricts the senior user to the actual geographical market it developed, thus furthering a policy in favor of rewarding those who seek federal registration. *In re Beatrice Foods Co.* (1970). As a result, there is a potential conflict.

In some cases, the prior user obtains nationwide registration and the second user merely has the right to work the mark in the limited areas in which it has developed the market. In another case, the junior user actually has been awarded a concurrent registration even though the senior user's rights became incontestable. *Old Dutch Foods, Inc. v. Dan Dee Pretzel & Potato Chip Co.* (1973). In one case, the court allowed the parties to settle by agreement how the rights to nonuse areas would be allocated. The court insisted, however, that since concurrent registrations should be awarded based on the likelihood of confusion, mistake, and deception, the allocation should be determined on the basis of likelihood of *expansion*. Apparently, the court reasoned that the public might be confused if it had expectations that one party or the other was more likely to expand into a particular area of the country. Since confusion would result based on that perceived likelihood, the court reasoned, the allocation also should be decided accordingly. *In re Beatrice Foods Co.,* supra.

Another case held, at least by implication, that registration raises certain presumptions even in favor of a second user, if the registration has become incontestable. In such a case, the court seems to have held that the second user, by being the first to register, is entitled to nationwide registration. The prior user, by failing to register, is relegated to whatever common law rights it actually had developed. *Wrist-Rocket Mfg. Co. v. Saunders Archery Co.* (1978).

The various procedural postures in which concurrent rights can be raised include opposition proceedings, interference proceedings, cancellation proceedings, *de novo* concurrent registration proceedings, as well as infringement actions in which a defense of concurrent use is raised. The results often depend upon the procedural situation.

Under section 1063, a person may oppose the registration of a mark if he would be damaged by the registration. Opposition proceedings must be commenced within thirty days after publication in the *Official Gazette* (which always precedes registration), although there is the possibility of extensions. At least with respect to junior users, the position of the PTO seems to be that an opposition proceeding is not a legitimate device by which to claim concurrent registration. In both *Hollowform, Inc. v. Delma AEH* (1975) and *American Security Bank v. American Security & Trust Co.* (1978), the Court of Customs and Patent Appeals applied a presumption in favor of the prior user, holding that it is entitled to nationwide registration and that any concurrent registration can be accomplished only through a concurrent registration proceeding. In *Hollowform,* however, the junior user had not started use until after the senior user already had applied for registration and thus was barred from commencing a concurrent registration proceeding because such proceedings are available only to users who have established some rights prior to the filing of an application, see § 14.1, supra. 15 U.S.C.A. § 1052(d). Thus, the only remedy available to such an opposer in terms of obtaining concurrent registration is a *judicial* decree since section 1052(d) does not require use prior to application for judicial relief. In that event, the Commissioner is authorized to grant concurrent registration after final judicial determination of the issue. However, the holdings in *Hollowform* and *American Security* are that, absent a judicial determination, the Commissioner cannot grant concurrent registration to a junior user who commenced use after application by the senior user, and may not grant relief other than in a concurrent registration proceeding to any other junior users. *Rosso & Mastracco, Inc. v. Giant Food, Inc.* (1983).

It also has been held that a cancellation proceeding commenced by a prior user against a registrant is not appropriate for the issuance of a concurrent registration as an alternative to complete cancellation of the registrant's rights. In *Selfway, Inc. v. Travelers Petroleum, Inc.* (1978), the court held that until incontestability, the junior user registrant is vulnerable to complete cancellation despite the policy favoring nationwide registration as a reward for promptly seeking federal registration. Thus, within five years of registration, the trademark is subject to cancellation. It is not appropriate for the junior user-registrant to seek a restricted registration in the form of a concurrent registration in a cancellation proceeding. Instead, the junior user-registrant must seek concurrent registration only through a concurrent registration proceeding.

## § 14.5  Abandonment

Trademark rights can be acquired only through use rather than adoption or appropriation in gross. Trademark rights therefore are a function of commercial reality. Thus, just as absence of use is a bar to the acquisition of legal rights, failure to use a mark after the acquisition of legal protection may constitute a bar to continued protection. The latter context is called abandonment.

To constitute abandonment, an owner either must discontinue use of the mark with the intent not to resume use, or the owner must do something or fail to do something that causes the mark to lose its distinctiveness. The first might be termed actual abandonment, since it is a subjective inquiry relating to the actual intention of the owner. The second might be termed constructive or legal abandonment since it applies irrespective of the owner's actual intent. To avoid a finding of actual or constructive abandonment, the Trademark Law Revision Act of 1988 ("TLRA") requires actual commercial use, not token use. In other words, the statute demands "bona fide use of a mark in the ordinary course of trade." 15 U.S.C.A. § 1127.

Section 1052(d) provides that a previously used mark can be appropriated if the earlier owner has abandoned the mark. Thus, abandonment may be a defense to the claim that registration either should not be granted or was granted improperly. Also, abandonment is one of only nine legitimate defenses to a claim by a user whose rights have become incontestable.

In a registration proceeding, a claim by the applicant of a prior user's abandonment may be challenged by that prior user insisting that it still has the right to the mark. Similarly, in an opposition proceeding, or in an interference declared by the PTO, an applicant may have to answer the claim by a prior user that the mark never had been abandoned. More frequently, the issue of abandonment arises in a cancellation proceeding in which the government or a rival party seeks to cancel the registration of a user who allegedly has failed to exercise the federal rights conferred by registration. It also may arise in a judicial proceeding, most often involving infringement, when a user defends its use of a mark by claiming that the plaintiff abandoned the mark.

Actual abandonment does not occur simply by nonuse. In addition there must be an actual intent to discontinue the use. If a person is forced to discontinue use merely because of economic pressures but has no intention to discontinue the use permanently, it is excusable nonuse and does not constitute abandonment. *Miller Brewing Co. v. Oland's Breweries [1971] Ltd.* (1976). If a person fails to use a mark for three years, it is presumptively abandoned. Upon proof of nonuse, the burden shifts to the registrant to show excusable nonuse. Nonuse is excusable when it constitutes what a reasonable business person having intent to use the mark would do. *Rivard v. Linville* (1998). Because of the two part test, presumptive abandonment can be rebutted by proof of intent to resume use, although this must be distinguished carefully from the lesser, and insufficient, standard of intent not to abandon the mark. *Exxon Corp. v. Humble Exploration Co.* (1983).

Since federal registration is nationwide, abandonment also must be national. It is not abandonment simply to stop using the mark in a particular area; in fact, it is not abandonment to stop using the mark everywhere except for one small locality. If a mark has been federally registered, even the most geographically limited of interstate uses is enough to counter any claim of abandonment. Use of a registered mark in just one area constructively notifies all others on a national scale. Therefore, although at common law a user could lose the right to protection in every area from which it withdrew, federal registration prevents that result. If a user were to withdraw, however, to only one *intrastate* use, that apparently would be an effective abandonment, since use for federal registration must be *interstate,* and withdrawal would be nonuse when viewed from that perspective. The language of *Dawn Donut Co. v. Hart's Food Stores, Inc.* (1959), stating that so long as a registrant uses the mark "anywhere" it is not abandoned is probably too broad, unless it is read to state that use "anywhere" at least must be interstate or have interstate effect.

Acts or omissions that cause the mark to lose significance include a failure to police it. When a registrant allows the mark to be used in such a way that it loses its distinctiveness, legal abandonment may occur even though there was no intent to discontinue use. In fact, a registrant may attempt to maximize the profitability of the mark by licensing its use by many other individuals. Such a registrant has an undeniable intention to continue using the mark; it evidences a desire to *extend* the mark. But if the registrant proceeds to make use of the mark so enthusiastically that he does not carefully control its use, the registrant may be held to have effectively abandoned the mark. When a registrant authorizes others to use the mark without any regard for either how it is used or with what products it is used, this "naked licensing" will work an abandonment. Similarly, the failure of a registrant to exercise reasonable controls over its licensees also can constitute abandonment, if it results in a loss of distinctiveness due to the use by others of the mark in connection with inappropriate products or services. *Universal City Studios v. Nintendo Co.* (1983).

Control of licensees is central to constructive or legal abandonment. However, the level of control necessary to defend against a claim of abandonment will vary according to the circumstances. Merely losing control over a few out of hundreds or thousands of licensees is not abandonment, especially if the registrant demonstrates that it has attempted to regain control. *United States Jaycees v. Philadelphia Jaycees* (1981). The loss of control can be measured over time as well as over numbers so that the loss of control for a short period of time, even though it involves all licensees, still is not abandonment. Even what constitutes a short period of time can vary according to the circumstances so that the loss of control for a number of years, in appropriate circumstances, may not constitute abandonment. *Sheila's Shine Prods., Inc. v. Sheila Shine, Inc.* (1973).

The variability of loss of control is illustrative of the central concern of legal abandonment, which is the loss of distinctiveness. The loss of control over a few licensees may not affect distinctiveness at all, if there remain a substantial number of effectively controlled licensees to affect public perception of the significance of the mark. Also, the loss of control over all licensees similarly will have different effects depending upon the circumstances so that with respect to a very strong mark complete loss for a period of time also may have no effect upon the mark's distinctiveness.

## § 14.6 Incontestability

Incontestability is one of the defining features of the federal registration system and represents, along with nationwide constructive notice and the intent-to-use provisions, the major departure from the common law effected by the Lanham Act. Indeed, the Supreme Court has noted that incontestability, along with constructive notice and the section 1064 protection against cancellation after five years, is evidence that Congress intended the Lanham Act to alter the substantive law of trademarks. *Park 'N Fly, Inc. v. Dollar Park & Fly, Inc.* (1985).

Essentially, incontestability allows a registrant who has complied with the incontestability provisions of section 1065 to bring an infringement action against another and foreclose the defendant from defending on the basis of any defense other than those listed in section 1115(b). It also allows the registrant to plead incontestability in response to the claims of another, either by way of judicial lawsuit or a PTO cancellation proceeding, thereby precluding cancellation.

Among other things, incontestability means that a registrant cannot be deprived of registration except on the stated grounds of either section 1064 (the cancellation provisions) or section 1115(b) (the incontestability defenses). In such a situation, the party seeking cancellation usually claims some kind of right to use the registrant's mark. The mere existence of rights in others is not enough to cancel the mark. Naturally, if one of the specific defenses of section 1115(b) can be proved, incontestability itself can be destroyed. It has been noted, however, that incontestability and grounds for cancellation probably should be distinguished because the protection offered by the cancellation provisions to a registrant after five years actually is greater than incontestability. *Union Carbide Corp. v. Ever–Ready Inc.* (1976). Section 1064 only allows cancellation under certain conditions and after five years the conditions are quite limited. This is true even if the registrant does not take the procedural steps to acquire incontestability because section 1064 depends not upon incontestability but only upon the passage of five years after federal publication.

Incontestability has some rather striking effects on a registrant's rights. The most common situation involves the use of a mark that has descriptive qualities. The doctrine has the effect of expanding federal trademark rights far beyond common-law doctrine, allowing the incontestable registrant to forbid competitors from using descriptive and competitively useful terms.

For many years, various circuits and even the Trademark Office applied a defensive/offensive distinction between a registrant who might permissibly resist cancellation with an incontestable though descriptive mark and a registrant who sought to enforce such a mark offensively against another. These offensive attempts were resisted by jurisdictions applying the distinction. That distinction, however, has been firmly rejected by the Supreme Court. *Park 'N Fly, Inc. v. Dollar Park & Fly, Inc., supra.*

Incontestability cannot be acquired if a mark is the "generic name" of the product. 15 U.S.C.A. § 1065(4). If incontestability applies, an infringing defendant can still successfully avoid liability if the mark is useful "only" to describe the product (that is, generically), since that is one of the nine enumerated defenses to incontestability. 15 U.S.C.A. § 1115(b)(4). Nevertheless, there is a difference between *the* generic name of a product used "only" to describe it, and a mark that may have descriptive qualities. It is with respect to that difference that incontestability has its greatest significance. The difference is between genericness and descriptiveness. A registrant with a generic mark never can successfully plead incontestability. But a mark that merely has descriptive qualities will not necessarily defeat a registrant's right to protection because of the presumption of secondary meaning.

Whether a mark is generic is tested by its significance to the relevant public. If its significance is merely that it identifies a product, it is generic. In other words, if it is synonymous with the goods or services, it is generic, not distinctive. What looks, at first blush, like rather peculiar language was added to the statute to cure a potential problem created by dictum in a case which stated that, if those who purchase Tide detergent are not motivated to do so because of any concerns about Proctor & Gamble, Tide might not be a good trademark. *Anti-Monopoly v. General Mills Fun Group, Inc.* (1982). Congress reacted to the furor this created by enacting the following language: "the primary significance of the registered mark to the relevant public rather than purchaser motivation shall be the test for determining whether the registered mark has become the generic name of goods ... in connection with which it has been used." 17 U.S.C.A. § 1064(c).

What this means is that a court can ask whether the mark means no more to the public than the goods or services but it cannot ask whether those goods or services are preferred because of the identity of the source. That is, their motivation in preferring the source is not an issue. Nevertheless, it still is clear that the purchasers must understand the mark to be, or at least use it as, a trademark, even though they are not motivated by the particular identity or character of the source. If they identify the mark with the goods, however, as opposed to a particular source, no matter how anonymous, the mark is plainly generic.

The most important feature of incontestability is its relationship to the presence or proof of secondary meaning. Since it is only genericness that is a defense to incontestability, proof of descriptive qualities will not defeat an incontestable right. The effect of incontestability, then, is to confer a conclusive presumption of secondary meaning upon a mark, since it is only secondary meaning that ordinarily could otherwise preserve a right to a descriptive mark. Incontestability thus substitutes for proof of secondary meaning. Unless a person contesting a registrant's incontestable right can prove actual genericness, mere proof of descriptiveness will not suffice. It is in this sense that the doctrine of incontestability effectively broadens federal protection beyond that available at common law.

In a sense, incontestability is very much a matter of proof. The doctrine requires that a defendant must go all the way and prove actual genericness. Merely proving that the public does not necessarily associate the mark with the plaintiff will not succeed. Instead the defendant must prove that the public associates the mark solely with the product: that it is generic.

A mark that is primarily merely a surname ordinarily is ineligible for federal registration. See § 12.5, supra. But because that defect is not one of the defenses to incontestability specifically enumerated in sections 1065 and 1115(b), an infringement defendant cannot plead the surname doctrine as a defense if incontestability is applied. *John R. Thompson Co. v. Holloway* (1966). Those specifically enumerated defenses include, for instance, fraud, abandonment, misrepresentation, good faith descriptiveness, certain good faith prior uses, antitrust violations, functionality, and various equitable defenses.

It should be noted that the "fair use" defense does avoid some of the harshness of incontestability as applied to descriptive marks. Even though a registrant can enforce a descriptive mark without secondary meaning through the incontestability doctrine, "fair use" will allow use of the mark in limited circumstances. Even incontestability, in other words, does not allow a registrant to prohibit the use of a descriptive term absolutely when it is used in a descriptive manner. See *Car-Freshener Corp. v. S.C. Johnson & Son, Inc.* (1995).

# CHAPTER 15

# TRADEMARK PRACTICE

## § 15.1 Overview

The procedures by which an applicant secures federal trademark registration are arranged in somewhat chronological order in the Lanham Act. By requiring "ownership" before registration, the Act, except for the "intent to use" provisions established by the TLRA, requires that the applicant use the mark first, thereby gaining some common law rights of ownership in the mark before federal protection is available. 15 U.S.C.A. § 1051.

The Lanham Act, as modified by the TLRA, allows registration in two ways. The first, under section 1051(a), requires "ownership" of the mark before registration. By demanding "ownership" before registration, the Act insists that the applicant use the mark first, the so-called requirement of "use in trade," thereby gaining some common law rights of ownership in the mark before federal protection is available. The second, under section 1051(b), the new intent-to-use section, allows a form of contingent registration prior to any use at all.

The intent-to-use provisions of the Lanham Act allow an application for registration to be filed prior to any actual use, provided the applicant demonstrates a "bona fide intention to use the mark in commerce." 15 U.S.C.A. § 1051(b). Filing a section 1051(b) application constitutes "constructive use" as of the filing date, 15 U.S.C.A. § 1057(c), and thus establishes priority against all others except those who either used the mark prior to filing or had filed earlier themselves. Allowance by the Trademark Office of this application is effectively a contingent registration that ripens into actual registration if the applicant files a statement of actual commercial use within six months, extendable to twenty-four months, as provided in section 1051(d)(2), after issuance of the notice of allowance.

The Act includes the requirement that the applicant state under oath "to the best of his knowledge and belief" the essential facts necessary to registration, and fraud during the application process will invalidate the registration. Among the elements to which the applicant must swear are its belief that there is nobody else entitled to the mark and that it does not confusingly resemble any other mark. The application must be accompanied by a drawing or reproduction of the mark so that the contents of the application can be examined by the trademark office. 15 U.S.C.A. § 1051.

Because the application must demonstrate that the applicant has satisfied the essential requirements for registration, the registration process frequently involves disputes over those very requirements. Ex parte proceedings initiated by the Office may raise these issues and they eventually are resolved through an examiner's decision, which, in turn, can be appealed administratively and then to the Court of Appeals for the Federal Circuit, or sometimes to a federal district court. Alternatively, inter partes proceedings can be initiated by interested parties, although not everyone has standing to raise an objection.

Ex parte proceedings involving only the applicant and the Office are the most frequent. They usually result from a dispute between the examiner and the applicant over registrability. As with patents, see § 7.4, supra, the examiner must reexamine a refused application at least once. After the examiner issues a final refusal, the applicant may appeal the decision to the Trademark Trial and Appeal Board ("TTAB") which consists of the Commissioner, the Assistant Commissioners, and selected examiners appointed by the Commissioner. It is usual for a panel of three from the TTAB to hear appeals.

If the applicant is *unsuccessful* before the TTAB, it may then appeal according to one of two mutually exclusive procedures described in 15 U.S.C.A. § 1071(a) and (b). Subsection (a) provides for appeal from the TTAB or Commissioner to the Court of Appeals for the Federal Circuit. By doing so, the applicant waives its rights under subsection (b) to a de novo judicial trial. An applicant who elects to proceed under subsection (a), however, may be divested of the right to do so if any adverse party files a notice within twenty days objecting to proceeding under subsection (a). Thus, in those proceedings that are not ex parte, an applicant who elects to proceed by way of subsection (a), appealing directly to the Court of Appeals for the Federal Circuit, is subject to the risk that some other party may object and shift the appeal into subsection (b). In other words, a party can elect to waive a de novo judicial trial and proceed by way of subsection (a) directly to the Court of Appeals for the Federal Circuit only upon the tacit or express agreement of all other adverse parties.

The *prevailing* party in a TTAB proceeding has some rather attractive options. It can allow an unsuccessful party to appeal the decision to the Court of Appeals for the Federal Circuit or it has the option of forcing that party to institute an original proceeding in a district court by exercising its subsection (b) right. Importantly, an original action is termed "de novo," implying that the party instituting the lawsuit has the opportunity to retry the entire TTAB proceeding. It is true that a de novo proceeding allows the plaintiff—and the defendant—to introduce evidence that never was introduced into the TTAB proceeding below. In that sense the trial is truly de novo. However, the parties are bound significantly by the previous proceedings because "findings of fact made by the [TTAB] are given great weight and not upset unless new evidence is introduced which carries *thorough conviction.*" *Material Supply Int'l. v. Sunmnatch Indus. Co.* (1998).

After an application has been examined and approved the mark is published in the Official Gazette of the Office. 15 U.S.C.A. § 1062. Within thirty days, "[a]ny person who believes that he would be damaged by the registration" may initiate an opposition proceeding. 15 U.S.C.A. § 1063. Since they are inter partes proceedings, this goes directly to the TTAB and follows the normal pattern of appeal thereafter for these proceedings.

Finally, after a mark is registered, "any person who believes that he is or will be damaged by the registration" may initiate a cancellation proceeding upon various grounds and subject to a number of rather severe limitations. 15 U.S.C.A. § 1064. As an inter partes proceeding, cancellations are heard directly by the TTAB and appeals follow the usual course.

## § 15.2   First Use in Commerce

As stated in § 15.1, supra, registration now can be acquired in one of two ways—through the new "intent-to-use" route of the TLRA, or through the traditional "actual use" route. The new intent-to-use method was adopted to avoid the burdens, and the abuses, of the actual use method. Although it is probable that intent-to-use eventually will supplant all, or almost all, of actual use applications, it is instructive to understand the history of actual use, and thereby to understand better the significance of intent-to-use.

Under actual use, rights to registration should turn on priority of use. The definition of "use," however, must go beyond the plain meaning of the word. Because, even before the TLRA, use must have been "in commerce," simple use that was not in commerce could not qualify. The product must have been marketed. The requirement that the product be marketed meant that internal sales between various levels of one organization should not have qualified as "in commerce." Collusive or contrived attempts at marketing should similarly have been unacceptable. Thus, a fabricated shipment or sale to a cooperating party who returned the product to the applicant should not have qualified even under the most minimal test of use in commerce. Some bona fide interstate shipment or sale should have been required. *Blue Bell, Inc. v. Jaymar–Ruby, Inc.* (1974). On the other hand, even a single use was sufficient to satisfy the test of a use "in commerce." Since a single use was sufficient, placing the product on the market and contacting one customer was deemed enough, if not collusive or contrived. Widespread use in commerce certainly was not required nor did it have to gain significant consumer attention.

Normally, internal shipments were not enough. However, the Trademark Trial and Appeal Board, largely because of the absence of, and apparently a felt need for, an intent-to-use route, eventually approved even intra-organization shipments as being "in commerce" provided, apparently, that they were accompanied or at least followed by a real intent to engage "in trade." But the earlier shipments were required to be bona fide efforts to further that trade. The Board and courts effectively modified the requirement of full-scale use prior to registration by allowing for token transactions accompanied by good-faith intent to exercise the mark actively. Thus, a token transaction that was accompanied by an "intent to engage in continuing commercial use in the future" was held to qualify. *Blue Bell, Inc. v. Jaymar–Ruby, Inc.,* supra. In other words, at least for registration purposes, as long as actual use "in trade" followed the first use "in commerce," it did not matter that the first use did not satisfy both the "in commerce" and "in trade" tests. *Standard Pressed Steel Co. v. Midwest Chrome Process Co.* (1976). See also *Blue Bell, Inc. v. Farah Mfg. Co.* (1975). This simply recognized the great expenditures involved in developing products prior to the screening process, which could take place only after application had been made. Clearly, *Standard Pressed Steel* came close to creating judicially an "intent to use" statute by recognizing an intracorporate shipment outside of real trade as sufficient use.

The increasing liberality with which courts treated the requirement of a use in commerce was more than the simple lifting of technical statutory requirements and, in fact, represented a profound alteration in the nature of the Lanham Act. Because of the fundamental distinction between use in commerce and use in trade, the tendency of courts to liberalize both of these requirements, without distinguishing between the two, had the effect of transforming the law of federal trademarks from that based upon the traditional common law rights flowing from actual use of the mark in trade to that of the European doctrine, which allows business persons to claim rights in marks simply by establishing an intent to use the mark. Although it may not always be obvious, this transformation is immediately apparent, however, through an understanding of that fundamental distinction.

The requirements of use in trade and use in commerce have their origins both in the Lanham Act and in outside sources. The outside source for the use in trade requirement is state common law; the outside source for the use-in-commerce requirement is the Commerce Clause of the Constitution.

Use in trade was required by section 1051, prior to the TLRA, which allowed registration to the "owner" of a trademark. This immediately raises common law issues because ownership of a trademark, at common law, requires the proprietor to use the device in trade. Thus, unless an owner actually had established a state common law right of ownership in the mark, he could not comply with the requirement in section 1051 that he be an "owner." This, then, is what is called the use in trade requirement.

Use in commerce was and is required similarly by section 1051, which allows registration of a trademark "used in commerce." This requirement exists because there is no trademark clause in the Constitution. In fact, early attempts to regulate trademarks federally under the Patent and Copyright Clause were rejected as unconstitutional. *Trade-Mark Cases* (1879). The Lanham Act gains constitutional legitimacy because it is founded upon the Commerce Clause, under which federal regulation of commerce is legitimate if, and only if, the regulated activities are interstate. Thus, unless an owner has used its mark in interstate commerce, it cannot comply with the requirement in section 1051 that the mark be "used in commerce." This, then, is what is called the use-in-commerce requirement.

Since both requirements had the same statutory source, it is not completely surprising that courts treated them similarly, despite the fact that their external sources, one being common law, the other being constitutional, were profoundly different. In constitutional law, there was a steady liberalization of the interstate requirement in all areas of Commerce Clause legislation for many years. *Wickard v. Filburn* (1942). As a result, trademark cases have held that equally minimal interstate contacts are sufficient to satisfy the use-in-commerce requirement. *Application of Silenus Wines, Inc.* (1977). However, an apparent confusion between the use in commerce and use-in-trade requirements led the courts blindly to treat both as identical, without regard to the different results liberalization of each may have. This confusion was more understandable, however, upon examination of the Lanham Act itself, which, prior to the TLRA, defined use in commerce in terms confusingly similar to those that are relevant only to use in trade. Thus, although cases have minimized the interstate requirements, following the development of constitutional law generally, it seems to have gone unnoticed that to liberalize the use in trade requirement in a similar fashion had an extraordinary effect on the basis of the marks being registered, with respect to ownership, property, and common law issues generally.

It therefore seems entirely appropriate for courts to have liberalized what was referred to as "registration use," which was a euphemism for use in commerce, since this was and is, in fact, a very minimal constitutional requirement. When courts proceeded, however, to accept minimal and even token uses also to satisfy the use in trade requirement, they were effectively transforming the common law basis of the Lanham Act, which required state ownership of a mark before registration could be obtained. In European and other civil law jurisdictions, it often is possible for a business person to register *and own* a mark without actually using it in trade first, simply by having the intent to use it and complying with the applicable registration procedures (including a search of existing registrations). But, under the Lanham Act, prior to the TLRA, to equate what should be a substantive use in trade with a grossly liberalized and minimized use in commerce effectively created something quite similar, if not identical, to an intent-to-use statute.

The courts, at times, recognized this danger. To avoid it, when they allowed a minimal use to satisfy both use in trade and use-in-commerce requirements, they occasionally would warn that the use would not necessarily afford full protection if a dispute arose with a nonregistrant who, in fact, did establish a real use in trade and that, generally, the "liberal policy" only would be applied in cases "in which a dispute as to priority of use and ownership of a mark is not involved." *Standard Pressed Steel Co. v. Midwest Chrome Process Co.*, supra. A minimal use that ordinarily would allow a proprietor to register his mark, therefore, would not necessarily protect against the claims of another who actually used the mark in trade. One might say that registration use provided only a presumption of ownership and that the liberalized rules for registration use were ineffective when there was a dispute over ownership of the mark.

As an example, in *La Societe Anonyme des Parfums Le Galion v. Jean Patou, Inc.* (1974), Patou owned the registration to the mark SNOB for perfume that Patou "never made a serious effort to merchandise" and sold in only minimal amounts. In fact, the court interestingly found that the real purpose of registration was to reserve the name for future use as part of a "trademark maintenance program." Although this token use might be sufficient to gain registration, it was insufficient to establish a lasting claim to ownership. "Adoption and a single use may be sufficient to entitle the user to register the mark, ... but more is required to sustain the mark against a charge of nonusage."

Mere secret uses, conception of the mark, internal shipments, or anything else that signifies the attempt of an applicant to reserve a mark for *future* use without anything more was always insufficient for federal registration. Use in trade was axiomatic to trademark rights. Without some trade involving actual customers, close cases were resolved against the applicant. *Blue Bell, Inc. v. Farah Mfg. Co.*, supra.

Thus, until the TLRA, the distinction between use in trade and use in commerce was central to the Lanham Act. As a corollary, most courts, and perhaps especially the Trademark Office, minimized what should have been the substantial requirements of use in trade in order to allow registrants to secure protection based on truly minimal, even token, use. With the advent of the intent-to-use provisions of the TLRA, it no longer is necessary to recognize such minimal uses. Instead, the Lanham Act, as modified by the TLRA, offers what is effectively a contingent registration for a limited time prior to any use at all. The kind of use required for permanent registration, with or without the intent-to-use provisions, however, now clearly is commercial, that is, bona fide use in the ordinary course of trade, not token use. This modification thus has made it unnecessary for jurisdictions to fabricate legally cognizable use from what otherwise would be insufficient trade activity.

With the advent of intent-to-use, there is no longer any need for courts to give legal significance to minimal uses. See *Blue Bell, Inc. v. Jaymar–Ruby, Inc.*, supra; *Standard Pressed Steel Co. v. Midwest Chrome Process Co.*, supra; *Blue Bell, Inc.*

*v. Farah Mfg. Co.*, supra. The earlier judicial acceptance of minimal uses, not requiring what the TLRA now makes clear must be—and always should have been—truly bona fide use in the ordinary course of trade, was caused by a confusion between use in commerce and use in trade. Use in commerce, which is and always was merely a federal jurisdictional requirement, always should have been treated, as all interstate commerce requirements are, as a justifiably minimal requirement. Use in trade, however, from the beginning, were it not for the absence of an intent-to-use statute, always should have required true commercial transactions to support registration. Although, in theory, courts should now be more demanding of such use, the precedential force of cases decided before intent-to-use continues. See *Allard Enterprises, Inc. v. Advanced Programming Resources* (1998).

The "in connection with" requirement, set out in sections 1051(a)(1) and 1051(b)(1)(A), means that registration can be obtained only with reference to whatever goods or services actually were used in commerce. The sale or transport of apples in commerce under the mark "Sweet–Test," for instance, will not allow the applicant to claim registration for that mark for later shipments of peaches or pears. In addition, the mark actually must be used as a mark and not in some ineligible sense. For instance, the sale of "Sweet–Test" apples in interstate commerce with the promise that any bruised apples could be returned under a "bruise-free" guarantee would not qualify the term "bruise-free" as the trademark of the goods sold. The term "bruise-free" would not be in connection with the sale of the goods, but in the marketing of the guarantee. In one case, it was held that the term "Syncom," which identified a computer that was used by the trademark owner to test speakers but that was not actually sold to the public could not qualify as a trademark for the speakers that were tested by the computer, even though, apparently, only those speakers were tested by the computer. However, had the applicant submitted proof that the term was affixed to each loudspeaker, even though the term referred to the testing system, "Syncom" might have been registrable as a mark used in connection with the speakers instead of in connection with the computer. *In re Bose Corp.* (1976).

## § 15.3   Standing

An opposition can be based only on a claim that the applicant's mark is somehow ineligible for registration because it contravenes an express provision of the Lanham Act. The courts have been flexible in granting standing to interested parties in opposition proceedings, depending upon the exact nature and grounds of the opposition. For instance, the provisions prohibiting registration of a mark that has been used by another could be raised only by that other owner of the mark. Yet, other provisions of the Act are not designed to protect such narrow interests in so particular a fashion. In other words, standing to initiate an opposition proceeding is determined by examining the interests protected by the provision of the Lanham Act upon which the opposer relies. When narrow private interests are involved, standing may be similarly narrow. When larger public interests are protected, representatives of that larger public legitimately may initiate an opposition.

For instance, 15 U.S.C.A. § 1052(a) prohibits the registration of marks that are immoral, deceptive, or scandalous, or that defame persons, institutions, beliefs, or national symbols. See § 12.5, supra. An examiner might not know of the significance of certain symbols to certain sects, for instance, and it is logical that a member of a small religious sect has standing to oppose the registration of a mark that might be contemptuous of that religion. Although, in the past, objections have been raised in *ex parte* proceedings by examiners sensitive to the religious significance of certain marks, *In re Riverbank Canning Co.* (1938), members of the public have standing to oppose registration. In fact, the Board "has a duty to obtain the views of the affected public." Marks that have offended women, Native Americans, and Christians, for instance, have been held to confer standing on members of those groups. The interest need not be commercial, since the interest protected by section 1051(a) is in being free from contempt, immorality, scandal, and other noncommercial consequences. An opposer need not have an interest different from the public at large to have standing, as long as he shares a trait that is affected by the proposed mark. *Ritchie v. Simpson* (1999).

# CHAPTER 16

# SUBJECT MATTER

## § 16.1  Overview

The Lanham Act is divided into two discrete parts. One consists of all those sections regulating the issuance of federal registration to a wide variety of marks, words, phrases, and other devices that can fulfill the functions of a trademark, service mark, collective mark, or certification mark. The other consists solely of 15 U.S.C.A. § 1125, commonly termed section 43. Whereas the registration sections of the Lanham Act offer trademark protection, section 43 constitutes a federal law of unfair competition, forbidding false statements in connection with interstate commercial activities, as well as acts of dilution of famous marks and Internet domain registrations of others' marks or personal names.

In addition to traditional trademarks, the Lanham Act allows registration of service marks. Service marks are identical to trademarks in all respects except that they are intended to indicate the origin of services, rather than goods. The Lanham Act also provides for certification and collective marks. Certification marks are usually those allowing an organization to indicate that goods or services meet certain quality or regional origin standards, thereby excluding all others from making the same claim with the same or similar marks that might cause confusion. Collective marks generally provide a device by which a number of individuals can identify themselves as members of a particular group.

## § 16.2  Certification Marks

A certification mark is used in connection with goods or services to indicate that those products or services originated in a particular region, or that they are of a particular nature, quality, or characteristic, or that they were produced by a member of a particular organization, usually a labor union. 15 U.S.C.A. § 1127. In other words, the mark is used to certify a characteristic of the goods or services that is significant to consumers and about which it is important to avoid confusion. Certification marks share a distinctive feature with collective marks in that the owner of the mark may not be the producer or provider of the services or products with which the mark is used. This, of course, is radically different from trademarks and service marks with respect to which any use of the mark by one other than the owner is severely restricted. See § 14.5, supra. In fact, engaging in actual production or marketing of the goods or services is expressly grounds for cancellation of a certification mark. 15 U.S.C.A. § 1064. The owner of a certification mark must maintain control over its use, however, just as the owner of a trademark must take care not to allow it to be used indiscriminately.

Because a certification mark may expressly be used to certify the geographic origin of goods or services, the bar against geographical names applicable to most trademarks does not apply to certification marks. Because certification marks cannot be owned by any person who actually produces goods or services with which the mark is used, the danger of preemption by the owner of geographical terms does not exist, especially because the owner of a certification mark may not deny use of the mark to anyone who maintains the characteristics that the mark certifies. Any discrimination is a ground for cancellation of a certification mark. *In re Monsanto Co.* (1978). Thus, ownership of a certification mark does *not* convey what ordinarily are thought of as exclusive rights; to the contrary, the rights must be available to all.

Certification marks are subject to all other requirements of trademark law, including the requirement of distinctiveness. Thus, even if a certification mark is a geographically descriptive term, it must be distinctive of a geographical region or otherwise distinctive to signify and identify the possession of the particular characteristics for which the mark stands. Therefore, the bar against the use of generic or descriptive (other then geographically so) names is often as applicable to certification marks as it is to any other trademark. Thus, it is possible for a geographically descriptive term to become ineligibly generic or simply nongeographically descriptive and thus lose registrability. For instance, if the term "Roquefort" no longer identified cheeses originating in that province of France but, instead, became either descriptive of a particular type of blue-veined cheese or generic as indicating a very general type of cheese, then the French owners of that mark would have no right to registrability. *Community of Roquefort v. William Faehndrich, Inc.* (1962).

The bar against ownership by the producer or provider of the goods or services with which the certification mark is used does not mean that there can be no connection between the owner and the goods. For instance, a union that owns a mark indicating that goods are manufactured by its members possibly has a close connection with the employers. The bar only means that the union could not actually produce the goods on its own. Likewise, the bar does not mean that the manufacturer of particular raw materials cannot own a certification mark indicating that certain manufactured goods contain its products. For instance, an agricultural cooperative might own a certification mark indicating that products contain cotton or wool that they cultivate. As long as they do not manufacture the finished products, they are free to register the mark. In fact, the cooperative also might own a bona fide trademark to indicate the origin of cotton or wool that it actually sells. It is essential, however, that these two activities be kept separate.

Therefore, if an owner has both certification and trademarks, they cannot be identical. To the extent they are similar, they must be distinguishable so that consumers are not deceived into believing that the products sold under the trademark are somehow of the quality that the certification indicates. For example, the mark "Good Housekeeping" serves to indicate the origin of a particular magazine. The mark "Good Housekeeping Seal of Approval" indicates that particular products or services meet the standards set by the owners of that mark (and of the magazine). The marks must be distinguishable, however, to prevent the magazine from appearing to meet the certification standards and thus achieve an unfair advantage over other magazines. Since trademarks indicate origin and certification marks indicate a guarantee of a certain characteristic, a common owner must be careful to ensure that the marks are distinguishable. *In re Monsanto Co.* (1978) (use of the term "WearDated" to indicate the particular fiber as well as manufactured items incorporating the fiber).

The use of certification marks closely intersects the use of trademarks by "related companies." 15 U.S.C.A. § 1055. A trademark owner may allow "related companies" to use the mark—such as in a franchising arrangement—even though the origin of goods then becomes somewhat dispersed. In these cases, the trademark represents the good will of the owner more than it designates origin as such. The use of certification marks approaches the "related companies" doctrine except for one crucial distinction: a certification mark owner may not discriminate among users as long as they adhere to the appropriate level of quality. A traditional trademark owner, however, may choose to license its use to related companies in any way it chooses, short of antitrust violations. *Siegel v. Chicken Delight, Inc.* (1971).

## § 16.3 Collective Marks

A collective mark indicates either that goods or services are produced by members of a collective group or simply indicates membership in a particular group. 15 U.S.C.A. § 1127. Thus, there are two forms of collective marks: collective trade (or service) marks and collective membership marks. Collective trademarks or service marks are traditional marks in the sense that they do indicate origin— that is, that the source is a member of the group. They are nontraditional in the sense that ownership of the mark is vested not in the producer or provider but in a group of which each producer or provider is a member. Collective membership marks, however, are completely nontraditional since they do not serve any origination function. The mark is not used to indicate origin but simply membership.

However, both collective membership marks and collective trademarks share a common characteristic: the mark indicates association with a group. It is this characteristic that primarily defines the collective mark and distinguishes it from certification marks. A certification mark generally certifies a characteristic of the product; a collective mark merely indicates association of its producer with a group.

Collective marks and certification marks tend to become coextensive when membership in the group is founded upon or relates in some way to certain standards relevant to quality or regional origin. For instance, a group of producers who base their membership requirements on regional location may obtain a collective mark indicating association with the group. But membership in the group, because of the qualifications for membership, inherently involves an identification of regional association. The mark would then indicate both that the producer was a member of the group (the function of the collective mark) and also that the product originated in a particular region (theoretically the only function of a certification mark). Thus a collective mark, to the extent that membership is premised on particular standards, in effect may certify the presence of those standards.

Although collective marks commonly are used by members of a collective group and not by the group itself, there is no bar, similar to that applicable to certification marks, against use by the owner. For instance, a club or group may register its mark for use by members but *also* may apply the mark to its stationery, publications, or news releases. Although the Trademark Office will allow the owner of a collective mark to use the mark on such things as stationery, see Hancock, *Notes from the Patent Office,* 46 T.M.R. 1341 (November, 1956), there are other indications that this is a matter of degree. If the collective group actually manufactures and markets goods or provides services, it may be entitled to a collective mark for its members but may have to obtain its own trade or service mark for those particular activities. *Aloe Creme Laboratories, Inc. v. American Society for Aesthetic Plastic Surgery, Inc.* (1976); *Huber Baking Co. v. Stroehmann Brothers Co.* (1958).

Although it is not clear how a court or the Trademark Office would respond to the use of a collective mark in what is essentially a certification activity, service marks have been cancelled when they effectively function as collective marks. The cancellation in *National Trailways Bus System v. Trailway Van Lines, Inc.* (1965) was based on fraud in representing that the applicant provided the service of bus transportation when, in fact, it was a membership organization. Only the members, not the applicant, actually provided the services. It is possible that an applicant who gained a collective mark and, by limiting membership rights, effectively certified the quality or origin of goods or services in a discriminatory way could be held fraudulent in applying for a collective mark when the mark identified and distinguished quality instead of membership.

## § 16.4 Service Marks

Service marks are essentially trademarks that are used in the sale of services instead of goods. 15 U.S.C.A. § 1127. Otherwise, trademarks and service marks are in all respects identical. There is some question whether a service mark is registrable as such when the service is primarily promoting the sale of specific goods. For instance, the use of "Weathervane" as a mark indicating the service of promoting sporting events was questioned when the owner also sold "Weathervane" clothing and it seemed clear that sponsorship of the sporting events was intended to promote the sale of the goods. It was decided, however, that as long as the service is a bona fide one and the effect on the sale of goods is only incidental, there is no reason to refuse registration. A correlative holding is that an owner may own a mark as both a service mark and a trademark if it is used in both ways. *Ex parte Handmacher–Vogel, Inc.* (1953).

That issue is directly addressed in the Lanham Act because of a 1962 amendment expressly allowing the registration of television or radio program titles as service marks despite the fact that the programs are used in the promotion of specific goods. 15 U.S.C.A. § 1127. That amendment was a response to *Ex parte The Procter & Gamble Co.* (1953), which held that the applicant could not register the name of its radio program, "Ma Perkins," as a service mark because the title was not used to identify the program so much as to promote the sale of goods. The decision did hold, however, that entertainment was a legitimate service that could satisfy the Lanham Act. It is not clear that the amendment to the Act to allow registration in *Procter & Gamble* creates a narrow exception to a broader bar against the registration of services that primarily function to advertise goods or whether it states, by way of example, a broad rule that such activities generally are registrable as service marks.

To constitute a service mark, a word, phrase, or device must be something more than simply the business name of an enterprise. This does not mean that the business name cannot also be the service mark but mere status as a business name is not enough to qualify as a service mark. The test is the use to which the mark is put; the mark must do more than identify the enterprise as a business organization—it must identify and distinguish the service rendered. *In re Unclaimed Salvage & Freight Co.* (1976).

## § 16.5 Primary Purpose

To be registered, a trademark actually must be used to identify and distinguish goods or services. Merely because a device is capable of so identifying or distinguishing goods or services does not automatically qualify it for registration. Sometimes, a device capable of identification and distinction is simply part of the trade dress of the goods. A device, including a name or design, that simply accompanies the goods and is merely a necessary part of their packaging or is otherwise a necessary but collateral component of the sales process and that does not *primarily* serve to distinguish and identify the goods, is ineligible for registration. But trade dress legitimately can serve as a trademark if it actually identifies and distinguishes the service or goods with which it is used.

Since all goods have physical structure and many goods need to be packaged, attempts to register some feature of the structure or method of packaging may fail under the *primary-purpose* test. However, the test is not whether the device is a feature of the goods' physical structure, nor whether it is an element of the packaging. It is, instead, whether the device has as its *primary purpose* merely to structure or package the goods. If a structural feature or packaging method is distinctive enough so that in the marketplace its primary purpose is to serve as a trademark, registration should not be denied merely because it *might* have a nontrademark purpose in other circumstances or even that it does have nontrademark purposes as well.

In *In re Mogen David Wine Corp.* (1964), the court held that it was immaterial that the design claimed as a trademark was also the subject of a design patent. The distinctively fluted shape of the wine bottles that the applicant claimed as a trademark device might be eligible for trademark registration as well as a design patent, said the court, if the design in fact "functions as a trademark to indicate origin." The test is not whether a structural or packaging feature has other functions as well, but whether the packaging or structure (which might *also* have trade dress functions) "does in fact identify appellant's goods and distinguish them from those of others." *In re World's Finest Chocolate, Inc.* (1973). If the primary purpose of the device is to distinguish and identify, it is no bar to registration if it also has structural or packaging functions.

The primary-purpose rule also controls devices that may have other purposes beside structure or packaging. Trademarks consisting of arbitrary or fanciful elements also may have ornamental value. When a mark consists of a number of elements, it is possible that analysis of each individual element could yield the conclusion that each element alone is merely ornamental. A finding to that effect would prohibit ownership of any of those individual elements but would not affect registration of the device as a whole. Actual use of the complete device as a trademark would support registration of the whole. The key is whether the component elements actually are used as a device to identify and distinguish.

Each separate element of a composite mark consisting of several elements nevertheless may be registered if each satisfies the requirement of actually fulfilling the purpose of a trademark. When, for instance, the word "Sterno" was the registered trademark of a solid fuel and the word was used on the barrel-shaped torso of a fanciful bear, it was found that both the word and the figure were registrable separately because each served the purpose of identifying and distinguishing the fuel from others. *In re Sterno, Inc.* (1963). When the element becomes no more than a fanciful animal figure, however, the determination of whether it serves by itself the purpose of distinguishing and identifying the goods is more difficult and involves closer questions. The presence of alternating black and white stripes on batteries was held to be "mere 'dress,' " the purpose of which was simply design and ornamentation. *In re Burgess Battery Co.* (1940). On the other hand, two horizontal polka-dot bands bordering other elements including words and fanciful figures were held to be registrable separate from the other elements. The test was not whether the elements served some ornamental purpose but whether they were "recognized by the public as a primary means of identification." *Application of Swift & Co.* (1955).

It always is difficult to determine whether a device is merely ornamental or whether it serves to distinguish and identify. However, one case seems to imply that when the device commonly is used by others as ornamentation, it is presumed ornamental absent proof that the mark is perceived by consumers as distinctive. In other words, with a design that is commonly ornamental in similar surroundings, proof of secondary meaning is necessary. *In re Soccer Sport Supply Co.* (1975).

## § 16.6   The Functional Bar

A device that is solely functional cannot be registered. Goods having such a device could not be identified or distinguished from other goods performing the same function for they would then have to share the same device. To grant registration would be to register not only a trademark but also to exclude others from the function as well, thus converting trademark registration into something approximating patent protection. In holding that the appearance of generic drugs is at least partly functional, since it allows the user to identify the appropriate medicine at the appropriate time, the Supreme Court has said, "a product feature is functional if it is essential to the use or purpose of the article or if it affects the cost or quality of the article." *Inwood Laboratories, Inc. v. Ives Laboratories, Inc.* (1982).

Mere possession of functional attributes, has been, historically, insufficient to bar registration. The Lanham Act states that a functional device is ineligible for registration only if it is functional "as a whole." 15 U.S.C. § 1052. The question is not, courts have said, whether the device is functional but whether its *sole* purpose is utilitarian. Therefore, a device only becomes nonregistrable if its elements have solely functional significance and have been chosen to perform some utilitarian function. Jewelry in a particular shape having trademark significance may be registrable, even though jewelry normally performs its own function of appealing to aesthetic sensibilities. When pendants, cuff links, and bracelets were in the shape of the Penthouse key logo, the court held that, despite the fact that jewelry normally performs the aesthetic-utilitarian function, when it actually serves to identify and distinguish on the basis of origin, there was no reason to bar registration. *In re Application of Penthouse Int'l Ltd.* (1977).

One court has articulated the test as being whether the device is "primarily utilitarian." *Rolls-Royce Motors Ltd. v. A & A Fiberglass, Inc.* (1977). In that case an infringer claimed that the famous Flying Lady on the Rolls–Royce radiator and its Classic Grill consisting of vertical louvers were non-registrable. The defendant attempted to force the plaintiff into the untenable intersection of the functional bar and the ornamental purpose doctrines, saying that the grill and radiator cap were functional or, alternatively, if the plaintiff succeeded in showing that they served no function at all, therefore were merely ornamental and equally unregistrable. The defendant was mistaken in thinking that this presented a Hobson's choice, however, because the bar does not require devices to be completely nonfunctional and nonornamental, but instead, only requires that they not be "primarily" functional or ornamental.

Some courts have stated that buildings, despite functionality, could serve as trademarks if they possessed elements that served to distinguish and identify goods or services. Registration would be limited, however, to the distinctive elements (although the entire building might qualify in some cases). *Fotomat Corp. v. Photo Drive–Thru, Inc.* (1977). Other courts have held that the stitching on mattresses was registrable when it was done in a distinctive vertical double arrangement and when it was not "inherently functional"—which seems to be another way of saying it is not *solely* functional. *Application of Simmons Co.* (1960). This is a good illustration of a multiple purpose device. Clearly, stitching is necessary to hold a mattress together. But when the manufacturer adds something arbitrary, such as a particular way of performing double stitching in a vertical format that is unrelated to its function, then the mark is registrable to the extent of that nonfunctional element.

The Lanham Act bars from registration a mark that "comprises any matter that, as a whole, is functional." The Act also provides for cancellation of any marks that are functional, even if they have become incontestible. 15 U.S.C.A. §§ 1052(e), 1062.

Whereas a design patent does not bar trademark registration and, in a sense, reinforces it by attesting to the nonutilitarian characteristics of the element, a utility patent acts as a complete bar. Even after expiration of a utility patent, the fact that a claimed distinguishing element is eligible for registration effectively is rebutted by the earlier patent, which demonstrates persuasively that the element was adopted primarily for utilitarian reasons. In *In re Shenango Ceramics, Inc.* (1966), a set of ribs on the bottom of a ceramic plate had been patented for their vibration-damping utility and also for their handling utility. Even after the patent expired, the evidence of utility resulting from the patent was fatal to any claim under trademark that functional utility was not a primary purpose of the ribs. When a patent expires, the patented features enter the public domain. Since all have the right to use the feature, the applicant could not identify and distinguish its goods by use of the formerly patented feature. *TrafFix Devices, Inc. v. Marketing Displays, Inc.* (2001). However, merely because a patent "reads on" one feature does not necessarily mean that such a feature is so functional as to bar its trademark registrability. *Cable Electric Products v. Genmark, Inc.* (1985).

## § 16.7   Color

The Supreme Court has held that color alone can serve as a trademark even though for many years there was a judicial rule against this. *Qualitex Co. v. Jacobson Products Co.* (1995). Nevertheless, color cannot serve as a trademark when it serves a functional purpose. Thus, for instance, black is not available as a mark for outboard motors when it would provide a competitive advantage because black is compatible with a wide variety of boat colors. *Brunswick Corp. v. British Seagull Ltd.* (1994). On the other hand, one decision has held that "mere taste or preference" does not constitute functionality. *The L.D. Kichler Co. v. Davoil, Inc.* (1999).

One factor, however, that the Supreme Court did not fully resolve is that of "color depletion." Recognizing that there may be far fewer colors available than other symbols or devices, the Court nevertheless refused to treat color differently. The Court held that this "occasional problem" could be addressed, when it arises, by applying the functionality bar. However, by the time available colors for a particular product or service are exhausted, it seems too late, as a practical matter, to resolve the problem since it would require either the massive cancellation of existing marks, or the continued recognition of color in existing registrants but denying it to future registrants. It may be that the Court assumed that in today's economy there will never be that many competitors in particular product or service lines.

## § 16.8 Section 43

Section 43(a), 15 U.S.C.A. § 1125(a), provides protection in the *absence* of trademark rights, or at least without regard to them. Its effect is to create a federal law regulating unfair trade practices. Limited to activities subject to the constitutional interstate Commerce Clause, it provides a broad civil remedy for these practices. Section 43(a) dispenses with intent, requiring only deception about a product, that is, false advertising. It also provides a wide range of equitable remedies, and it does not require proof of actual loss. The importance of section 43(a) aside from the creation of a federal "common law" of unfair competition is that it provides federal subject matter jurisdiction even in the absence of federal trademark registration. This means that trade dress—the appearance or even packaging of a product—can be protected without Lanham Act registration. *Two Pesos, Inc. v. Taco Cabana Int'l.* (1992). However, whereas trade dress that is only packaging need not have secondary meaning, trade dress that is part of product design needs secondary meaning to be protected. *Wal-Mart Stores v. Samara Brothers* (2000).

Common law remedies at first were limited to false designations of origin, but any false statements of fact suffice for a section 43(a) civil action. Statements need not be false on their face but can be false by implication, or by consideration of all surrounding circumstances. When a defendant claimed it was producing "potato chips," when, in fact, they were processed potato products, it was held to violate section 43(a). *Potato Chip Institute v. General Mills, Inc.* (1971). When a defendant manufactured artificial fur and used terms in its advertising such as "Normink," "platinum," and "the warmth and beauty of mink," it was held that there were deceptive representations despite the possible argument that there was no actual false statement of fact. Creation of a "false impression" was sufficient for a section 43(a) violation. *Mutation Mink Breeders Ass'n. v. Lou Nierenberg Corp.* (1959). The TLRA effectively has reversed those earlier cases that held that the requirements of section 43(a) are not met when a defendant makes false claims about the plaintiff's competing products.

The statute has been construed narrowly to provide a remedy to "commercial parties" only. *Johnson & Johnson v. Carter–Wallace, Inc.* (1980). Thus, it cannot serve as a general consumer protection statute. Within the context of "commercial parties," section 43 prohibits the use of false designations, descriptions, or representations in connection with goods or services in commerce. This prohibits deceptive descriptions of one's own or others' goods or services and provides a civil remedy to certain persons injured by the deception.

The statute also prohibits "palming off" by which a competitor deceives buyers into believing that its product or service is that of another. In "palming off," the injured party may be the purchaser if the purchased goods are inferior to the goods that they were represented to be. In addition, the competitor as to whose goods the bogus products were misdescribed has a remedy for assumed loss of business. Although section 43(a) is not simply "palming off," especially since the TLRA expanded the action to include not only false statements about the plaintiff's products or services but also competing ones, it still is true that "palming off" is one of its paradigms. However, to prevent collision between trademark and copyright law, it has been held that a section 43(a) action cannot be based on a misrepresentation of authorship of a noncopyrighted work, and that the "origin" of goods within the meaning of 43(a) does not extend to the orign of ideas contained within those goods. *Dastar Corp. v. Twentieth Century Fox Film Corp.* (2003).

There is no necessity to prove actual damages. When a defendant has made claims about its product that are false and the sales of which threaten to deprive a plaintiff of profits unfairly, the plaintiff is not required to prove that actual sales have been diverted to the defendant. Upon proof of the false statements and the likelihood of injury, the plaintiff is entitled to injunctive relief without proving any more than likelihood of injury. For monetary damages, however, the plaintiff must prove actual losses to avoid a windfall. *Johnson & Johnson v. Carter–Wallace, Inc.,* supra. Note, however, that in the new "cyberpiracy" provisions of section 43(d), statutory damages of up to $100,000 per domain name may be available. 5 U.S.C.A. § 1117(d).

If a defendant has profited unfairly by false statements, or if there is the threat that this might occur, a plaintiff is entitled to injunctive relief and perhaps damages without proving that the defendant acted intentionally. *Int'l. Election Systems Corp. v. Shoup* (1978).

The section 43(a) cause of action also has been limited with respect to standing to sue. Although there are cases that indicate the plaintiff need not be a direct competitor and that only a direct pecuniary interest is necessary, consumers have been held to have no standing despite the "any person" language in the statute. *Colligan v. Activities Club of New York, Ltd.* (1971). But see *Waits v. Frito–Lay, Inc.* (1992).

Section 43 is still developing. The TLRA revisions have added a prohibition against false advertising without any requirement of any showing of confusion, mistake, deception, or their likelihood. 15 U.S.C.A. § 1125(a)(2). Other, more recent amendments have prohibited the importing of products that violate the section, as well as acts of dilution, see § 13.6 supra, and so-called "cyberpiracy," 15 U.S.C.A. § 1125(b)-(d). Section 43(a) also has been used as a vehicle for asserting something close to copyright moral rights. See §§ 27.3–27.4, infra. One court has characterized section 43(a) as articulating "an affirmative code of business ethics." *Gold Seal Co. v. Weeks* (1955).

The provisions against "cyberpiracy" allow damages and injunctive relief against the bad faith registration of internet domain names that are confusingly similar to the marks of others, including personal names. Bad faith is determined by several factors, including the offer to sell the name to the owner without having any intention to use the name in a bona fide manner, or even a "pattern" of merely attempted sales of internet domain names. A broad exception prohibits a finding of bad faith when the registrant had a reasonable belief that she was engaged in fair use or otherwise lawful conduct. 15 U.S.C.A. § 1125(d).

# CHAPTER 17

# INFRINGEMENT

## § 17.1   Overview

The touchstone of trademark infringement is "likelihood of confusion." By requiring only a likelihood of confusion, a plaintiff's case is less burdensome. Since only a likelihood rather than a reality of confusion is necessary, the ambit of what constitutes confusion inevitably is widened, relaxing the need for proof of damage, absolute identity of the marks, identity of markets, and similar considerations.

There are specific inquiries probative of the likelihood of confusion:

(1) the similarity of the marks with respect to appearance, sound, connotation, and impression;

(2) similarity of the goods or services;

(3) similarity of "trade channels";

(4) conditions of sale—that is "impulse" v. considered purchases;

(5) strength of the competing marks;

(6) actual confusion;

(7) number and nature of similar marks on similar goods;

(8) length of time of concurrent use without actual confusion; and

(9) variety of goods with which each of the marks is used.

*In re E.I. DuPont DeNemours & Co.* (1973).

Prior to the 1962 amendments to the Lanham Act, proof of confusion as to purchasers was required. Now, likelihood of confusion need be demonstrated only in some significant respect; it need not be demonstrated as to purchasers. If a confusingly similar mark is likely to deceive or confuse any significant number of persons, infringement exists.

With dissimilar marks, there is little likelihood of confusion. All other things being equal, the more similar the mark, the more likely it is that confusion will exist. Those other things, however, are important. Among them are the strength of the mark, the similarity of the goods or services, the similarity and character of the markets, and the presence or absence of intent. *Chester Barrie, Ltd. v. Chester Laurie, Ltd.* (1960).

The last element, intent, clearly does not affect similarity or the likelihood of confusion *per se*. It is partly evidentiary and party equitable. As an evidentiary function, intent may be relevant in the close case. When an intentional act is involved, a court might justifiably conclude in a close case that confusion is likely. As an equitable measure, it is an important factor that the defendant acts in bad faith, so that the presence or absence of intent may determine whether an injunction will issue.

## § 17.2   Similarity of Marks

Marks may be confusingly similar based on physical design, sounds, psychological, commercial, or social connotations and significance, color scheme, or linguistic characteristics. These elements are interrelated so that (1) they are additive—that is, there is a greater likelihood of confusion as more of these different bases of similarity coexist—and (2) they are each independently sufficient, although not necessarily so—for example, the more similar or identical the physical design, the less necessary it is that they be similar in sound, connotation, or color.

Most words have a number of homonyms and all words of more than one syllable are composed of elements that exist in only a finite number. Because of the inevitability that the most basic elements of a mark will consist of the basic elements of a language (or, when applied to visual impact, the basic elements of spatial design, such as straight or curved lines), similarity cannot be measured solely by analysis of each of the elements of which the mark is composed. On the other hand, marks that are similar when taken as a whole cannot be distinguished by analyzing the separate elements to find one distinguishable element in a complex mark that, when examined as a whole, is confusingly similar to another. Courts will not "dissect and analyze trademarks'' to allow an infringer who is using a generally similar mark to avoid liability or to allow an owner to enjoin use of a generally dissimilar mark that happens to share some common elements with that of the owner. *Simoniz Co. v. Permanizing Stations of America, Inc.* (1931).

Since the inquiry is into the *similarity* of mark, rather than *identity* of mark, the test involves evaluating the *degree* of similarity. When the mark is fanciful or arbitrary, less actual replication of each linguistic element is necessary for similarity to be found. This is at least partly due to a suspicion about striking similarities involving fanciful words and the inference that the similarity is intentional. With respect to a fanciful mark, the presence of a different element—for instance, a different prefix or suffix—often will be insufficient to defend a claim of infringement. In such a case, there is no difference of meaning or connotation that might help distinguish two similar fanciful marks. Thus, with respect to fanciful or arbitrary names that carry no connotative substance but have only a distinctive sound, similarities of sound will be very persuasive—since sound is the only substance the mark has. *G.D. Searle & Co. v. Chas. Pfizer & Co.* (1959).

Courts, however, do examine the elements. The test is whether the marks will confuse the relevant consumers. Infringement of similar sounding marks will be determined on the basis of a balancing process that considers whether the market is composed of sophisticated customers who will take the time to analyze similar marks, whether the goods are similar, and other factors that logically relate to the likelihood of confusion in the marketplace.

When the marks are not fanciful or arbitrary, and thus have meanings that may help to distinguish them from each other, courts are likely to require much greater similarity of sound. However, the scale may be tipped by one of the other related factors. When similar sounding marks are involved, a most important factor is whether purchases are made in circumstances in which sound rather than appearance or spelling is decisive. Thus, in *Singer Mfg. Co. v. Morse Sewing Machine & Supply Corp.* (1955), the registration of the term "styleomatic" was refused on the opposition of the owner of "dialomatic." Although the terms had different substantive meanings, they had nearly identical sounds. The fact that the items frequently were ordered over the telephone and might be advertised on radio was decisive: since the market for the items was one in which sound dominated, similarity of sound was enough to create a likelihood of confusion despite the differences in content and appearance. But one court, finding "Lexis" and "Lexus" distinguishable in radio advertising, held that the appropriate standard is not "everyday spoken English," but "ordinary, reasonably careful speech." *Mead Data Central, Inc. v. Toyota Motor Sales, U.S.A.* (1989).

## § 17.3   Similarity of Goods or Services

To the extent that the marks may not be very similar, similarity of goods or services may be so great as to tip the balance. On the other hand, marks that are very nearly identical may be found noninfringing if they are used on entirely unrelated, dissimilar, goods or services. It is realistic to expect that consumers will be confused by only slightly dissimilar marks when the goods are absolutely identical. A famous example is the "Dramamine" case in which the identical goods—motion sickness medicine—were marketed under somewhat similar marks, "Dramamine," and "Bonamine." *G.D. Searle & Co. v. Chas. Pfizer & Co.* (1959). It is possible that the use of the identical mark "Dramamine" on a completely dissimilar and nonrelated product would not give rise to infringement. This certainly is true in the case of nonfanciful names that, unlike an arbitrary mark like "Dramamine," have considerably less strength. Thus, if the motion sickness pills were named "Steady" pills, it is unlikely that the manufacturer of "Steady" typewriters would be liable for infringement. There is no likelihood of confusion even with identical marks in completely unrelated markets for unrelated goods or services.

Of course, judging the similarity of goods or services is not so simple as determining whether the goods are exactly the same. Once goods are not absolutely identical, measurement of *how* similar they are must proceed from an understanding of the purpose of the inquiry.

Similarity of goods or services is determined by inquiring whether the products or services are similar in the eyes of the average consumer. From the standpoint of the consumer, goods are similar when they serve the same purposes, relate to the same activities, or fulfill the same needs. For instance, although dog food and dog vitamins are dissimilar in form, appearance, function, and many other ways, they serve the same purpose of nourishing domestic pets, relate to the activity of caring for animals, and fulfill the need of maintaining the health of those creatures. When a dog food manufacturer marketing its product under the mark "Doggie Dinner" opposed the registration of "DogEDite" as the mark for dog vitamins, it was successful despite the substantial dissimilarity of the marks because of the close similarity of the products and their purposes. *S.E. Mighton Co. v. La Pryor Milling Co.* (1960). It is thus the likely reaction of the average consumer that is determinative.

For instance, in a case involving the sale of products used for the growing of roses marketed by a registrant who opposed the registration of a similar mark to an applicant who marketed veterinary products, the court noted that, even though both parties manufactured insecticides, they were used differently enough to preclude confusion since the customers of the rose company "would probably be sickened by scenes depicted in Plaintiff's exhibit . . . of herds of ticks on the rear end of a steer. . . ." *Conard-Pyle Co. v. Thuron Industries, Inc.* (1978).

Determining similarity of goods may involve defining the goods, as well as the relevant market. In a way, this process is closely related to the problem of defining the product and market in antitrust cases. See Gellhorn & Kovacic, *Antitrust Law and Economics in a Nutshell, 4th ed.* The broader the market and product definition are, the more likely it is that goods will be found similar. For instance, in a case involving the marketing of men's clothing by a prior user of the mark "Hyde Park" who claimed infringement by a later user of the identical mark on women's clothing, the court found no infringement, largely by determining that men's clothing is not similar to women's clothing. *Hyde Park Clothes, Inc. v. Hyde Park Fashions, Inc.* (1953). Had the court defined the goods as clothing instead of men's clothing, the goods would have then been identical and the result may well have changed, for it would be difficult to deny infringement in a case in which both the goods and the mark are absolutely identical.

## § 17.4 Character and Similarity of Markets

Whether the average consumer is likely to be confused by similar marks applied to similar products or services may depend upon the consumer and his environment. When dealing with "impulse" buying in a supermarket, for instance, where goods are stocked closely together, and in which the consumer may be relatively inattentive, confusion may be a likely and common phenomenon. When considering purchases of expensive automobiles or highly technical equipment in which consumers exercise sophisticated judgments, confusion may be an almost nonexistent phenomenon. Similarity of goods and similarity of marks are weighed in a scale that is adjusted by considering the character of the market; the scale is recalibrated as the sophistication of the market changes. The "discriminating purchaser" theory frequently is decisive. For instance, in an opposition between a registrant of the mark "Climatrol" for air conditioning equipment and an applicant for the mark "Climematic" for identical equipment, the court held that the marks were not confusingly similar, considering the expensive nature of the products and the probable care that purchasers would use in making purchases. *L. J. Mueller Furnace Co. v. United Conditioning Corp.* (1955).

Equally important is whether the products or services are marketed in similar channels of trade. For instance, it is unlikely that confusion will result if very different consumers purchase the two different goods or services. The sale of products by one party solely in wholesale channels to other businessmen under a certain mark might reach such a different body of customers from that of the sale of the same or finished products to retail customers that there could be no infringement even if the marks and products were very similar. In *Dawn Donut Co. v. Hart's Food Stores, Inc.* (1959), the court held that the division between retail and wholesale markets was important in finding that there was no infringement. Similar issues have occurred in cases involving the sale by one party of books being purchased for very young children and the sale by another of books being purchased for older children, *Field Enterprises Educational Corp. v. Grosset & Dunlap, Inc.* (1966), and sales of furniture to the trade by one party and sales of furniture at retail by another party, *Habitat Design Holdings Ltd. v. Habitat, Inc.* (1977), although in the latter case the different marketing characteristics were not sufficient to avoid a claim of infringement when the supposedly "trade" showrooms actually were open to the public so that the retail customers also were significantly involved in the trade purchases.

That the parties market their products in wholly different ways, that is, retail and wholesale, may mean that confusion is impossible because definably different classes of customers exist. Of course, it also is true that there is no competition in such a case. If separate categories of customers exist who are aware of the different products or services and who may tend to associate the two in a general way, a court may decide to protect the deserving mark through a doctrine of expanded rights, despite the fact that there is no real confusion. A lack of competition is not necessarily decisive. Many modern courts find that irrelevant when trademark rights are subject to dilution. In these cases, courts tend to equate, perhaps illegitimately, similarity with confusion. *World Carpets, Inc. v. Dick Littrell's New World Carpets* (1971). However, this position seems supported by a literal reading of the present Lanham Act, in which the former language, requiring confusion as to the source of goods or services, was amended, abandoning any requirement for confusion as to source and, instead, requiring mere confusion.

This leaves it up to the courts to decide the critical issue: confusion as to what? Those courts that have decided that the statute thereby treats as sufficiently confusing any mark that is visually or sensorially similar have collapsed the requirement of confusion into similarity, a step not clearly mandated by the statute, and one that moves trademark perilously close to copyright. *Boston Professional Hockey Ass'n. v. Dallas Cap & Emblem Mfg., Inc.* (1975). Many courts, however, still use concepts originally derived from the former language of the Act, and require confusion as to origin or an implication of "association between the goods or sponsorship of the allegedly infringing goods." *Lindy Pen Co. v. Bic Pen Corp.* (1984).

The "related goods" doctrine recognizes that, despite differences in goods, products, or market channels, consumers may tend to *associate* different goods if there is a public expectation that these goods might emanate from the same source. This doctrine includes within the category of similar goods all those goods that a consumer might expect to be produced by the same manufacturer or provider of services. The effect of this doctrine is that seemingly totally unrelated goods may be found to be either similar or related, so that the use of a similar mark may be held infringing even though the owner of the mark does not produce or provide goods or services that are in any way similar to those of the alleged infringer.

For instance, in an action for infringement by the owner of the mark "Minute Maid" used for frozen fruit juice concentrates against a defendant who used the identical mark on frozen meats, the court found infringement because the same customers purchased the same categories of goods (frozen foods) in the same locations (food retail stores). Since both parties sold frozen food products and the customers legitimately might expect that one source was responsible for both products, there was a strong likelihood of confusion. The court noted that the danger of allowing similar marks on such related goods is that the good will of the registered owner might be harmed by association with that of the infringer, even though, naturally, there was no evidence of inferiority of goods. See § 13.4, supra. In this case there was evidence of actual confusion. *Pure Foods Inc. v. Minute Maid Corp.* (1954).

On the other hand, there are courts that reject this kind of monopolization by which a registered owner attempts to forbid all use of the mark by any other party, whether or not in competition and irrespective of actual confusion, simply by defining the category of goods or services so broadly that it effectively prohibits the use of the mark by any other person. For instance, one court called the attempt by the owner of "Sunkist" in connection with the marketing of fruits to prohibit the use of that mark in the marketing of bread products an "unconscionable" attempt to "monopolize the food market by the monopoly of the word 'Sunkist' on all manner of goods sold in the usual food stores."

*California Fruit Growers Exchange v. Sunkist Baking Co.* (1947). The court noted that in modern society marketing is accomplished in supermarkets and similar establishments in which many different products are sold under one roof. To call all these products "related goods" would broaden trademark rights so wide as to destroy the concept of trademark protection as a right appurtenant to actual use.

Therefore, in the application of the "related goods" doctrine, it seems that a finding that the articles or services merely share the same marketing environment should be insufficient to find the goods similar or related. There should be more evidence of likelihood of confusion than that the products or services are provided through a common mass marketing system because that is so characteristic of modern society.

## § 17.5 Subsidiary Evidence of Likelihood of Confusion

The most decisive factors probative of likelihood of confusion and therefore of infringement are the similarity of marks, similarity of goods or services, and the character and similarity of market conditions. However, the relative strength of the mark, the intent of the alleged infringer, the nature of the mark, and the existence of *actual* confusion can be persuasive. The factors are interrelated. Thus, the nature of the mark may interact with the relative strength of the mark; for instance, a fanciful or arbitrary mark may receive more protection than a common phrase, partly because there is less of a public interest in preserving public rights in a fanciful mark than there is in a word or phrase that is a part of our language. At the same time, it is possible that a fanciful or arbitrary mark may become a much stronger mark than will a common phrase or word, simply because it is more recognizable and distinctive. Likewise, because intent is persuasive, intentional infringements of fanciful or arbitrary marks frequently are enjoined, because it is a justifiable inference that a second-comer did not just "happen upon" a fanciful mark.

Finally, there can be little better evidence of a likelihood of confusion than evidence of actual confusion. When the dispute is over whether any customers really will be confused, proof of actual confusion quickly disposes of the central issue. On the other hand, the difficulty of proving a negative means that a defendant will not frequently succeed in disproving the likelihood of confusion by presenting a few witnesses who claim they were not actually confused. This does not mean that negative evidence always is unsuccessful, however, because occasionally evidence of lack of actual confusion can support a finding of noninfringement. *California Fruit Growers Exchange v. Sunkist Baking Co.* (1947).

For equitable relief, intent is logically relevant because it is directly related to considerations such as good faith that are of concern to a court of equity. However, the decision to grant relief can come only after a finding of infringement. In effect then, courts tend to take intentional actors at their word, concluding that if the infringer thought he would succeed in his attempt to gain business by imitating another's mark, there is nothing unfair about enjoining him. This resembles estoppel. The court treats that as a kind of admission that the infringer cannot easily deny.

Intent has an indirect relationship to the likelihood of confusion, based wholly on the accuracy of the infringer's judgment. The infringer's judgment is substituted for that of the court, which otherwise normally would conduct the complicated inquiry into the likelihood of confusion by examining such things as similarity of the mark, of the product or service, and of the character of the market. There are some intentional uses, however, that do not justify such an approach. For instance, when an innocent infringer is notified of the infringement but continues to use the mark intentionally only because it has developed the mark in its own locality, the infringer is then not attempting to profit by another's mark but is only trying to protect its own investment. *Straus v. Notaseme Hosiery Co.* (1916). Thus, the intent element must be evaluated carefully.

Some courts have accurately termed the significance of intent as raising a presumption that the infringer's acts successfully created deception. The effect of a finding of intent, in other words, is that the infringer must demonstrate that it failed in its attempt. The finding of intent is so important, in fact, that occasionally an appellate court will reverse a trial court's finding of an absence of likelihood of confusion based on a judicial skepticism that the infringer could have been mistaken; these courts imply that it is more likely the trial court was mistaken about the likelihood of confusion than was the infringer who intentionally adopted a course of action aimed at using another's mark successfully. *Harold F. Ritchie, Inc. v. Chesebrough–Pond's Inc.* (1960).

## § 17.6   Defenses—Fair and Collateral Use

Since trademark law is equitable, it utilizes the traditional equitable defenses with the added element of a presumption favoring the registrant. Whereas in most equitable cases the court considers the public interest generally, the scale is usually tipped considerably in trademark cases in favor of the registrant, who not only has the statutory license to use the mark but comes equipped with the presumption of validity that registration confers. Nevertheless, the equitable doctrines of laches, estoppel, and unclean hands are all applied in appropriate trademark infringement cases.

Fair use allows fair comment that incidentally involves use of the mark for a purpose other than that normally made of a trademark. Collateral use allows the use of goods that bear a preexisting mark, resembling the repair-reconstruction doctrine in patents. See § 8.6, supra. The parallel between collateral use and repair-reconstruction is striking in some cases. When a party uses a trademarked item as a component of a more complex product, the doctrine of collateral use allows the party to so identify the component by its trademarked name without fear of being liable for infringement. This is true, however, only insofar as the party does not deceive the public into thinking that the product, as sold, actually is marketed by the owner of the trademark. Thus, the reprocessor can use the trademark in a nonconspicuous way solely to identify the component, but not to misattribute the finished product to the trademark owner. *Prestonettes, Inc. v. Coty* (1924). When the mark is already on the product that is repaired or reprocessed, it need not necessarily be removed therefrom.

In such cases, then, the reprocessor does not necessarily commit infringement merely by failing to remove the mark. Any deception would occur, if at all, only if the reprocessor sold the items as new. In that event, however, it would not be a case of trademark infringement so much as a case of consumer fraud. Unless the seller claims that the item is new, the situation is no different than the seller of a used car who is not required to remove the nameplate of the manufacturer before selling it to avoid trademark infringement. *Champion Spark Plug Co. v. Sanders* (1947). On the other hand, one court preliminarily enjoined sales of stale cough drops, even though their expiration date would have accurately indicated that fact, when the manufacturer exercised quality control efforts aimed at keeping stale product off the market. *Warner-Lambert Co. v. Northside Dev. Corp.* (1996).

Fair use also involves the use of the mark in a "fair comment." The situation most often arises in some kind of advertising circumstance in which the alleged infringer's product or service is claimed to be comparable to that of the trademark owner. In the case of an imitation or copy the second-comer has the right to use the mark to identify the object imitated as long as precautions are taken to avoid deception or confusion. However, the risk of a certain amount of confusion may be necessary to use the mark, and the mere likelihood of confusion is not a bar to the fair use defense. *KP Permanent Make-Up, Inc. v. Lasting Impression I, Inc. et al.* (2004).

Especially because of the patent-law doctrine that unpatented products should be in the public domain, when parties attempt to copy unpatented items, the doctrine of fair use prevents trademark protection from becoming the equivalent of illegitimate patent protection. The courts have held that to disallow fair use would prevent the copier from informing the public about the availability of a substitute. Of course, if a party makes untrue claims of equivalence instead of engaging in mere comparison, or makes claims implying that a used product is new, that may constitute a violation of section 43(a). See *Smith v. Chanel, Inc.* (1968).

Parody has been held a legitimate form of trademark fair use, and, in fact, the subject is informed by the Supreme Court's treatment of copyright parody in *Campbell v. Acuff–Rose Music, Inc.* (1994).

See § 23.7, infra. But it is not fair use when a claimed parody is used to promote competitive goods or services. *Harley-Davidson, Inc. v. Grottanelli* (1999).

## § 17.7 Gray Market Goods

So called "gray market" goods bear valid trademarks, are imported into the United States, and compete with domestically manufactured or marketed goods bearing the same, equally valid, trademark. The term "gray market" is used to imply that something is wrong with them or their marketing, although their trademark status is often perfectly legitimate, which is why they are certainly not "black market" goods. Domestic parties complain that these lower-priced "parallel imports," for one reason or another, compete unfairly with their own products. However, it is clear that trademark law does not give a party the right to exclude the sale of most gray market goods. The fact that the gray market trademark was authorized by a legitimate trademark owner is enough to remove any claim of trademark infringement. The dispute over parallel imports usually is not one of trademark law, but one of international trade law sometimes bordering on protectionism. It requires, at least, particular legislation because trademark law alone offers no comfort when the trademark is legitimate. The Tariff Act of 1930 forbids the importation of a very limited category of parallel imports, 19 U.S.C.A. §§ 1301 et seq. The Supreme Court upheld the Customs Service position that the statute does not apply when there is common control, that is a relationship of parent, subsidiary, or sibling subsidiary, between the domestic and foreign party. 19 C.F.R. § 133.21(b) (1987). Only when the gray market producer is not subject to common control, but merely an authorized independent party, is there any legislative remedy—and at that, it is not a trademark remedy but one of international trade law. *K Mart Corp. v. Cartier, Inc.* (1988). However, when the gray market goods differ in a materially significant way from those sold domestically, they are excludable under 19 U.S.C.A. § 1337 as trademark infringements unless sufficiently labelled to mitigate consumer confusion. *Gamut Trading Co. v. United States* ITC (1999).

## § 17.8   Eleventh Amendment Immunity

Although Congress attempted to abrogate the states' Eleventh Amendment immunity by defining "person" in sections 43(a) and 1127 to include states and their instrumentalities, the Supreme Court has held, in a section 43(a) action, that this is constitutionally invalid absent a pattern of state trademark infringement, similar to its reason for rejecting immunity in the patent law context. See §§ 9.5, 10.1, supra, and § 26.6, infra. *College Savs. Bank v. Florida Prepaid Postsecondary Educ. Expense Bd.* (1999).

# CHAPTER 18

# REMEDIES

## § 18.1 Overview

The remedies for infringement under the Lanham Act are statutory and consist of: (1) injunctive relief, (2) an accounting for profits, (3) damages, including the possibility of treble damages when appropriate, (4) attorney's fees in "exceptional cases," and (5) costs. 15 U.S.C.A. § 1117.

Importantly, these remedies are cumulative so that a plaintiff may recover not only the defendant's profits, but damages, as well. In addition, both damages and profits can be adjusted by the court above those actually proven—damages to an extent three times that demonstrated, and profits to an amount that the court finds appropriate.

## § 18.2 Injunctive Relief

The normal equitable principles apply to trademark law, including the standard defenses. However, in awarding equitable relief, the general rule that the public interest is to be considered has a particular cast to it since the Lanham Act is considered a statement of the public interest. Thus, the grant of equitable relief usually protects not only the plaintiff from infringement but also the public from deception. On the other hand, there are instances when relief might create an effective monopoly in the plaintiff over the product as well as the mark. Therefore, the public interest tends to cut both ways. See *Crossbow, Inc. v. Glovemakers, Inc.* (1967).

Otherwise, the grant of preliminary and permanent equitable relief mirrors other areas of the law. In trademark cases, equitable relief must be carefully framed in an affirmative manner so as to prohibit illegitimate infringement while allowing legitimate competitive activity. A plaintiff may well demand that the defendant cease all activity but courts are exceedingly careful to recognize that some of the activities of defendants that cost plaintiff business nevertheless may be the results of legitimate competitive practices. For instance, when a plaintiff demanded that defendant be enjoined from competing, the court instead affirmatively required that the defendant conspicuously notify all prospective purchasers that the defendant's product was not the same as the plaintiff's, thereby prohibiting the infringement but continuing fair competition. *William R. Warner & Co. v. Eli Lilly & Co.* (1924).

## § 18.3 Accounting

Accounting is a traditional equitable remedy available to recover profits unfairly gained from another's property. Under the Lanham Act, plaintiffs are entitled to an accounting *in addition to damages.* The burden is upon the defendant to prove items of cost; all the plaintiff has to demonstrate is defendant's gross income. In other words, the plaintiff in a Lanham Act action only has to prove the total amount of defendant's sales and need not worry about what portion of those gross sales are attributable to the cost of the items, advertising, administrative costs, and any other expenses that are deductible from gross amounts to determine profits. The defendant must prove to the court whatever expenses it wishes to claim are appropriate.

Additionally, the plaintiff does not have to demonstrate that, had the defendant not made these sales, the consumers would have purchased from the plaintiff instead. In other words, plaintiff does not have to prove that defendant's sales directly competed with plaintiff's. In order to vindicate the public interest in preventing deceptive trade practices, it is deemed appropriate to allow the plaintiff to be the beneficiary and receive the profits rather than defendant. It effectively allows the trademark plaintiff to be a private attorney general. *Monsanto Chem. Co. v. Perfect Fit Products Mfg. Co.* (1965).

Finally the court is entitled to adjust the award of profits either up *or down* when, despite the proof offered by plaintiff and defendant, the court is satisfied that the amounts demonstrated are either oppressive or inadequate when measured by a compensatory rather than punitive standard. A court must be certain that the accounting for profits does not yield a result that is so high as to work a punishment on the defendant rather than as a compensation to the plaintiff for any losses. The court also must guard against the possibility that the accounting fails to consider factors that unfairly deprive the plaintiff of what is justly his. *Caesars World, Inc. v. Venus Lounge, Inc.* (1975).

## § 18.4  Damages

The Lanham Act provides that a plaintiff is to recover damages and, according to the "circumstances," the court may award any amount up to three times the demonstrated damages. However, the Act concludes by stating: "Such sum ... shall constitute compensation and not a penalty." 15 U.S.C.A. § 1117.

Thus, a recurring question has involved the propriety of exemplary or punitive damages in Lanham Act infringement actions. The better reasoned cases conclude that the final sentence of section 1117 expressly precludes the award of punitive damages. The phrase therefore is interpreted to provide for three times a showing of *actual* damages when there is some demonstration that the plaintiff's proof did not include all of his actual losses. *Caesars World, Inc. v. Venus Lounge, Inc.* (1975).

## § 18.5  Attorneys' Fees

At one time, the traditional American rule against the award of attorney's fees to the successful party was good law in trademark cases. The Supreme Court held that there was no reason to vary the rule absent statutory authorization. *Fleischmann Distilling Corp. v. Maier Brewing Co.* (1967). However, in 1975, Congress amended the Lanham Act to include the award of attorneys' fees in "exceptional cases." 15 U.S.C.A. § 1117. This mirrors the provision in the Patent Act, 35 U.S.C.A. § 285, also allowing attorneys' fees in the identical circumstances. See § 9.4, supra. It is fairly certain that attorneys' fees are to be awarded on a party-neutral basis, although there may be some reason to favor prevailing defendants. *Fogerty v. Fantasy, Inc.* (1994).

# PART III

# COPYRIGHT

## CHAPTER 19

## FOUNDATIONS OF COPYRIGHT PROTECTION

### § 19.1 Origins and Development of Copyright Law

The development of copyright law in England was shaped by the efforts of mercantile interests to obtain monopoly control of the publishing industry—similar to those of the guilds that were instrumental in shaping patent and trademark law. The history of copyright law is largely the story of judicial and statutory reactions to the resulting monopolistic restraints. In addition to the interest of publishers in having a monopoly over the production of books similar to the interest of medieval guilds in having control over the production of new technology, the development of copyright law also was uniquely influenced by those with an interest in controlling the *content* of new works of authorship. The most significant interest of this character was the church, which sought to restrict the dissemination of anticlerical and reformation publications.

This interest, however, has left few important legacies; by far, the most enduring influence on the development of copyright law was that of the publishers themselves.

During the late seventeenth century, the control that the publishing groups exercised over the printing of books was challenged by authors and others wishing to share in the commercial rewards of publishing. In 1710, Parliament enacted the Statute of Anne, which purported to limit the formerly perpetual rights held by publishers to a period of years. Thus, copyright law has been shaped since at least 1710 by practices and laws intended to limit as well as to create monopolistic copyright protection.

The growth of legal protection for bookbinders and printers illuminated an important commercial distinction between the author and the publisher that existed at least as early as the eighteenth century. Although the author had some ill-defined legal rights to his work prior to publication, after the work was distributed the publisher gained the publication rights. This distinction between pre and postpublication rights that originated in the distinction between the two interests involved—authors and publishers—survived until recently in slightly altered form.

American copyright law came to distinguish between the "common law" right of an author to his unpublished creations, and the statutory copyright that might be secured upon publication. Until recently, therefore, an author had a perpetual right to his creation, which included the right to decide when, if, and how to publish the work, but that common law right terminated upon publication at which time statutory rights became the sole rights, if any, to which the author was entitled. This distinction was altered by the Copyright Act of 1976 (the "new Act"), which shifts the line of demarcation between common law and statutory copyright from the moment of publication to the moment of fixation of the work into a tangible form.

Article I, section 8, clause 8 of the Constitution states: "The Congress shall have Power ... To promote the Progress of Science ..., by securing for limited Times to Authors ... the exclusive Right to their ... Writings...." See § 1.1, supra. Under this clause, Congress has the power to enact any legislation consistent with the intent of the Constitution to provide copyright protection for limited times. There is no requirement however, that this power be exercised. This point undercuts any claim of an author for protection that does not appear in the Act itself. In fact, Congress has exercised its power since 1790.

Although Congress need not exercise the constitutional power at all, if it does, it must do so within the wording of the clause. Perpetual rights probably would be unconstitutional, therefore, because the grant in Article I, section 8 is only for "limited times." But exactly how to implement that term, and perhaps the entire constitutional clause itself, seems to be within a virtually unassailable Congressional discretion. *Eldred v. Ashcroft* (2003). Also, the subject matter of copyright protection is somewhat loosely circumscribed by the use of the words "Authors" and "Writings." As will be seen, the word "writings" has been very broadly construed, so as to include even such things as sculpture, videotape, notated or recorded choreography, and computer programs. On the other hand, the Supreme Court has invalidated an attempt to enact trademark legislation under this clause, see § 11.1, supra, because trademarks are not writings.

Copyright, at least in Anglo–American jurisprudence, never has developed a procedure of administrative examination before registration as is true of both patent and trademark law. Instead, copyright has developed the doctrine that expressive works are entitled to protection without examination— and, in fact, largely without registration. At common law, prepublication protection would have been impossible, of course, if prior examination were required since one of the purposes of protection was the author's privacy. Registration is significant to modern American copyright law but the basic doctrine of this country's copyright law is to protect authors without requiring it.

## § 19.2 The Copyright Acts

Pursuant to the constitutional clause, Congress adopted a copyright statute in 1790 and, since that time, has substantially revised or rewritten the copyright law four times—in 1831, 1870, 1909, and 1976. More limited amendments, typically to deal with specific issues, have been enacted from time to time. As new forms of expression became commercially important, the copyright law was revised or rewritten to protect the exploitation of those technologies. In 1802 Congress added prints to the works subject to protection. The 1831 law added musical compositions to protected subject matter and the 1870 revision added such things as paintings, sculpture, and other fine arts to the list of copyrightable works.

The 1909 Act is primarily important today because it is the last act that maintained the distinction between prepublication and postpublication rights. Although the 1976 Act abandoned that distinction, the 1909 dichotomy is still significant with respect to the immense body of protected works that originally were governed by the 1909 statute and in certain respects continue to be despite the 1976 revision. See § 24.7, infra.

All of the Acts have required deposit or registration of the protected work in one form or another either with a United States District Court, the Secretary of State, or, as is presently the case, the Register of Copyrights. At one time deposit was a prerequisite to protection but by 1909 deposit was merely a formality and became mandatory only to initiate an infringement suit. Registration has experienced a similar decline in significance.

Thus, the history of copyright protection is in many respects a history of decreasing formalities. Just as deposit and registration achieved lesser importance until they finally became merely formal prerequisites to the initiation of a lawsuit, so did virtually all other formalities.

Perhaps most importantly, the United States' accession to the Berne Convention in 1989 was accompanied by extraordinary revisions of the Act that essentially made copyright notice completely elective. Virtually its only significance now is that it bars a defense of innocent infringement. But because we are now a member of the Berne Convention, United States authors have gained more rights and advantages in the international copyright arena.

Until recently, the United States always had granted protection in multiples of fourteen years. The 1909 Act had an initial term of twenty-eight years followed by a possible renewal for another twenty-eight years. The 1976 Act, however, adopted a lifetime-plus-fifty-years (now a lifetime-plus-seventy-years) period.

The present Act extends protection to just about anything that can be expressed in tangible form. Some works receive less protection than others— most notably sound recordings, which lack what are called "performance rights," except for digital transmissions thereof.

## § 19.3 The Common Law–Statutory Copyright Distinction and the 1976 Act

The historical distinction between the rights of an author to his unpublished creation and the rights of the publisher—whether an independent printer, bookbinder, or the author himself—to exclusive control of the exploitation of the copying enterprise found a sturdy and long-lived home in the American copyright statutes and the body of common law rights that developed around them. The distinction produced two separate concepts of copyright. The *common law copyright* became the right of an author to exclude all others from his unpublished works. Someone who purloined another's unpublished manuscript, produced copies of another's unpublished artistic creation, or published the score of an unpublished musical composition could be sued for infringement of the creator's common law copyright. The common law copyright was perpetual and an author who decided not to publish and keep her creation to herself could prevent others from copying the work forever. In fact, the creator's heirs likewise could prevent others from copying the work and until an authorized person actually published it—at which time it potentially entered the domain of *statutory copyright*—others could be prevented from copying it in perpetuity.

However, once the work was published, the common law copyright was extinguished. From then on, protection was afforded only through statutory means. Instead of being perpetual, statutory copyright was limited—a maximum of fifty-six years under the 1909 Act, for example. Under common law copyright, the creator had perpetual protection but could not exploit it because if he published the work, common law copyright would be extinguished. Thus, in exchange for the privilege of publicly exploiting their work and making a profit from it, authors bargained away their perpetual rights and accepted a limited monopoly period to disseminate their work publicly, gaining protection that they would not have had otherwise upon abandoning their common law protection.

For many years the distinction between common law and statutory protection was perceived to be burdensome. For one thing, the system of dual protection made it difficult to predict exactly when common law privileges would be extinguished and when statutory protection would start. Many of the difficulties arose in connection with the definition of publication—the point at which common law protection died and statutory protection potentially began. The issue became more complicated each time a new medium of communication—theatre, motion pictures, radio, television—came into existence. Many felt the need for a single unified system of protection that would not depend upon the somewhat unpredictable concept of publication. As a result, the 1976 Act attempted to abolish all significant aspects of common law copyright and created a unified protection system by beginning statutory protection as soon as the work was reduced to a concrete form. 17 U.S.C.A. § 102(a).

## § 19.4  Copyright Basics

Under the 1976 Act an author is protected as soon as a work is recorded in some concrete way, since the Act protects all expressions upon fixation in a tangible medium. 17 U.S.C.A. § 102(a). Protection under the 1976 Act is secure until seventy years after the death of the author. 17 U.S.C.A. § 302(a). Certain exclusive rights belong to the author, to her assigns, or sometimes to her employer if the work is a "work for hire." 17 U.S.C.A. § 203(a)(b)(d). The author or copyright owner has the exclusive right to make copies of the work, 17 U.S.C.A. § 106(1), and anyone who produces copies without authorization is subject to an infringement suit, which provides damages, sometimes attorneys' fees, and injunctive relief. It is also a criminal act to violate the federal copyright laws. 17 U.S.C.A. § 506. In addition to the right to make copies, copyright protection also allows the owner to control derivative works—such as plays, motion pictures, or other adaptations of the basic work, 17 U.S.C.A. § 106(2)—and to sue for damages and injunctive relief against anyone basing any other work on it that is substantially similar. The owner also has exclusive rights, with respect to most works, to display and perform the work publicly. 17 U.S.C.A. § 106(4)(5).

Just as patent protection extends to any useful, nonobvious, novel, *application* of an idea, copyright protection centers fundamentally upon the original *expression* of an idea, whether literary, artistic, commercial, or otherwise. The expression is the key because only the expression is protected by copyright. For example, the idea of a Civil War family besieged by the terrors and hardships of internecine conflict cannot be copyrighted. But the *expression* of that idea in a complex dramatic story, such as *Gone With The Wind,* is accorded important copyright protection.

The basic concept of copyright is *originality.* The parallel in patent law are the concepts of novelty, nonobviousness, and utility, and, in trademark, distinctiveness. An invention, to be patentable, must be new or novel; it cannot have been invented previously by another. A copyrighted work, however, need not be novel. The author need not demonstrate that he was the first to create the particular expression embodied in his work. Since his work need not be novel, all that is needed to obtain copyright is originality—that the work have *originated* with him; the author cannot have copied it from another. 17 U.S.C.A. § 102(a). Therefore the author's ideas and themes may have appeared in earlier works. Indeed much of the expression may have been produced before, but copyright will be available to the second author if his is a work of independent creation.

Thus, the twin concepts of *expression* and *originality* are the fundamental building blocks of copyright protection. An original expression is copyrightable provided that the copyright act protects the particular form of expression. Section 102 of the statute provides eight categories of protected subject matter: literary works, musical works, dramatic works, choreographic works, graphic works, audiovisual works, sound recordings, and architectural works. However the Act indicates that these forms are only listed by way of example, and are not meant to limit the more general definition of copyrightable subject matter, which is meant to extend to any "original works of authorship" fixed in a tangible medium whether within or without the listed categories.

# CHAPTER 20

# THE SUBJECT MATTER OF COPYRIGHT

## § 20.1  Originality

The essence of copyright is originality, which implies that the copyright owner or claimant originated the work. By contrast to a patent, however, a work of originality need not be novel. An author can claim copyright in a work as long as he created it himself, even if a thousand people created it before him. Originality only implies that the copyright claimant did not copy from someone else. From that definition of originality comes the common but true example that an author could gain a copyright on the *Romeo and Juliet* story as long as he made it up himself and did not copy it from Shakespeare. The resulting copyright would prevent anyone else from copying the work of the copyright owner (but it would not prevent others from copying Shakespeare's creation since that is in the public domain).

It is important to understand the genesis of the originality requirement. The copyright grant depends in the first instance upon an understanding of the constitutional language. The constitutional grant only states that "authors" may have protection for their "writings." The only constitutional restrictions on copyrightability, implicit or otherwise, must be provided by whatever connotations the words "author" and "writings" possess. Historically, these restrictions have been relatively minimal, and the requirements for copyright protection have been far less than the requirements for patent protection. The one enduring requirement over the past two hundred years has been that of originality, since it seems almost self-evident that one cannot be an author unless one originates something. The requirement of originality is therefore a direct result of the requirement of "authorship" provided by the language of the Constitution itself.

This is not to imply, however, that there never has been controversy as to the limits of copyright protection because of the requirement of "authors" and "writings." For instance, whether copyright protection could extend to anything more than a literal writing was an early issue, and was resolved quickly when one of the first copyright statutes provided protection for works of fine art. Once it became clear, however, that literality was no limit on copyright protection and that "writings" could also include paintings, sculptures, and other works of art, it also became clear that "authors" might include more than just literary artists and that, in fact, just as they need not be literary, they might not even be artists. Once the breadth of the constitutional words was accepted, it became obvious that a very minimal standard of originality was all that could be erected as an outer limit on copyright protection. In other words, only the minimal limit of originality—that protection could apply to anything a person created (originated)—remained.

Nevertheless, controversy has arisen over the limits of originality itself. Courts have wavered throughout the years over what was a suitable standard. In *Bleistein v. Donaldson Lithographing Co.* (1903), the Supreme Court held, that copyright was not limited to the fine arts and that it was outside both copyright law and the competence of courts to attempt to assess the artistic merits of original creations. The Court articulated a broad concept of originality, refusing to weigh the creative or artistic merits of lithographs against their more mundane commercial functions. As long as the work fit the statutory category of copyrightable matter and as long as the claimant originated it, there was no bar to copyrightability. A work had originality if it was "one man's alone."

At least since the Supreme Court's decision in *Burrow-Giles Lithographic Co. v. Sarony* (1884), for instance, photographs of real-life situations and objects have been copyrightable. The justification for protection was that the photographer had invested his pictures with serious artistic consideration and creative effort. But after *Bleistein,* such a claim seemed unnecessary and photographs are deemed copyrightable not because of any artistic creative effort but simply because they are the work of "one man alone." The fortuitously taken Zapruder film of the Kennedy assassination had the requisite originality for copyright protection. *Time Inc. v. Ber-*

*nard Geis Associates* (1968). The combination of happenstance and fate that led to shooting those films amplify the fact that originality is minimal, indeed. Seemingly, all that the owner added that was "one man's alone" was a push on the camera's button.

A reproduction is essentially a copy. The source of its subject matter did not originate with the reproducer but with the original author. Nevertheless, the copyrightability of reproductions of works of art is well-established. *Alfred Bell & Co. v. Catalda Fine Arts, Inc.* (1951). This accepted conclusion is based on the fact that the copyist has originated the reproduction, if nothing else. Although the underlying public domain subject matter is not, of course, protected—since others are free to copy the original—the copyist is protected against those who might attempt to gain a "free ride" by simply reproducing the reproduction instead of investing the effort required to copy the original.

The copyist must demonstrate that he has contributed something to the final reproduction. Thus, some courts speak of a distinguishable or substantial variation between the reproduction and original that satisfies the requirement of originality. As long as the variation between original and copy is more than merely "trivial," the requirement of originality is satisfied. *Alfred Bell & Co. v. Catalda Fine Arts, Inc.,* supra.

Until relatively recently, the so-called "sweat of the brow" doctrine supplied requisite originality to works that clearly had no artistic merit and often were simply aggregations of public domain material such as maps, charts, and telephone directories. The "sweat of the brow" doctrine only demanded that the author demonstrate the investment of some "original work" into the final product. However, the doctrine was firmly rejected by the Supreme Court in *Feist Publications v. Rural Telephone Service* (1991), which held that originality requires at least "some minimal degree of creativity," a standard not met by the simple alphabeticization of names in the white pages telephone book.

Without the "sweat of the brow" doctrine, many simple fact compilations once considered copyrightable, such as judicial case reporters, have been found unprotected because such simple things as pagination are not minimally creative enough. *Matthew Bender & Co. v. West Publishing Co.* (1998). Similar economically valuable fact collections, such as straightforward computer databases, seem uncopyrightable, leading to pressures to enact *sui generis* database protection statutes, as has the European Union. Whether these statutes will be effective or constitutional, or even any more desirable than other *sui generis* schemes that, more often than not, turn out to be ill-considered, is an open question.

Another open question is the continuing viability of the notion that a different standard of originality applies to bare fact works as opposed to the standard for fiction. It seems that all works must satisfy the minimal degree of creativity demanded by *Feist*

*Publications.* But how much creativity is required by *Feist* in a particular context remains unclear as the federal courts continue to struggle with the Supreme Court's decisions.

## § 20.2   Copyrightable Works

The constitutional limits and powers of the Copyright Clause are not necessarily coextensive with the powers and limits defined by the copyright statutes. The Constitution first defines the outer limit of protectability but Congress must expressly grant protection. Under the 1976 Copyright Act, the statute appears coextensive with the constitutional power, since although it lists, as previous statutes did, specific forms of works subject to copyright, it also states that copyright protection "subsists ... in original works of authorship fixed in any tangible medium of expression, *now known or later developed....*" 17 U.S.C.A. § 102(a) (emphasis supplied). In addition, the specifically listed categories are introduced by the phrase that copyright is to "include" those categories, thus demonstrating that copyright is not to be limited merely to the specifically listed categories. As nearly as it could, Congress attempted in the 1976 Act to extend copyright protection to all major categories of works cognizable under the Constitution. See § 20.4, infra.

The boundaries of copyright thus are not defined by the statutorily listed categories of works in section 102. They are defined instead by the broader concepts of copyright articulated in the case law.

One of the most basic of those concepts is the distinction between utilitarian and nonutilitarian objects. Purely utilitarian objects are not subject to copyright protection. However, to the extent a work is nonutilitarian or with respect to those separable portions of a work that are nonutilitarian, there is no reason to deny copyright protection, assuming it is statutorily authorized. For instance, in *Mazer v. Stein* (1954), the Supreme Court allowed the copyright of lamp bases, in the form of statuettes, despite the fact that the lamp itself was functional and clearly utilitarian.

One reason the courts are unwilling to grant copyright protection to purely utilitarian works is that patent protection is reserved to works of utility. Because copyright protection lasts longer than patent protection and also because copyright protection is granted upon the very minimal showing of originality as opposed to the rigorous demonstration of novelty, nonobviousness, and utility required for patent protection, courts attempt to keep the borders between copyright and patent well-defined and clear. Thus, to allow copyright protection for a utilitarian object would allow monopoly control over something that might more appropriately be subject to the very different protection of patent law but probably could not satisfy the demanding prerequisites of the Patent Act (and the constitutional Patent Clause) to qualify for protection.

A similar argument is posed by the problems of the copyrightability of forms, systems, contest blanks, tests, and similar items. Once again, a basic copyright concept is at work. The federal courts have made it clear that copyright is reserved for the *expression* of an idea; it does not extend to the *idea* itself—courts are reluctant to grant protection when the expressive elements of the work seems to be coextensive with the underlying idea. For instance, in *Baker v. Selden* (1879), the copyrightability of an accounting system was at issue. The Supreme Court held that since the defendant's account books were arranged differently than those of the original author, it was not infringement to use the principles or ideas expounded by the original author. The Court emphasized the difference between the "art," or subject matter of the book, and the "description" of the art, or its expression. The idea underlying Selden's system of accounting was not copyrightable, although its expression was. Thus, if there had been literal copying of the original author's forms of account, it would have been infringement. Since the defendant's account books were arranged differently, all that had been taken from the author was the idea, or the "art," which is not protectible under copyright.

Naturally, the most fundamental issue involved in *Baker v. Selden* is the copyrightability of ideas. Since all are free to borrow the idea (it cannot be monopolized), there is very little protection available to the original author of a similar system of accounting or business methods generally except the protection against copying the original explanation of the system. As a result, numerous fields have very little protection, other than against literal copying of the works themselves. In *Continental Casualty Co. v. Beardsley* (1958), the Court held that insurance forms and instruments are copyrightable but found that the scope of protection of forms varies according to the degree of variation in expression inherently available to potential competitors. In other words, to the extent that a form can be expressed in many different ways, an original author will be protected against copying. However, as the form becomes more simple and the possibilities of expressing the underlying idea in different ways become fewer, only a strictly literal reproduction would constitute infringement, if at all.

The scope of copyrightable subject matter is determined, therefore, by two basic principles: the utilitarian-nonutilitarian or functional-nonfunctional dichotomy, and the idea-expression dichotomy. Thus, the explanation of Selden's bookkeeping method was copyrightable, although the method itself was not. In *Beardsley,* however, the only issue was the forms themselves but both the utilitarian function and the expressive function were united in them. The court could not separate the two as it could separate the sculptured base from the functional lamp bases in *Mazer v. Stein.* Thus, the court had two options: it could hold that when the utilitarian function and the nonutilitarian were inseparable, there could be no protection or, alternatively, that when they were so inseparable, protection should not be completely denied. Opting for the latter, the court distinguished the insurance forms from the *Mazer* lamps and, in order not to extend copyright protection unduly far, chose to limit its scope rather than ban it completely on subject matter grounds.

As idea and expression merge or as the difference between utility and nonutility narrows, the court is faced with that same choice. When there are few possible ways to express an idea, the doctrine of *merger* often applies to preclude copyrightability, as it does to many features of computer programs. *Lotus Development Corp. v. Borland Int'l., Inc.* (1995), affirmed by an equally divided Supreme Court. With respect to boxtop contests, it has been held that when the manner of expression of the rules incidental to an uncopyrightable game merges with the idea of the contest itself, copyright is not appropriate. *Morrissey v. Procter & Gamble Co.* (1967). Similarly, fabric designs, fashion designs, and jewelry designs have questionable copyrightability. To the extent that the design is separable from its utilitarian aspect, such as a simple pattern upon bolts of cloth, copyrightability has been upheld. *Peter Pan Fabrics, Inc. v. Martin Weiner Corp.* (1960). To the extent that copyright is sought in the end product itself, such as a dress by drawing a picture of the dress, copyright has been denied. *Jack Adelman, Inc. v. Sonners & Gordon, Inc.* (1934).

Blueprints of structures are themselves copyrightable but until recently, constructing a building that duplicated the plans did not necessarily violate the architect's copyright. *Imperial Homes Corp. v. Lamont* (1972). The 1976 Act's legislative history distinguished between functional structures such as houses and buildings and nonfunctional ones such as monuments and statues, under which the latter were protected but the former were not. But, in 1988 and again in 1990, the Act was amended, partly due to our accession to the Berne Convention, to extend copyright to architectural plans and their embodiments in the form of, for instance, the very buildings themselves but does not include "individual standard features." This is probably meant to exclude copyrightability from the functional elements such as doors, windows, and standard hardware but to recognize protection in the architectural elements of design. Additionally, it is explicitly not an infringement to photograph a copyrighted building that is "ordinarily visible from a public place." 17 U.S.C.A. § 120(a).

Whether a work is protected or not will depend not only upon the idea-expression dichotomy and the utilitarian-nonutilitarian dichotomy, but also on the availability of other types of relief. For instance, the availability of patent protection or of design patent protection may influence a court in denying copyrightability. Although there is no legal bar to simultaneous protection, the availability of patent protection, for instance, may be decisive to a court in determining where on the functional-nonfunctional continuum a particular work lies. The more likely it is that patent protection is available, the more likely it is that a court will hold a work to be functional rather than nonfunctional. *Brown Instrument Co. v. Warner* (1947). The same is true of design patents, although the functional character of such works is reduced significantly and, thus, the likelihood that copyright will be denied also is lessened. In *In re Yardley* (1974), the court held that design patents and copyrights both can exist in the same work.

## § 20.3   Noncopyrightable Works

Since, under the 1976 Act, any original work of authorship fixed in a tangible medium from which the expression can be reproduced is copyrightable, there are few works remaining that are outside the scope of the Act. However, one area—intangible (unfixed) expressions—still is clearly beyond the Act. One important example of this type of work is choreography. To the extent that a choreographer creates a dance or series of movements and does not reduce it to a tangible medium of expression, there is no federal statutory protection under the copyright laws. However, if the choreographer films his work, or reduces it to choreographic notation, there is no question that protection exists.

The same analysis holds true for oral presentations. A speech, lecture, or other vocal performance, to the extent it is not reduced to tangible form, is outside the Act. Protection must come from the common law. Again, if the author reduces it to writing or to any other fixed form, protection subsists.

Typefaces undeniably are tangible, but lie outside the Act largely for historical reasons and perhaps because of their functionality. Typefaces never were accepted for registration by the copyright office, although it now accepts computer programs that design typefaces. *Adobe Systems v. Southern Software, Inc.* (1998).

## § 20.4   Writings and Fixation

Since constitutional protection is afforded only to "writings" of "authors," it is clear that it would be unconstitutional to afford protection to works that are undeniably not "writings," at least under the Copyright Clause. However, the term has been given very broad construction beginning at least as early as 1865 when photographs were included in the copyright statute.

Under the new Act, the analog to the constitutional term "writings" is "works of authorship." One issue is whether anything can qualify as a work of authorship beyond the notion of a writing. Because of the broad construction given the term "writing," however, as "any physical rendering of the fruits of creative, intellectual or aesthetic labor," *Goldstein v. California* (1973), and because of the equally broad definition of originality, it is unlikely that the constitutional clause will be a realistic barrier to any tangible item that an author may claim to have originated. Congress has explicitly denied that the language "works of authorship" was intended to be coextensive with the constitutional term "writings," but it is unlikely that there are substantial areas in which copyright coverage is doubtful merely because of the wording of the statute. To avoid taking a firm position with respect to new technologies, Congress explicitly limited the term "original works of authorship" to something less than the full scope of the word "writings" as used in the Constitution. However, it is difficult to identify those works that would constitute writings but that would not be original works of authorship. This problem never may arise judging by the historically broad judicial construction of the word "writing," and the open-ended character of the key provisions of the Copyright Act.

Despite the extremely broad manner in which "writings" has been construed, such things as computer programs, phonorecords, and dramatic personalities, have at times been denied protection. Even today no matter how much is invested in developing a dramatic character for a public performance, it is not copyrightable unless it is at some point reduced to a physical expression. In *Columbia Broadcasting System, Inc. v. DeCosta* (1967), the plaintiff had developed a character called "Paladin," consisting of a western cowboy personality dressed in black who would appear at public occasions on horseback and hand out a calling card with the statement "Have Gun Will Travel—Wire Paladin" on it. The plaintiff claimed that the defendants had stolen his character and developed it into a television series called "Have Gun Will Travel" in which the character bore a striking resemblance to the one he had created. Because he had never reduced his creation to a fixed form, however, the court found that he had no copyright protection. The mere development of such an evanescent thing as a dramatic character did not fulfill the constitutional or 1909 Act's requirement that copyright could exist only in "writings," despite the otherwise broad construction of that term. This does not leave the author completely unprotected, however, because state common law remedies still offer substantial protection against unfair competition and other tortious conduct.

Similarly, there were some doubts as to the copyrightability of computer programs based on a number of objections, one of them being the writing requirement. Whether a computer program is a writing in the constitutional sense was questioned in part because, by itself, the program has little or no expressive capacity. A program's significance is when it is operated in conjunction with a machine and, therefore, its status as a writing is somewhat vitiated and it seems to be a utilitarian work. Nevertheless, prior to the 1976 Act, the Copyright Office decided to accept deposit of programs. The Act, as a result of a 1980 amendment, now explicitly accepts protection for programs. 17 U.S.C.A. § 117. See § 20.5, infra.

The concepts of "writings" and "fixation" have been tied to the notion of "copy" for almost a century. In *White-Smith Music Publishing Co. v. Apollo Co.* (1908), the Supreme Court held that player piano rolls were not copies for purposes of infringement because a copy, according to the Court, had to be something that others could directly perceive and from which the underlying work could be reproduced. Although the direct-perception test of *White-Smith* has been expressly rejected by the 1976 Act, its basic reproduction requirement is still good law. The 1976 Act broadened copyright protection to include anything tangible from which the author's work can be reproduced, but the requirement that the work be tangible reflects the constitutional limit that copyright extends only to "writings."

## § 20.5　Computer Programs

Computer programs were accepted by the Copyright Office for copyright registration for a number of years before the Copyright Act specifically addressed their status. Mere registration did not make them copyrightable, of course, but did reflect the view of many respected persons both within and without the Copyright Office that programs were writings and have sufficient originality and authorship to be copyrightable and do not suffer from the fatal defects of the utility-nonutility or idea-expression dichotomies.

As a result of a 1980 amendment, section 117 recognizes the copyrightability of computer programs. Section 117 is the fruit of the National Commission on New Technological Uses of Copyrighted Works (CONTU), which made three recommendations: (1) that computer programs be copyrightable, (2) that the new Act apply to all computer uses of copyrighted programs, and (3) that owners of copyrighted programs be allowed to copy those programs to the extent necessary to use them effectively without incurring liability for infringement. The present section 117, as amended, constitutes almost verbatim the recommended statutory language proposed by CONTU. It thus is reasonable to conclude that the intent embodied in the CONTU Report accurately reflects the intent of Congress.

Although computer programs clearly are copyrightable subject matter by virtue of section 117, some programs may be ineligible for copyright not because they are computer programs but because they either (a) lack minimal originality, being so simple and basic as to reflect an inadequate investment of labor to merit copyright protection, or (b) constitute the only way of accomplishing a particular result so that the program can be characterized as embodying an idea, under the merger doctrine, rather than as one way among many of expressing that idea.

The current important issues with regard to copyright protection of computer programs now seem to be the extent and scope of the resulting protection, especially with respect to the merger doctrine as well as the distinction between the literal and nonliteral components of programs. The Act defines a computer program as "a set of statements or instructions to be used ... in a computer." 17 U.S.C.A. § 101. This has been taken to apply to both the literal components of a program and, although less clearly so, to the nonliteral elements as well.

The literal components include the source code—code that is in a form readily understandable by the programmer—and the object code—code that is understandable to the machine and more recently, microcode which is the instruction set built into a microprocessor essentially giving the microprocessor its "vocabulary." Source and object code, perhaps because they seem analogous to "literary" material, generally have enjoyed copyright protection. *Apple Computer, Inc. v. Franklin Computer Corp.* (1983).

The nonliteral components include the sequence, structure, and organization of the program, as well as the screen output or user-interface, sometimes called the program's "look and feel." The courts have been more cautious in protecting these nonliteral components, partly because they seem to be more closely analogous to the program's "idea" than its "expression" and therefore arguably, fall within section 102(b). *Computer Associates Int'l., Inc. v. Altai, Inc.* (1992). They also may raise tangible fixation problems, their nature often depending upon transitory interactions with the user.

"Whether the nonliteral components of a program, including the structure, sequence and organization and user interface, are protected depends on whether, on the particular facts of each case, the component in question qualifies as an expression of an idea, or an idea itself." *Johnson Controls, Inc. v. Phoenix Control Systems, Inc.* (1989). But when the on-screen appearance depends upon interaction with the user, the appearance may owe so much to the transitory choices of the user that the lack of tangible fixation for any one screen may be a bar to copyrightability of the screen images. Whether it is protected, then, may depend upon whether the program's resulting interaction with the user is tangibly fixed, as in, for instance, user-created files. *Micro Star v. FormGen Inc.* (1998).

But some obstacles to full copyrightability may be peculiarly common to computer programs because of their need for routine and convention. For instance, standardized features—almost like the buttons and knobs on a television—may be uncopyrightable because they are too close to ideas. Thus, a program such as "Windows" that uses various icons and a "desktop" appearance has been held uncopyrightable to that extent because it is an idea. *Apple Computer, Inc. v. Microsoft Corp.* (1994). Similarly, the Lotus "1–2–3" menu command hierarchy has been held uncopyrightable because of the "method of operations" bar in section 102(b), *Lotus Development Corp. v. Borland Int'l., Inc.* (1995). Furthermore, even the literal components of a program do not always merit protection. Although it relates more to infringement than subject matter, the fact that computer programs depend on convention and routine steps means that, despite the principle that programs are copyrightable, merger and similar doctrines will exclude vast portions of computer programs from copyrightability. *Computer Associates Int'l., Inc. v. Altai, Inc.*, supra.

It is unclear whether the copyrightability of computer programs will have any effect on attempts to increase protection for them through other means—notably patent law. See § 2.8, supra. Although it seems logical to expect some such relationship, the shifting trends in both areas seem too uncoordinated to sustain any prediction at this time.

## § 20.6  Semiconductor Chip Protection Act

The Semiconductor Chip Protection Act of 1984, 17 U.S.C.A. §§ 902 et seq., although found in the copyright title of the United States Code, is a kind of hybrid, borrowing from both copyright and patent law to provide protection for the physical "chips" upon which computer technology presently depends. The Chip Act protects mask works fixed in a semiconductor chip product—primarily against photographic processes. In a way, the Chip Act protects computer code in the form of circuitry, including, therefore, code fixed in ROM (read-only-memory) chips. Before the Chip Act, this type of code was not universally protected under copyright law by the courts.

Protection begins upon registration or commercial exploitation, whichever occurs first. Commercial exploitation means distribution of a semiconductor chip embodying the mask work to the public for commercial purposes or a written offer to sell or transfer such a chip already in existence. The Chip Act contains a requirement of originality and excludes mere ideas. Thus, the Chip Act borrows heavily from copyright. Specifically excluded are any "procedure, process, system, method of operation, concept, principal, or discoveries." Furthermore, protection does not extend to "designs that are staple, commonplace, or familiar in the semiconductor industry," a concept the Act borrows heavily from the patent doctrines of novelty and nonobviousness.

The Chip Act provides an exclusive right to reproduce the mask work by any method, as well as to import or distribute a semiconductor chip that embodies the mask work. However, it is not an infringement to "reverse engineer" the mask work for most purposes. Further, one may incorporate the results of such analysis in a new mask work so long as the new mask work meets the originality requirement. There is a distinction between the physical object and the exclusive right to copy so that sale of a chip embodying the mask work does not convey the right to reproduce it.

Protection lasts for ten years, assuming the chip is registered within two years of commercial exploitation. Although this may seem a short term, given the rate at which chip innovations occur, it actually is considered a substantial term. Notice, although not required, affords certain procedural protections and is indicated by the words "mask work," the symbol *M*, or the letter M in a circle.

## § 20.7 Sound Recordings

Although music and sheet music have long been copyrightable subject matter, recordings of music have had a long history of doubtful copyright status.

Three different categories of parties have an interest in the copyrightability of sound recordings. Composers obviously have an interest in profiting from the fruits of their labor. Equally interested are those persons and institutions that produce the recordings. The third are the performers. Each of these categories of parties has a different interest, although their positions sometimes may merge; each of these categories also has different legal protection.

Until just shortly before the enactment of the new Act, in 1972, when the 1909 Act was amended to provide increased protection, producers and performers had no copyright in the sound recording. This was primarily because of an early Supreme Court decision, *White-Smith Music Publishing Co. v. Apollo Co.* (1908), which held that piano rolls were not copies of the underlying musical composition they caused a player piano to reproduce, because piano rolls could not be read or deciphered by the naked eye. *White-Smith* was extended to sound recordings. Thus, from 1908 until shortly before the 1976 Act, sound recordings had no copyright protection and could be reproduced by "pirates" with relative immunity from federal copyright laws.

However, the 1909 copyright revision gave some protection to the composers of underlying musical works in order to vitiate part of the harshness of *White-Smith*. Although not going so far as to reject *White-Smith* by declaring sound recordings or piano rolls to be copies and thus subject to complete regulation by the copyright law, the 1909 legislation gave composers the exclusive right to authorize a sound recording. Once having authorized a sound recording, however, the composer was subject to a statutory license and royalty. Any other producer was free to manufacture his own sound recordings upon payment of the statutory fee—which was two cents per copy. Congress adopted this compromise position between *White-Smith* and full copyrightability because of fears that if full copyright protection were granted, the producer of piano rolls, a company that effectively monopolized the recording market at the time, would dominate the market. Thus the compulsory license was seen as an ameliorative device while the composer's right to determine initial production was seen as granting the composer what was just.

Because of the compromise nature of the congressional response to *White-Smith*, there was a gap between the composer's right to a per-record royalty and the undefined positions of the publisher of the records and the performers. Since these devices could not be copyrighted, others were free to record their own versions of them subject only to the obligation to pay the statutory fee to the composer for the underlying musical composition. Eventually, record piracy became a serious problem. Rival manufacturers would simply obtain masters or copies of the authorized producer's phonorecords and proceed to reproduce and sell pirated copies, merely paying the small statutory royalty to the composer of the underlying musical composition or paying nothing to anyone. The performers and producers had no copyright that was infringed; likewise, the composer only had the right to the statutory royalty and, upon payment, had few other remedies. The manufacturer, of course, had no copyright at all, since his product was not a copyrightable work.

Recognizing this untenable situation, Congress finally granted record companies a copyright in their phonorecords in 1972 and empowered them to bring infringement actions against pirates. Under the 1976 Act, sound recordings and phonorecords are not treated differently from other mediums of expression with respect to being copyrightable subject matter. 17 U.S.C.A. § 102(a). Since a phonorecord is a fixation in tangible form of the underlying musical composition, composers have copyright protection under the current Act with respect to sound recordings and phonorecords. Since phonorecords also are granted copyright protection as independent works, producers likewise have some, although severely limited, copyright protection.

The 1976 Act makes it clear that the old method of piracy that effectively immunized a pirate upon the payment of the compulsory fee no longer would defeat the composer's or the producer's rights. Under section 115(a)(1), a producer cannot duplicate (meaning the making of a literal and slavish copy of the electronic signals of) another's sound recording without the express consent of the owner of the copyright in the sound recording. Nevertheless, sound recordings still suffer from severely limiting provisions that restrict the rights that their owners have as compared to other copyright proprietors.

The most important limitation upon sound recordings aside from the existence of the compulsory license of the composer's work is the limitation upon exclusive rights. Owners of copyright in sound recordings have only the right to prevent literal copies. Whereas most copyright owners have all of the applicable rights listed in section 106, owners of copyrights in sound recordings—meaning basically producers of sound recordings—do not have, for instance, the right to exclude others from performing the work (the recording) publicly. This means that once a sound recording is produced, purchasers are free to perform the recording publicly (such as radio broadcasts) without paying the producer or performers any fee (although the composer of the underlying work has full rights over such performances). Additionally, the other exclusive rights listed in section 106 are also eliminated by section 114. The rights to exclude others from reproducing the work or from preparing derivative works are limited in the case of sound recordings to the production of literal copies. Thus, the owner of a sound recording can prevent others, for instance "pirates," from actually reproducing a particular phonorecord or from preparing a derivative work by using the actual sounds of its recording in a rearrangement or other derivation using the actual sounds of the phonorecord. But the copyright owner cannot prevent others from simulating his recording or derivations "even though such sounds imitate or simulate those in the copyrighted sound recording." 17 U.S.C.A. § 114(b).

In terms of the current Act, it is important to distinguish between two components of a typically recorded work. First, the underlying musical composition is a separately copyrightable work of authorship, unaffected by the various perambulations of the Act under section 114 unless and until the composer authorizes the use of the composition in the production of a sound recording. Then, his control is diminished significantly (although just with respect to his inability to prevent others from making recordings of the composition) by virtue of the compulsory license. Second, the sound recording is another separately copyrightable work of authorship, being the sounds that are fixed by the process of recording. If the sound recording makes use of a composition, it may be a work of more than one author—that of the underlying composer, the producer, and, perhaps of the performers. If the sound recording fixes other, nonmusical, sounds such as bird songs, automobile races, or ocean waves, for instance, its author most likely would be just the producer of the recording. In such a case, no underlying composition would be involved. The phonorecord is simply the tangible medium in which the sound recording is expressed, the author of which, despite the possibility that it may embody an underlying musical composition or other work, is solely the manufacturer who created the physical object and who has the right to prevent others from duplicating it—a right absent under previous laws at least until the 1972 amendments.

Thus, a phonorecord may embrace two separate copyrightable works of music—the sound recording embodied in the phonorecord the producer of which is the person or persons who recorded the sounds, and the musical composition if the phonorecord is a recording of such a composition.

## § 20.8 Copyright Formalities—Registration and Notice

Since the United States' accession to the Berne Convention in 1989, the copyright formalities, especially with respect to works published or distributed after accession, have lost almost all their legal significance, which already had been reduced by the 1976 Act. Now, notice of copyright, whatever its practical value may be, has virtually no legal significance. Its only legal effect is that including a notice on the copyrighted work can prevent an infringer, except for some kinds of fair users, from pleading innocent infringement. 17 U.S.C.A. §§ 401(d), 402(d). Even without notice, of course, the burden of proving innocent infringement still would be on the accused infringer. That is, the absence of notice does not make resulting infringements automatically innocent. Similarly, registration has almost no legal significance. There is only one somewhat substantive effect of registration in that attorneys' fees and statutory damages are only recoverable for postregistration infringements. The only remaining procedural effect of registration is that United States authors must register before bringing suit. 17 U.S.C.A. §§ 411, 412.

With respect to older works under the 1976 Act that were published or distributed prior to United States accession to the Berne Convention, notice still has some importance, and those works are treated as they were before the Berne amendments to the Copyright Act. Basically, with respect to those works, copyright can be lost if notice was omitted and that omission was not cured within five years of publication, by registration and affixation of the notice to the remaining copies. 17 U.S.C.A. § 405.

# CHAPTER 21

# EXCLUSIVE RIGHTS

## § 21.1  Introduction

The exclusive rights are systematically presented in the current Act in section 106. But, first it should be noted that of the six exclusive rights—(1) the reproduction right, (2) the derivative work right, (3) the distribution right, (4) the performance right, (5) the display right, and (6) the digital transmission performance right—the last four are limited to the *public* exercise of those rights. The first two are infringed whether done publicly or privately. "Publicly" is defined by the Act as a performance or display to a "substantial number of persons" outside of family and friends. 17 U.S.C.A. § 101. Also, nowhere does the Act limit an owner's right to exclude only commercial exploitations. Thus, it is no defense *per se* that a copy was made for no commercial purpose, or that a performance was done by a nonprofit group, although these factors may well become relevant for some defenses involving fair use. And, second, the reader should understand that, in the sections following section 106, the statute is replete with a large number of very specific limitations upon the copyright owner's exclusive rights embracing a diverse set of circumstances—ranging from the right of record stores to play selections for promotional purposes, which would otherwise infringe the performance right, 17 U.S.C.A. § 110(7), to the right to make a temporary copy of a computer program in order to maintain or repair it, which would otherwise infringe the reproduction right, 17 U.S.C.A. § 117(c). These statutory limitations upon a copyright proprietor's exclusive rights cannot be generalized in summary form.

## § 21.2  Reproduction

The most basic and historic exclusive right is that of reproduction. It allows the copyright owner to *exclude* all others from reproducing the work in the form of a copy or phonorecord. The statute specifically adds the exclusive right to produce phonorecords because phonorecords are not defined as copies. See § 21.4, infra. Without this addition to the list of exclusive rights, others would be free to produce phonorecords embodying the owner's work.

Although the reproduction right is basic and seems obvious, the statute must be referred to for the definition of a copy. A copy is any material object from which, either with the naked eye or other senses, or with the aid of a machine or other device, the work can be perceived, reproduced, or communicated. 17 U.S.C.A. § 101. Because phonorecords are specifically *excluded* from the definition of copies, section 106 specifically adds producing them as one of the prohibited means of reproduction.

There are statutory exceptions to the exclusive reproduction right, relating to high technology. The first allows "transmitting organizations," which are commonly radio, television, or cable television companies, to record works temporarily for later transmission. 17 U.S.C.A. § 111(b)(c). Since even a temporary recording constitutes a violation of the exclusive right of reproduction, the statutory exception was necessary to allow such companies to delay transmission for time zone purposes and similar uses. The second statutory exception allows owners of computer programs to make what technically would be copies in order to utilize, repair, and maintain the program effectively. 17 U.S.C.A. § 117. Both of these sections require that the user erase or otherwise destroy the exempted copy within a certain time except for archival purposes.

## § 21.3 Derivative Works

A copyright owner has the right to exclude all others from creating works based on his own. This right safeguards a copyright owner from what otherwise might be an unduly narrow interpretation of the reproduction right, which would permit another to vary elements of the work sufficiently or change the medium of presentation and then assert that it is not actually a copy. In addition to safeguarding the reproduction right, however, the Act's grant of the exclusive right to prepare derivative works has enormous independent significance. 17 U.S.C.A. § 106(2).

The statutory definition of a "derivative work" is extremely comprehensive, including such things as translations, arrangements, dramatizations, fictionalizations, films, recordings, abridgments, condensations, "or any other form in which a work may be recast, transformed, or adapted." 17 U.S.C.A. § 101. The breadth of this definition is best understood in terms of history. Prior to the 1976 Act, the courts had acted somewhat inconsistently by holding that certain kinds of adaptations or derivations were infringements but that others, seemingly identical from a functional perspective, were not.

For instance, translations at one time were held to be new works that did not infringe the underlying translated work. *Stowe v. Thomas* (1853). This result was reached by viewing copyright narrowly; it reflected the notion that copyright subsisted only in the exact expression that the author had created. Since such a narrow view of copyright did not cover the underlying concepts, ideas, or essence of the book, it was natural, recognizing the great effort required to translate a large work, to conclude that the translation was therefore an independent creative work that was not technically a "copy," and therefore not an infringement of the author's exclusive right to produce copies. Likewise, a book of plot outlines has been held not to constitute a copy of the original works, which, of course, it does not if the definition of "copy" is held to include only an exact duplicate of the original. *G. Ricordi & Co. v. Mason* (1912).

It is clear that a translation, which, at the time of *Stowe,* avoided liability because of a gap in the law (filled by congressional action in 1870), would be held infringing today under the statute's broad definition of derivative works since it expressly includes translations. It is not so clear, however, that the kind of plot outlines involved in *G. Ricordi* would be barred by the current Act, although the prohibition of any derivative form "in which a work may be recast, transformed, or adapted," is considerably broader than previous statutes and arguably could encompass such outlines. As an example of the potential breadth of the new derivative right, one court has held that the alteration (by attachment to ceramic tiles) of photographs removed from a copyrighted book is infringing because the result is a "version" of the original, despite the fact that the author had parted with title to the actual pictures through sale of the book. *Mirage Editions, Inc. v. Albuquerque A.R.T. Co.* (1988). Another, probably better-reasoned, decision has found such treatments to be noninfringing, because of the first-sale doctrine, see § 21.4, infra, as well as the fact that such a broad application of the derivative right would create an American moral right broader than any European version, something Congress certainly never intended. *Lee v. A.R.T. Co.* (1997).

## § 21.4  Distribution

The third of the enumerated exclusive rights guaranteed to the copyright owner is the right "to distribute copies or phonorecords ... to the public by sale or other transfer of ownership, or by rental, lease, or lending...." 17 U.S.C.A. § 106(3). Since the reproduction and derivative work rights secure to the copyright owner all or most of what conceivably could form the basis of any public distributions, the distribution right might be thought of as more of a limitation than a grant of an exclusive right. In that sense, it accurately has been called the "first-sale" doctrine. *American Int'l. Pictures, Inc. v. Foreman* (1978).

The first-sale doctrine assures the copyright owner that, until she parts with ownership, she has the right to prohibit all others from distributing the work. On the other hand, once a sale has occurred, the first-sale doctrine allows the new owner to treat the object as his own. Thus, although a copyright owner might transfer ownership to a buyer and impose certain conditions, it is not a violation of copyright for the buyer to sell the work to another, even if the copyright owner had conditioned the sale upon a promise of no resales. Copyright law and the distribution right only secure to the copyright owner the right to control the first transfer of ownership. A statutory exception to the first-sale doctrine, enacted at the behest of the computer and record industries, forbids the commercial rental, lease, or lending, or anything "in the nature of rental, lease, or lending," of phonorecords and computer programs. 17 U.S.C.A. § 109(b)(1).

Under the current Copyright Act, the "first-sale" doctrine is incorporated into section 109. Subsection (c) limits the use of the doctrine to persons who acquire ownership rather than mere possession of the work. Thus, the first-sale doctrine would apply to a buyer who acquired title to a motion picture film, even though the buyer was meant to destroy the film after use. Sale of a film, however, by a person who merely acquired possession for screening purposes would not qualify for the first-sale doctrine, even if a rental fee were paid for the screening privilege, since "ownership," or acquisition of some title, is a prerequisite to the first-sale doctrine.

The first-sale doctrine authorizes continuing sales or other transfers of a copy or, for that matter, the original. But it does not authorize further copying of the work or of the copy. Thus, the distribution right and the first-sale limitation upon it merely apply to the chattel (a copy or a phonorecord) that has been sold or otherwise transferred. The copyright owner is still protected against unauthorized copying of the work by the reproduction right. The reproduction right would probably not exclude, however, modifications to the physical work itself, to which title has passed. *Lee v. A.R.T. Co.* (1997).

Two consequences flow from the distribution right. First, because the first-sale doctrine is designed to prevent restraints on alienation, it is likely that attempts to make an actual sale resemble something less than that—for instance, a rental— will be unsuccessful. Second, the first-sale doctrine has important effects upon third-party purchasers. Since scienter is not always necessary for infringement, at least in the civil context, it is possible for an innocent third party to be liable for infringement if no first sale ever took place. This may explain why courts are reluctant to analyze a transfer of possession in a way that makes it something less than a transfer of ownership, since to do so would subject all later good faith purchasers to unpredictable copyright consequences.

## § 21.5  Performance

Largely due to the highly developed and profitable communications and entertainment industries and technologies of the twentieth century, the right of the copyright owner to exclude all others from publicly performing his work has become one of the most important rights secured by the copyright laws. Because large segments of our population now receive copyrighted information through mass media, electronic motion pictures, television tapes and discs, radio broadcasts, and a host of other technologies by which information is delivered *to* the consumer—or, in other words, publicly *performed*—the right of public performance has become extremely valuable to a copyright proprietor.

The statute specifies that the public performance right applies only to literary, musical, dramatic, choreographic, pantomime, motion picture, and other audiovisual works. 17 U.S.C.A. § 106(4). Except for purely pictorial, graphic, and sculptural works— what might be loosely termed the visual arts—and sound recordings, this list exhausts the field of what constitutes copyrightable works. Since it is difficult to conceive of a "performance" of a visual object, it probably is correct to say that, with the exception of sound recordings, the exclusive right of public performance is very comprehensive.

On the other hand, the exclusion of sound recordings from the performance right—except for digitally transmitted performances—is significant and important. In addition to being omitted from the grant of exclusive rights in section 106(4), sound recordings are omitted from the performance right by section 114, making it doubly clear that Congress intended to exclude sound recordings from this important area of protection. Nevertheless, section 106 still guarantees to the author of any underlying musical composition or other work captured on a sound recording the right to exclude others from public performance. Therefore, the omission of sound recordings from the public performance right simply means that producers of sound recordings have no right to royalties for public performance; the composers of the underlying work are not thereby affected. Apparently Congress felt that the economic conditions of the record industry were such that it would have been unwise to burden those who play sound recordings for the public—radio and television stations—with having to pay royalties to the record companies and their recording artists as well as to the composers. This is not true, of course, for digitally transmitted performances to which the performance right attaches. 17 U.S.C.A. § 106(6).

In addition to the exclusion of sound recordings from the performance right, one of the most significant effects of section 106(4) is the absence of any requirement that performances that allegedly violate the copyright owner's exclusive right be for profit. This represents a major departure from the law under the 1909 Act, which, although not imposing the profit requirement uniformly, limited the exclusive performance right for musical compositions to "for profit" performances. A good deal of judicial energy was invested in devising a broad enough definition of "profit" to allow musical composers control over performances that had few indicia of profit. In *Herbert v. Shanley Co.* (1917), Justice Holmes held that the requirement of "profit" for the public performance of musical compositions meant only that the musical performance had to have some connection with a profit-making activity; in that case it was playing music in a hotel dining room.

Under the 1909 Act, it had been held that the reception of radio transmissions by various establishments and the playing of those receptions to consumers, even without direct charge, constituted an impermissible performance, unfairly depriving the composer of royalties. Thus, in *Buck v. Jewell–La Salle Realty Co.* (1931), the Supreme Court held that a hotel that played radio broadcasts over loudspeakers in the public rooms for the benefit of its guests infringed the exclusive rights of the composers whose compositions were being aired by the radio station. Broadcasting, held the Court, did not exhaust the performance right of the composers and therefore the hotel was impermissibly performing the composers' works. In *Society of European Stage Authors & Composers v. New York Hotel Statler Co.* (1937), the Court held that even if a hotel confined the reception to the private rooms of guests, it still impermissibly infringed the composers' exclusive performance rights. More recently, however, in *Twentieth Century Music Corp. v. Aiken* (1975), the Court held that the owner of a fast-food chicken store did not infringe by playing a radio connected to four speakers in his establishment. That reception, said the Court, was not a performance that belonged exclusively to the copyright owner for a number of reasons. First, it distinguished *La Salle* by noting that the broadcasts in that case were totally unlicensed, whereas in Aiken's case the composers had granted licenses to the radio stations. Second, the Supreme Court held that policing these arguably public performances would be impractical and unenforceable. Finally, it held that the result was dictated by two prior cases, *Fortnightly Corp. v. United Artists Television, Inc.* (1968), and *Teleprompter Corp. v. Columbia Broadcasting System, Inc.* (1974), both of which essentially held that cable television retransmission of received signals did not constitute a separate infringing performance of the initial transmitted performance.

The need for this type of judicial hair-splitting seems to have been significantly reduced under the 1976 Copyright Act. Instead, section 110 exempts certain specified performances from the copyright owner's exclusive performance right, most of which coincide with the not-for-profit exceptions under the 1909 Act. The exemptions basically include "face-to-face" educational activities, religious worship, noncommercial, nonpublic performances for charitable purposes, limited reception on home-type receivers involving no admission charge (an attempt to codify the *Aiken* case), fairs, and performances by or for the handicapped. Most of the exceptions are not comprehensive but are limited instead to nondramatic literary or musical works so that, even if a performance is not-for-profit, it is not necessarily exempted if it does not fit the exact and rather particular situations specified in section 110. Moreover, the exemptions have become minutely detailed, addressing the number of speakers, the diagonal size of televisions, and the square footage occupied by restaurants, for instance.

In addition, and most importantly, the exemptions of section 110 closely parallel the requirements of the prior 1909 Act with respect to the rather expansive definition of what is "for profit." Under the current Act generally, activities are exempted only if performed "without any purpose of direct or indirect commercial advantage and without any payment of any fee or other compensation for the performance to any of its performers, promoters, or organizers. . . ." 17 U.S.C.A. § 110(4). Thus, as in *Herbert v. Shanley Co.,* supra, a performance is not exempted merely because there is no direct charge for the performance itself if the activity of which it is a part is a profit-making one.

Because of the problems inherent in reconciling the needs of divergent and often competing technologies, the current Act has resolved the questions posed by the reception of broadcast transmissions by specific statutory treatment. The special and difficult problems of cable television have been comprehensively treated in section 111 of the current Act.

Sections 110(5) and 111(a) of the 1976 Act allow limited receptions of electronic transmissions when the receiving apparatus is basically a private home-type device or when the reception is piped into the rooms of an apartment house, hotel, or similar establishment and no direct charge is imposed. Thus, instead of artificially construing the terms "performance," "public," or "profit," the Act directly treats the specific circumstances. Now, whether a restaurant or other establishment can share with the public the reception of an electronic transmission will turn on the type, number, and size of equipment used, the size of the premises, and on whether a direct charge is made for the service. Similarly, whether a hotel can pipe in music to its guests will turn on whether the signals are those within the local reception area and whether, again, a direct charge is imposed. Finally, under the current Act, the legitimacy of these receptions is not affected by the legitimacy of the original transmission—that is, whether the radio or television station obtained an appropriate license from the copyright owner.

## § 21.6　Display

The exclusive right of the copyright owner to display his work is relatively new. With the proliferation of computer networks, and the Internet, the statute has increasing applicability and importance. 17 U.S.C.A. § 106(5). The display right recognizes the potential development of new technological methods for exploiting works that do not amount to a performance or actual reproduction.

Section 109(b) allows the lawful owner of a copy to display one image of the copy at the place where it is located. When this provision is combined with the copyright owner's otherwise exclusive right to display, the exclusive right secured by section 106 amounts to the right to display multiple images at locations separate and apart from that in which the work or copy itself is located, such as over computer networks and the Internet.

Thus, the owner of a copy of a painting, a photograph, a microfiche or even a computerized memory of copyrighted materials might publicly display the work by showing the painting or photograph to others or by making the microfiche or computer terminal available to the public at one location and be immunized in doing so by section 109(b). But, in order to protect the authors of copyrighted works from having their products unfairly exploited by developing and future communications technology, Congress has granted the copyright owner the exclusive right to display the copy in a way that would make it available in either multiple images or to persons outside the actual physical location of the copy. Thus, any digital form of network or Internet transmission would constitute a public display that violates the copyright owner's exclusive display right and that is not immunized by the more narrow privilege granted by section 109(b) limited strictly to "no more than one image at a time, to viewers present at the place where the copy is located."

## § 21.7    Digital Transmission Performance

Many people believe that one of the most glaring—but historically based—anomalies of the 1976 Act is the absence of a performance right for owners of sound recordings. Because of established industry relationships that have developed out of reliance upon this feature of American copyright law, it has been impossible to alter despite occasional lobbying efforts to do so. With the advent of an entirely new sphere of music distribution and performance based on computer digital transmissions over the Internet, the opportunity was ripe to recognize these performance rights because of a lack of developed industry relationships in that sector that otherwise might have opposed legislation. The pressure to amend the Copyright Act succeeded in 1995. Thus, with respect to digital transmissions, sound recording copyright owners have full performance rights and now have the opportunity to negotiate over, and profit from, the fees paid for such performances.

## § 21.8    Other Rights in Advanced and Digital Technologies

The digital transmission performance right is only one portent of related new copyright developments. The growth of advanced, including digital, technology of which the new performance right is a part, has accelerated changes in the Copyright Act.

One of the earliest of these was the Audio Home Recording Act of 1992 that attempted to protect the rights of sound recording proprietors in digital recordings, because digital, unlike analog recordings, suffer no degradation as they are duplicated. In order to afford these proprietors rights against, and royalties in, such flawlessly accurate reproductions, various copy protection measures were adopted, including a prohibition on the distribution of digital recorders without special protective measures—the Serial Copy Management System. These measures make it possible to assess royalties on both the machines and the media—disks, tapes, and drives, for instance. 17 U.S.C.A. §§ 1001 et seq. A part of the Act was a compromise provision designed to assure that the major portions of the Act would not be used against private acts of sound recording duplication. That provision states that consumers who make noncommercial recordings in both analog and digital form cannot be sued for infringement, thus effectively legalizing "home taping" which, absent this compromise provision, would be infringing as an unauthorized reproduction of a sound recording. 17 U.S.C.A. § 1008.

The Intellectual Property and Communications Omnibus Reform Act of 1999 adopted further provisions respecting advanced technologies, many of which establish rights far broader than those of traditional copyright. These provisions make it unlawful to circumvent protection measures that control access to copyrighted works. Unlike traditional copyright, the 1999 law does not directly protect the expressions themselves, but, instead, the "technological measures" employed to prevent the expressions from being copied—forbidding descrambling, decrypting, or otherwise circumventing those measures. 17 U.S.C.A. §§ 1201 et seq. One collateral, perhaps unintended, effect of this legislation is that the measures—usually computer programs—that are meant to protect underlying works become, themselves, works that receive even greater protection than the underlying works receive from traditional copyright. The "technological measure" is protected from being deciphered, even though any other work protected by copyright is generally available to be read, examined, or otherwise understood. One objection to this heightened protection for these "technological measures" is that it may hinder the progress of the very area of technology—encryption—necessary for it to work.

Unsurprisingly, these rights have been judicially troublesome. One of the protections afforded by the Act is access to the encryption code as well as the underlying work. Codes which give access to the underlying function—such as opening a garage door, or a computer printer—instead of the encryption or the underlying work—have been held not infringing. *Chamberlain Group v. Skylink Techs.* (2004). *Lexmark Int'l. v. Static Control Components* (2004). Because encryption can protect otherwise unprotected, even uncopyrightable, works, there are constitutional arguments about whether they go beyond the legitimate purposes of the constitutional copyright clause, and whether a fair use privilege should be read into the Act.

# CHAPTER 22

# INFRINGEMENT

## § 22.1 Overview

Infringement—a word that is not defined anywhere in the Copyright Act—occurs whenever somebody exercises any of the rights reserved exclusively for the copyright owner without authorization. 17 U.S.C.A. § 501(a). Infringement need not be intentional. Liability for innocent infringement is well-established. *Carter v. Hawaii Transportation Co.* (1961). There even can be unconscious infringement in the sense that an author, in creating what he conceives to be his own original product, unintentionally and thus in a sense unconsciously, "borrows" the work of another. For instance, in *Bright Tunes Music Corp. v. Harrisongs Music, Ltd.* (1976), the court held that George Harrison of the "Beatles" singing group, had infringed a song previously recorded by the "Chiffons." The plagiarism, even though unconscious, was actionable. It seems Harrison had access to the earlier work (meaning he had heard it performed) and, because of the almost exact similarity between Harrison's work, "My Sweet Lord," and the earlier composition, "He's So Fine," the court concluded that, although Harrison did not plagiarize deliberately, and although he was not conscious of copying the earlier work, "his subconscious knew … a song his conscious mind did not remember."

The concept of innocent infringement is equally applicable to the rights of reproduction, derivation, distribution, performance, and display. Thus, in a situation similar to *Bright Tunes* it is possible that an author might create a work that is unconsciously based on a prior work and therefore impermissibly infringes the original copyright owner's exclusive right to prepare derivative works.

Although one who actually exercises an exclusive right without authority is a direct infringer, there is also indirect infringement, a civil variation of the criminal "aiding and abetting" element. One who actively and knowingly encourages another to infringe is an indirect infringer. In *MGM Studios, Inc. v. Grokster, Ltd.* (2005), the Supreme Court held that the way the defendant promoted its product and encouraged others to use its "peer-to-peer" network to download copyrighted music was evidence sufficient to support a finding of indirect infringement.

Contributory infringement exists as a judicial doctrine in copyright law just as it does, though in codified form, in patent law. See *supra*, § 8.5. In *Universal City Studios, Inc. v. Sony Corp. of America* (1979), the Supreme Court held that simply producing a device that infringes does not constitute contributory infringement so long as it has substantial non-infringing uses as well. See § 23.3, infra. In *A & M Records v. Napster* (2001) the court held that defendant's file sharing system contributed to its users' acts of infringement and therefore the defendant was a contributory infringer, without much examination of the assertions that, in fact, the system had some non-infringing uses, just as the device did in *Sony*. Instead of treating the noninfringing uses, if substantial, as an absolute bar to contributory infringement, the *Napster* court treated their inverse—the infringing uses—as evidence of constructive knowledge of users' infringements, in seeming contradiction with *Sony*.

There is also the doctrine of vicarious or related infringement. A person who profits from an infringing performance, for instance, and who somehow supervises or has the right to control or supervise the performance, is just as liable as the actual performer. The owner of a hotel or ballroom who employs a band to entertain its patrons is just as liable as the bandleader or instrumentalists who play copyrighted music without authorization even though those employees are independent contractors and the hotel or ballroom owner has no ability to determine the details of their work. In *M. Witmark & Sons v. Pastime Amusement Co.* (1924), the owner of a movie theatre was liable for the infringing performances of a band she hired to accompany the pictures on the screen. In *Dreamland Ball Room v. Shapiro, Bernstein & Co.* (1929), a dancehall owner was liable for the infringing performances of its hired band even though the band had the discretion to choose its music independent of the owner. On the other hand, in *Roy Export Co. Establishment v. Trustees of Columbia University* (1972), the defendant was not liable for infringing performances of Chaplin's *Modern Times* on campus even though Columbia University had the ability to control such performances and had been warned that the performances would occur. The missing ingredient was profit or benefit flowing to the University. The dual requirements for vicarious infringement are thus the right to control *and* profit potential. But there is now a statutory exception protecting Internet service providers from vicarious liability. 17 U.S.C.A. § 512.

## § 22.2   Proof of Infringement

To prove infringement, a party must establish ownership of the copyright and impermissible copying. *Ferguson v. National Broadcasting Co.* (1978). If it can be shown that the defendant actually copied protected portions of the original work, infringement is easily demonstrated. However, since direct evidence of plagiarism seldom is available, infringement usually is proven through circumstantial evidence. Infringement is commonly proven by demonstrating that the allegedly infringing work bears a remarkable resemblance to the original and that the alleged infringer had some opportunity for contact with the original prior to creating the alleged infringement. The combination of remarkable similarity and opportunity for contact with the original is persuasive evidence that the infringer must have copied the original. In other words, infringement is established by proof of *access* and *substantial similarity*. *Ferguson v. National Broadcasting Co.*, supra. Of course, those elements merely constitute another way of describing the requisite circumstantial evidence to justify an inference that copying actually occurred.

When the alleged infringement is a word-for-word—or literal—copy, this is highly persuasive proof of copying and the requisite proof of access will be concomitantly lower. Alternatively, the more variation there is between the original and the alleged infringement, the more persuasive must be the proof that the defendant actually made use of the access that was available. As the variations become more significant and substantial, proof of access must be more than the mere opportunity for access. It will have to be actual exercise of that access—in other words, proof of actual copying.

However, proof of access and substantial similarity does not involve a discrete *substantive* doctrine. It is merely an *evidentiary* method—a restatement of the circumstantial evidence needed to establish infringement, which means that illegitimate copying has occurred. In addition, of course, substantial similarity must relate to the copyrightable substance of the original, and not elements of the original that constitute uncopyrightable ideas or matters in the public domain. *Bleistein v. Donaldson Lithographing Co.* (1903) ("Others are free to copy the original. They are not free to copy the copy.").

Infringement usually is shown in a two-stage process. The first is designed to reveal whether copying occurred. The second is designed to decide whether that copying, if any, amounts to impermissible appropriation. With respect to the first, analytical, or dissection, stage, the defendant's evidence often will include an examination of related works in the public domain. The evidence is probative of at least two conclusions: first, that the defendant borrowed from the public domain instead of the plaintiff's work; second, that the plaintiff himself borrowed from the public domain and therefore is not entitled to copyright protection. *Novelty Textile Mills, Inc. v. Joan Fabrics Corp.* (1977). Sometimes public domain material is relevant to prove that the defendant copied from plaintiff because of remarkable coincidences between the defendant's and the plaintiff's work in light of much greater variation between works already in the public domain and the plaintiff's work. See *Eisenschiml v. Fawcett Publications, Inc.* (1957); *Greenbie v. Noble* (1957).

Evidence concerning the content of the public domain is less relevant to the copyrightability of the plaintiff's work than it is to a conclusion of copying. It is relevant, that is, "so far as it may break the force of the inference to be drawn from likenesses between the work and the putative piracy." *Sheldon v. Metro–Goldwyn Pictures Corp.* (1936).

Experts commonly are utilized in the first stage to analyze the original work and the allegedly infringing one to discover whether enough similarities exist to conclude that the alleged infringement is a copy of the original. However, expert testimony is not competent to prove the legal conclusion of infringement, which is entirely for the trier of fact when it determines whether the defendant actually appropriated the original author's protected expression. Whether through expert testimony, use of "analytic" means, or examination of the elements of similarity, the first stage really is no more than the application of the circumstantial evidence rule. The first stage leads to the conclusion that the defendant, using the available access, copied whatever elements exist in the original that are substantially similar to those of the alleged infringement. However, this proof of copying does not inevitably lead to a conclusion of infringement.

The second stage leads to the conclusion of infringement. Now, plaintiff must prove that, of the elements "copied" or "taken" from the original, at least some of them were those protected by copyright. Thus, there is a distinction between permissible copying and illicit copying or unlawful appropriation. *Arnstein v. Porter* (1946). The issue of illicit as opposed to permissible copying is a matter for the lay observer and not for expert witnesses nor for piece-by-piece analysis of the elements of the two works. Permissible copying includes the taking of ideas; illicit copying appropriates protected expression. *Nichols v. Universal Pictures Corp.* (1930). See also *Sid & Marty Krofft Television Productions, Inc. v. McDonald's Corp.* (1977). The "lay observer" test or "ordinary observer" test is the key to drawing this distinction. The ordinary observer is similar to the reasonable person standard and is meant to distinguish between those similarities in two works an observer would notice and those the ordinary observer would tend to disregard as immaterial and unrelated to the overall character of the two works. *Peter Pan Fabrics, Inc. v. Martin Weiner Corp.* (1960).

## § 22.3    Infringement of Musical Works

Because there are only a limited number of musical elements—the seven notes of the traditional western scale ("do, re, mi, fa, sol, la, ti") plus the five sharps or flats—certain similarities between musical works are expected and inevitable. The issue then becomes to decide at what point the inevitable repetitions become impermissible takings.

Since most, and quite possibly all, of the basic building blocks of musical compositions are already in the public domain, the concept of public domain work has special significance in musical infringement cases. When one adds to that the fact that adaptation, orchestration, and arrangement are art forms that are practically independent of composition,the significance of public domain material, both from an evidentiary and a substantive perspective, becomes even greater.

For instance, the presence of a certain series of notes in the public domain may indicate that the alleged infringer could as easily have made up the sequence as did the plaintiff. Conversely, the presence of a unique element of the plaintiff's work in the defendant's suggests copying. In *Heim v. Universal Pictures Co.* (1946), the court said that, even absent any proof of access at all, infringement could be proven if "a single brief phrase, contained in both pieces, was so idiosyncratic in its treatment as to preclude coincidence." Because of the limited basic musical elements, this "coincidence" defense has a certain plausibility, but when proof of access shows a closeness in time and space between the defendant's contact with the plaintiff's work and the creation of the alleged infringement, proof of possible coincidence frequently is overcome. *Fred Fisher, Inc. v. Dillingham* (1924).

A showing that the allegedly "borrowed" element exists in the public domain tends to support a defendant's contention that he independently or with the help of other works than the plaintiff's, created the work without infringing the plaintiff's work. *Heim v. Universal Pictures Co.,* supra. Sometimes, in fact, the defendant explicitly claims to have taken from the public domain—as when a composer claimed to have borrowed fourteen notes of a Dvorak sixteen note sequence, *Heim v. Universal Pictures Co.,* supra. In *Fred Fisher, Inc. v. Dillingham,* supra, the defendant claimed that the similarities between his work and the plaintiff's also were present to a certain extent in the public domain. The court found that the public domain did not include the precise figure found in both the plaintiff's and defendant's work but it did find similarities between the plaintiff's work and the public domain. The court then articulated two important principles with respect to public domain matter and musical copyright: the existence of a similar public domain work is no defense to a claim of infringement unless (1) plaintiff added so little to the public domain work that his work cannot be protected for lack of originality, or (2) defendant affirmatively shows that he, too, borrowed from the public domain instead of from the plaintiff. In a variation of the axiom that it is permissible to copy the original but not to copy the copy, the court found that the defendant's access to plaintiff's song made the coincidence theory so unlikely that copying from the plaintiff had been proven and copying from the public domain had not.

The significance of limited combinations and of prior similar works is usually that originality may exist *despite* similarities because they merely are coincidental. Coincidence, in other words, is more possible when only a limited number of combinations are possible. Musical compositions frequently are adaptations, variations, and arrangements of prior works. Assuming the arrangement is copyrightable, the relevance of prior similar works becomes even more important. Since the composer of an adaptation who claims infringement, for instance, has by definition taken something from the public domain (unless he has adapted a more recent work with authorization), the defendant will try even harder to prove that the author contributed little or nothing original to the unprotected work. If he fails, the defendant must prove that he, too, took from the public domain. See *Novelty Textile Mills, Inc. v. Joan Fabrics Corp.* (1977).

## § 22.4   Infringement of Literary Works

Just as the physical act of copying is the paradigmatic act of infringement, literary infringement seems to represent the paradigmatic subject matter of infringement. This is at least historically understandable, see § 19.1, supra, since in its beginnings copyright infringement involved nothing but literary works. With respect to the elements of an infringement action, literary infringement does not differ from any other copyright subject matter: illegitimate copying must be proven, usually by demonstrating access and substantial similarity. The application of the substantial-similarity test to literary works poses difficulties because so many writing elements inevitably are repeated from one work to the next. Since some elements will be common to numerous works, the courts have struggled to develop ways of distinguishing those aspects that can be taken with impunity from those that remain the author's. Those rather basic literary elements that essentially are fair game between authors are those constituting mere *ideas*. The greater detail that individual authors create, and which the courts are willing to protect, are their *expressions*. For instance, the story of the Civil War is fair game for any author. Aside from the fact that it is a series of historical events that is part of the public domain, the basic story of a nation or people divided over profound social issues and the resulting family, personal, and political divisions has been a basic building block or *idea* since before Euripides and extends past *Gone With the Wind*. But once the story is embellished with characters, incidents, and dramatic elements, the bare idea has matured into a protected expression.

The classic distinction between protected and unprotected elements of literary creations is that articulated by Judge Learned Hand in *Nichols v. Universal Pictures Corp.* (1930). Since literary properties consist basically of characters and sequence, it is necessary to identify the point at which either characters or sequence or a combination thereof become copyrightable. *Nichols* held that there is no clear and precise line but the point at which either incident or character becomes protected depends upon their complexity or development in the context of the individual work. "The less developed the characters, the less they can be copyrighted." Instead of articulating a particular point at which infringement occurs, *Nichols* identified a continuum along which the development of characters and sequence and other literary elements lie. This is called the "abstractions" test and is commonly adapted and applied by the courts in various contexts, even to computer programs. *Mitel, Inc. v. IQTel, Inc.* (1997).

With respect to sequence, the continuum runs from an unprotected idea, to a relatively unprotected theme, to an arguably protected plot, to a relatively protected incident, to an almost certainly protected dialogue or language. *Sheldon v. Metro–Goldwyn Pictures Corp.* (1936). With respect to characters, the point at which they become protected depends upon their stage of development in the work and their importance to it. The general idea of a character is unprotected. Stock figures, prototypes, or stereotypical figures likewise are unprotected, essentially constituting nothing more than ideas. Characters become more protected as they become more detailed and become the centerpiece of the story. But the attribution of general qualities to the character—such as strength—or emotional features—such as compassion—is not sufficient to gain copyright protection.

Although characters are less copyrightable than incident, the degree of protection depends on the context in which the character is developed and how prominently the character figures within the work. There is little but the character in some literary genres. Therefore, it is not surprising they tend to gain protection. The most typical example is the cartoon character who travels from one stock incident to another, but whose particular attributes are absolutely central to the comic book or strip. Thus, in both *Detective Comics, Inc. v. Bruns Publications, Inc.* (1940), and *National Comics Publications v. Fawcett Publications* (1951), it was held that protection extends to the character but only when combined with particular antics and appearance. When such a character thus assumes what might be called a "personality" as a result of both its attributes and antics in a graphic *appearance,* as is true of a Superman or a Snoopy or a Mickey Mouse, the character is protected. It is this combination of distinctive attributes with graphic appearance that makes the cartoon character especially protected.

Other fanciful characters are equally protected, especially when they are personified in particularly graphic form. For instance, in *Sid & Marty Krofft Television Productions, Inc. v. McDonald's Corp.* (1977), the plaintiffs had created "costumed characters," similar to puppets. These were substantially duplicated by the defendant who used them in commercial promotions of its products and services. The court held that these characters are protectible. Undoubtedly, the visual dimension of cartoon or fanciful characters makes them more eligible for protection than is true of most characters in written works.

The line between "stock" characters or stereotypes and protected developed characters is crossed whenever the author develops significantly more than the mere idea of a character. The expression of a nude figure would coincide with an idea. An author could not monopolize that concept. But, in the case of fantastic costumed characters or highly complex literary figures, the process of selecting from among the many possible combinations of elements makes the particular expression of the plaintiff's character idea copyrightable.

On the other hand, the simple title of a literary property is not subject to copyright protection—although it may be more than adequately protected under common law theories of unfair competition, misappropriation, or possibly even trademark law.

For instance, in *Warner Brothers Pictures, Inc. v. Majestic Pictures Corp.* (1934), the plaintiff sought to enjoin the defendant's use of the title "Gold Diggers of Paris" as the title of a movie because the plaintiff owned the rights in a script entitled "The Gold Diggers." The court denied the plaintiffs relief under copyright law, saying: "A copyright of a play does not carry with it the exclusive right to the use of the title." However, it granted an injunction upon common law trademark grounds, since the title had acquired secondary meaning, the public having come to identify it with the plaintiff's property. The possibility of public deception justified the relief.

# CHAPTER 23

# FAIR USE

## § 23.1 Overview

If copyright law is the "metaphysics" of law (see page one of the Introduction), fair use is its "semiotics." The boundaries of fair use are difficult to ascertain. Fair use is analogous to a privilege in tort law and, just as tort privileges are determined and justified by broad notions of policy rather than by strict statutory or common law definitions, so too is fair use. It is akin to a privilege because it is essentially a defense to a charge of infringement. As with a defense of privilege in a tort action, the defense of fair use acknowledges the elements of the tort but affirmatively raises other important issues and policies by way of mitigation or exoneration.

Fair use most commonly is raised in certain traditional contexts. These include educational activities, literary and social criticism, parody, and, importantly, First Amendment activities such as news reporting. Fair use almost invariably is a conclusion based upon the weighing of competing policies in terms of the specific facts before the court. The broad policies justifying the copyright monopoly always militate in favor of a finding of infringement. It is only because fair use allows an inquiry into the particular facts of a case that the opposite conclusion sometimes is reached. But because fair use requires such a specific inquiry, one cannot say that generally, for instance, educational activities or parody or some other activity is *per se* a fair use.

Prior to the current Copyright Act the fair-use doctrine was totally a matter of common law; section 107 of the Act purports to codify the common law: it simply says that fair use is a defense to infringement and goes on to give examples, but not a definition, of fair use. It states that "criticism, comment, news reporting, teaching . . . , scholarship, or research," are the types of purposes that may justify a finding of fair use. It also provides some general guidelines by which fair use may be ascertained. Those include the purpose of the activity, including whether it is profitable or not, the nature of the underlying work, the proportion of the material used, and the economic effect upon the copyright owner. The Act expressly states that those guidelines are not exhaustive.

## § 23.2 The Dynamics of Fair Use

Fair use involves a balancing process by which a complex of variables determine whether other interests should override the rights of creators. The current Act explicitly identifies four interests:

(1) the purpose and character of the use, including its commercial nature;

(2) the nature of the copyrighted work;

(3) the proportion that was "taken"; and

(4) the economic impact of the "taking."

17 U.S.C.A. § 107.

There are at least two additional interests relevant to fair use. First, although infringement need not be intentional and although the intent of the defendant is not determinative, the intent and motives of the defendant often are relevant. Second, a First Amendment interest often opposes the copyright monopoly. However, in *Harper & Row, Publishers, Inc. v. Nation Enterprises, Inc.* (1985), the Supreme Court found no inherent conflict between copyright law and the First Amendment, especially because of the very existence of the fair use defense. In *Harper & Row*, the *Nation* magazine had published excerpts from the memoirs of former President Ford before they were to be published in *Time* magazine, which then abandoned its plans to publish them. Minimizing First Amendment concerns, the Court held that the idea-expression dichotomy would have allowed the *Nation* to report the important facts of the memoir without "scooping" its very language and that, furthermore, there was no expansion of fair use based on a claimed "public figure" exception to copyright. The Court also emphasized the fact that the work had not yet had its "first publication," the significance of which apparently continues, even after the near-total replacement of common law copyright by statutory copyright through the 1976 Act, even though not as a prerequisite to protection as it had been under common law copyright, but as a fair use factor because of its arguably obvious economic impact.

In any case involving fair use at least one and usually more of these six interests are weighed against the interest in protecting the author's exclusive rights. To the extent that the user is not interested in profit but instead is using the work for educational purposes or for a completely private use, the demand that he be free of the copyright monopoly is more persuasive than it would be if he were profiting from his use. See *Sony Corp. of America v. Universal City Studios, Inc.* (1984). In *Sony*, a case complicated by the fact that the defendant was being sued not for direct infringement but for "contributory infringement" by selling its VCRs to purchasers who were videotaping television programs at home, the Supreme Court found home-taping to be fair use. The Court emphasized the fact that there was no demonstrated injury to the plaintiffs, owners of films and television programs, that were, after all, broadcast free to viewers. In that circumstance, said the Court, the private practice of home-taping came well within the limits of fair use.

Thus, the dynamics of the fair-use doctrine involve weighing the various, and typically competing, interests. These interests have ambiguous boundaries, cannot be measured with any precision, and overlap with one another. It should be no surprise, therefore, that fair use has been termed "the most troublesome in the whole law of copyright." *Dellar v. Samuel Goldwyn, Inc.* (1939).

## § 23.3   Purpose and Character of the Use

Included in the notions of purpose and character are the dual concepts of commercial versus noncommercial and public versus private uses. Because the dynamics of fair use involve interrelated rather than determinative factors, however, there is certainly no doctrine mandating that mere noncommercial purpose nor mere private use are automatically fair uses. Nevertheless, as decisions of the Supreme Court make clear, the noncommercial nature of a use as well as its private character is highly persuasive. *Williams & Wilkins v. United States* (1973); *Sony Corp. of America v. Universal City Studios, Inc.* (1984).

Much more explicit in recognizing a "private" fair-use doctrine was the trial court in *Universal City Studios, Inc. v. Sony Corp. of America* (1979), the famous "Betamax" case, in which the Supreme Court held that the private nature of a use contributes to a finding of fair use. The Ninth Circuit held, however, that privacy concerns are not legitimate components of fair use and are more appropriately addressed in the relief stage of copyright infringement litigation. Although some cases indicate that the explicitly commercial nature of a claimed fair use is highly and perhaps even presumptively important, the Supreme Court has held that this is only one factor, and that it establishes no presumption. *Campbell v. Acuff–Rose Music, Inc.* (1994).

Just as commercial purpose has been a basis for deciding against fair use, an educational purpose, especially a nonprofit one, has been a traditional basis in favor of fair use. Although the statute joins the terms nonprofit and educational, it is not at all clear that an educational fair use also must be nonprofit. The congressional history of the 1976 Act indicates that the legislative intent was to codify existing fair-use law. Prior case law does not require that an educational fair use also be a completely noncommercial one. At the same time, it should not be surprising that even when educational and nonprofit purposes coincide, fair use does not necessarily result. In *MacMillan v. King* (1914), the court rejected the fair-use defense when a teacher copied substantial portions of an economics text for use by his students. The nature of the work—a text whose market was only expected to be in the educational area—and the substantiality of the copying far outweighed the educational and nonprofit purposes of the defendant.

Likewise, in *Encyclopaedia Britannica Educational Corp. v. Crooks* (1978), the conjunction of an educational and a nonprofit purpose was insufficient to establish the fair-use defense even though the defendant was an exclusively educational governmental corporation and the duplicating of educational materials was intended merely to provide underprivileged citizens with educational assistance. The defense was rejected because the copying was total and because the only market for the educational copyrighted works was precisely the context in which the copying was done—education. However, *Williams & Wilkins v. United States*

(1973), supra, held that the educational purpose of the defendants' activities—massive copying and distributing of medical journals—coupled with its completely nonprofit character was enough to outweigh the interest of the copyright holder and establish a fair-use defense. *Williams & Wilkins* has been seriously criticized and despite the statutory language of section 107, which parallels parts of the court's opinion, the fact that the case stands in relative isolation, perhaps uniquely based upon a public policy of advancing medical science, should serve as a warning that nonprofit educational uses will not automatically establish a fair-use defense. See *Marcus v. Rowley* (1983).

To sum up, perhaps the most accurate way of highlighting the "purpose and character" test is to note that the profit motive almost inevitably vitiates a claim of fair use and what is claimed to be educational, critical, or otherwise legitimate, is likely, when done for money, to be seen by a court as "chiselling for personal profit." *Wainwright Securities, Inc. v. Wall Street Transcript Corp.* (1977).

## § 23.4   Nature of the Work

If a work is a form book or a book of quotations intended for use by others who are expected to incorporate a portion of the contents in other works, a defense of fair use seems preordained. On the other hand, the reproduction or performance of a poem or musical composition with no functional use and no expectations for later adaptation or incorporation would not so easily support a defendant's fair-use claim. The most difficult questions of fair use fall between those extremes and the results reached often turn upon the way the work's nature relates to the other variables of fair use, most particularly the nature of the defendant's use. Thus, a work whose nature is exclusively educational will not readily support a fair use that is itself educational. That is because the nature of the use relates intimately to the fourth statutory factor— the economic impact of the use. If the nature of the work is such that the defendant's use is in exactly the area in which the economic potential of the work lies, it will not readily support a fair-use defense. See § 23.10, infra.

The nature of the work thus relates to a form of implied consent theory. It is unlikely that an author would expect or consent to an uncompensated use when the author expects to exploit that use for her own benefit. But if the copyright holder authors a work that is intended to be utilized by copying, the defense of fair use amounts to little more than a conclusion that the author has consented to the use. Thus, in *American Institute of Architects v. Fenichel* (1941), a defense of fair use was recognized because "[w]hen the plaintiff put on the general market a book of forms, he implied the right to their private use. This conclusion follows from the nature of a book of forms."

The nature of the work sometimes is measured by the creativity and originality that the author has invested. A work that reflects a considerable amount of these characteristics is one that is less amenable to a fair use defense than is a work that is the product of sheer labor and of minimal or trivial creativity and originality. In *New York Times Co. v. Roxbury Data Interface, Inc.* (1977), the plaintiffs were denied a preliminary injunction that would have stopped the defendants from publishing a directory consisting of a list of all personal names appearing in the New York Times Index. The court considered the nature of the New York Times Index and instead of inquiring into the expectations of the New York Times in publishing the Index, considered whether the Index had an original or creative nature. According to the district judge: "Since the Times Index is a work more of diligence than of originality or inventiveness, defendants have greater license to use portions ... under the fair use doctrine than ... if a creative work had been involved."

Some cases held the unpublished nature of a work such as private papers and letters might be a decisive factor in applying the fair-use doctrine. *Harper & Row, Publishers, Inc. v. Nation Enterprises, Inc.* (1985); *Salinger v. Random House, Inc.* (1987). In response, Congress amended section 107 to declare that a work's unpublished nature need not bar fair use, as long as it is taken into consideration.

## § 23.5  The Proportional Amount and Substance of the Use

The reprinting of a sentence out of a full-length novel obviously is different from the same taking from a two-sentence poem. Likewise, the publication of a single picture of a frame from a multi-thousand frame motion picture obviously is different than the same publication out of a photographic exhibition or, worse, of a single artistic work of a major portrait artist. In other words, although the general principle is "the more the taking, the more the infringement," one must first define what "more" means. "More" can be measured meaningfully by the proportional substance or quality of the taking. By that measure, a wholesale taking of the entire background of the Mona Lisa (assuming it would be a protected work today and not in the public domain) might not be an infringement, whereas even a small but complete taking of a portion of the face or smile would be qualitatively, although not quantitatively, more serious. Moreover, the question of the proportionality of what is taken to the copyrighted portion of the plaintiff's original work must be distinguished from the question of the proportion the taken part bears to the entire work of the defendant. See *Walt Disney Productions v. Air Pirates* (1978). The latter might loosely be referred to as "reverse proportionality."

Both qualitative and quantitative measures are important under section 107 of the current Act. The Act specifies that proportionality is to be measured with respect to the copyrighted work and not the infringement. 17 U.S.C.A. § 107(3). Since, under the 1909 Act, the reverse proportionality also was measured with respect to the defendant's work, this measurement probably is still, although less, relevant under the 1976 Act because congressional history indicates that the Act is intended "to restate the present judicial doctrine of fair use, not to change, narrow, or enlarge it in any way." Notes of the Committee on the Judiciary, House Rep. No. 94–1476. Thus, it may be relevant that what is taken, even though only constituting a small proportion of the plaintiff's work—for instance one sentence out of a major literary work—constitutes a major part of the defendant's infringement—as would be true for instance when the single sentence is the entire work used by an advertising company in a promotional campaign. The emphasis in such an approach, that of the "free rider," clearly shifts from measuring how much of the plaintiff's efforts have been stolen by the defendant to a conclusion of unfair advantage or profit garnered by the defendant through work done by the plaintiff.

Although of quantitative, qualitative, and reverse proportionality only the first two are mentioned specifically in the current Act, all three have been used by the courts to determine fair use. In *Williams & Wilkins v. United States* (1973), the court rejected a straightforward quantitative measurement of proportional copying. It held that an entire taking of all of a plaintiff's work could be justified under fair use by other factors. Fair use neither is established nor precluded by a simple mathematical measurement. In *Robertson v. Batten, Barton, Durstine & Osborn, Inc.* (1956) the defendants used only portions of the plaintiff's song, but because those portions constituted "that ... upon which its popular appeal, and, hence, its commercial success, depends," such qualitative copying was held to be substantial enough to preclude the defense of fair use. In *Meeropol v. Nizer* (1977), the defendant copied verbatim twenty-eight letters the copyrights of which were owned by plaintiffs. The total amount of words copied, only 1,956, constituted less than one per cent of the defendant's entire work. However, on a qualitative basis, the court found that the nature of the *defendant's* work was such that these letters formed a key and prominent part of the work and its promotion. The court held that it was relevant to fair use that the qualitative proportion measured against the defendant's work was significant, thus applying the qualitative measure in a reverse manner.

One court has held that paraphrasing the original work will not avoid a claim of infringement nor necessarily uphold a fair use defense. Importantly, applying a kind of damned-if-you-do-damned-if-you-don't perspective, the court held that, in computing proportionality between the infringing and noninfringing portions, the paraphrased portions should be counted along with the literally copied portions. *Salinger v. Random House, Inc.* (1987).

## § 23.6 The Effect on the Original Author's Economic Market

Although all of the various measures of fair use are interrelated, the potential economic impact of the claimed fair use brings all of the other measures into play simultaneously. In fact, the Supreme Court has termed the economic effect, "the single most important element of fair use." *Harper & Row, Publishers, Inc. v. Nation Enterprises, Inc.* (1985). If the nature of the claimed fair use is for profit, there is at least a potential impact upon the author's economic market. Similarly, if the nature of the plaintiff's work is such that it invites, implies, or requires reproduction, it would be absurd to suggest that the author's potential market is not diminished since it would have been assumed to include all of the demand for copies, although the taking may be excused on a consent theory. See § 23.4, supra.

Likewise, the proportionality of copying, whether calculated qualitatively, quantitatively, or even in a reverse manner, bears intimately on the assessment of the original author's potential market. In this sense it is true that the more the copying the more the infringement, since it seems almost indisputable that if the plaintiff has anything to sell, it is worth correspondingly less as more of it is copied. Thus, although this factor may be the most important in the fair-use calculus, it is also the most circular since whether something has economic impact upon the author necessarily depends upon whether a court finds, in the end, that it infringes the author's rights.

Sometimes, a small part of a larger work can be its economic "heart," the infringement of which, despite its proportionally diminutive amount, will defeat a claim of fair use. *Harper & Row, Publishers, Inc. v. Nation Enterprises, Inc.,* supra. But, *Meeropol v. Nizer* (1977), held that the simple showing of an impact upon the plaintiff's market is not enough. The impact, implied the court, must be balanced against all of the other fair-use factors.

## § 23.7  Parody, Burlesque, and Satire

Since before Chaucer, utilizing earlier works for purposes of criticism has been a recognized literary technique. When applied to parody, burlesque, and satire, the test for fair use emphasizes purpose and economic effect over proportional, quantitative, or even qualitative measurements, whether reverse, or otherwise. The test is not simply how much was taken but, rather, the purpose served by the taking and the reasonableness of the taking in light of the purpose. *Campbell v. Acuff–Rose Music, Inc.* (1994).

For many years, the legitimacy of parody as fair use seemed to depend upon whether the parodist took any more than necessary to "conjure up" the original. *Berlin v. E. C. Publications, Inc.* (1964). In *Walt Disney Productions v. Air Pirates* (1978), the test for parody was thought to be related to the substantiality test, which required determining whether the taking was substantial *in the light of the legitimacy of parody* as an art form that necessarily must take a certain amount from the original work. The issue became whether the defendant did more than simply parody (which is only doing what is necessary to "recall or conjure up" the original) by taking more than necessary.

However, in a true judicial *tour de force*, Justice Souter, writing for the Supreme Court in *Campbell v. Acuff–Rose Music, Inc.*, supra, recast the parody test. He wrote that it is not a matter of how much is taken, but for what purpose is it taken and to what effect is it put that determines whether a parody is fair use. *Campbell* held that as long as the purpose is parody, the amount taken is not decisive. This is largely because the economic effect is negated by the fact that authors seldom if ever parody themselves or license others to do so. A parody does not act as a market substitute. Parody, said the Court in *Campbell*, is a true transformative use, creating a new work of a different character. Thus, it is not within the scope of the original author's expectations of profit. As a result, it does not even matter that the parodist takes the "heart" of a work—first, because a parody, to be effective, relies upon the very nature and "heart" of the original, and second, because "heart" or not, being parody it takes nothing from the economic expectations of the author. Further, the fact that parody or satire might affect the market—through negative criticism—does not make it infringing, since the question is not whether it legitimately suppresses demand through criticism but whether it unfairly usurps demand through substitution. Justice Souter's approach was applied in *Suntrust Bank v. Houghton Mifflin Co.* (2001), which held that a novel, *The Wind Done Gone*, which satirized *Gone With the Wind*, did not infringe, despite "wholesale" takings of characters, relationships, and events.

## § 23.8   Fair Use and Free Speech

In recent years, the First Amendment has been claimed as a defense in a number of infringement cases. The claim is strongest, of course, when raised in connection with matters of public interest or with respect to criticism or parody. Critics or parodists who take portions of another's original works often claim a right to do so based on either fair use, First Amendment considerations, or a combination of both.

One response to the defense is that the First Amendment creates no exception to copyright because, as a constitutional doctrine, it is opposed by an equally constitutional doctrine: the Copyright Clause. This response, however, has been dismissed by most courts and commentators as excessively simplistic for at least two reasons. First, a literal reading of the Constitution will show that since the First Amendment is an amendment to the Constitution and to the Copyright Clause itself, the amendment should control. Second, even if the Bill of Rights and the Constitution are taken as a whole, priority must be given to the specific protections contained in the Bill of Rights. To do otherwise would be to grant carte blanche under a number of general constitutional powers such as the Commerce Clause, thereby creating a risk of utterly destroying the rights granted by the Amendments.

The more accepted response to claims of First Amendment fair-use rights is found in the idea-expression dichotomy. Viewing the First Amendment as prohibiting any restraints on the free communication of ideas, courts have held that there is no constitutional violation as long as copyright merely restrains using a particular expression as opposed to the idea itself. However, matters of public interest sometimes become so important that copyright has been lost because the particular work is uniquely situated to convey the ideas. In *Time Inc. v. Bernard Geis Associates* (1968), the Zapruder films of the Kennedy assassination were held too important to be restricted by copyright claims. It may be thought that in such a case the idea and expression tend to merge. Generally, the courts have found the idea-expression line a convenient and workable way of resolving First Amendment claims. See *Sid & Marty Krofft Television Productions, Inc. v. McDonald's Corp.* (1977). The Supreme Court has dismissed the potential conflict between copyright and free speech because fair use and the idea/expression dichotomy constitute "built-in free speech safeguards." *Eldred v. Ashcroft* (2003).

First Amendment claims also have been evaluated under a rule of reason. In doing so, a court usually avoids the somewhat circular trap of the constitutional argument by acknowledging the constitutional right of criticism and fair use but insisting that the criticism and fair use be done reasonably. Using a greater amount of the copyrighted work than is reasonably necessary in reporting matters of public interest can defeat a fair-use defense. See *Zacchini v. Scripps–Howard Broadcasting Co.* (1977). Indeed, the idea-expression dichotomy dictates that even when there is a clear First Amendment right involved, such as the memoirs of an ex-President, the First Amendment does not override copyright interests when a lesser taking would communicate the same ideas and facts and satisfy First Amendment interests. Furthermore, the very existence of the fair-use privilege undercuts the notion that the First Amendment either conflicts with copyright or creates its own privilege such as, for instance, a public-figure exception. *Harper & Row, Publishers, Inc. v. Nation Enterprises, Inc.* (1985). The fact that copyright is content neutral also contributes to the argument that there is no inherent First Amendment conflict. *Universal City Studios, Inc. v. Corley* (2001).

First Amendment claims sometimes are avoided by defining copyright as a property right, and therefore not subject to significant free speech defenses. In cases involving fraud or piracy, courts have dismissed defenses based on freedom of speech by noting that the defendants have no interest in speech and are exercising no right to communicate but, instead, are attempting to take the property of others. *United States v. Bodin* (1974).

## § 23.9  Photocopying

Fair use under section 107 specifically allows for multiple copying of copyrighted works when done for classroom use under certain conditions. The exact scope of this permissible copying is not defined in the statute itself, however. Likewise, section 108 provides for a limitation on the copyright proprietor's exclusive rights and authorizes libraries to make copies of certain works. It also implicitly recognizes the right of others, under what presumably is fair use, to make photocopies in libraries having photocopying machines and immunizes libraries from any copyright liability if certain notices are posted.

Photocopying is thus to some extent a recognized partial exception to copyright, whether described as fair use or as a limitation upon the exclusive rights. This subject provoked a great deal of congressional discussion when the 1976 Act was being debated and never was finally resolved. However, an important agreement was reached among a group of publishers, authors, and educational institutions, which was published by Congress under the title, "Agreement on Guidelines for Classroom Copying in Not–For–Profit Educational Institutions," when it revised the copyright law. A similar agreement involving musical works also was published at that time.

The agreement allows limited copying of portions of works when used for scholarly purposes. The Guidelines specify that this copying must be characterized by brevity and spontaneity, implying that wholesale copying of entire works is not favored and that multiple copies are to be made only if another alternative is not possible due to time limitations. The Guidelines emphasize that fair use should not substitute for the purchase of materials that are otherwise available. Although this agreement does not occupy the status of law, it no doubt will be an authoritative source for both legislative intent and specific solutions to recurring problems.

With respect to library photocopying, section 108 echoes the same sentiments. Libraries and archives are allowed to make one copy of a work as long as it is not done for commercial advantage. However, this privilege is for the most part restricted to replacing damaged works or obtaining out-of-print works that otherwise are unavailable. Finally, libraries are immunized from liability when others make photocopies within their premises so long as photocopying machines provided by the library are accompanied by a notice warning that photocopying may be subject to the copyright law.

## § 23.10 The Functional—Equivalents or Transformative—Use Test

Implicit in fair use is a test that seeks to determine whether the defendant's work serves a function other than that which the original copyrighted work fulfilled and therefore does not interfere with, detract from, or unjustly deplete the plaintiff's expectations. However, this test sometimes is stated explicitly, especially when the economic impact of a claimed infringement is unclear. In that event, it is an attractive alternative for a court to pose the problem in these more abstract terms, based upon the "function" or the "intrinsic purpose" of the two works. A showing that a claimed infringement duplicates the original work's intended function can override even educational and nonprofit motives. *Marcus v. Rowley* (1983).

The test seeks to discover the function of both the original and the infringing works. It does not explicitly inquire into economic impact and so is useful when such questions are hopelessly speculative and circular. The conceptual characterization of the function of a work as "entertainment," or "parody," or "educational," is far easier to make than a determination whether a second work will interfere with the commercial prospects of the original. Thus the test directs the attention of a court towards the heart of fair use: whether an infringement serves a legitimate purpose not connected with that for which the original has been given protection under the copyright laws. If the new use is transformative—creating a new work satisfying an unrelated market—rather than superseding—thereby supplanting the market for the original—then it may be a fair use. This is the thrust of the Supreme Court decision in *Campbell v. Acuff–Rose Music, Inc.* (1994). See § 23.7, supra.

The advantage of the functional-equivalents test, aside from avoiding the speculative determination of economic impact, is that it dispenses with any requirement that the original and the infringement be in the same medium or share any other particular characteristic. Thus, a musical adaptation of "Gone With the Wind," even though it is a stage play performed in an intimate cabaret atmosphere, as opposed to the original's semi-serious novel form or later full-length motion picture derivation, cannot claim fair use if it fulfills the same function as the original—entertainment. *Metro-Goldwyn–Mayer, Inc. v. Showcase Atlanta Cooperative Productions, Inc.* (1979).

But the disadvantage of this test is that it is almost automatically answered at the definitional stage. To the extent the court broadly defines the copyrighted work's function, it is very likely that the challenged work will be found to fulfill the same function and thus preclude a fair-use defense. To the extent the court decides to define the function of the copyrighted work more narrowly, it is well on the way to allowing the fair-use defense. The test is thus somewhat result-oriented.

# CHAPTER 24

# OWNERSHIP

## § 24.1 The Copyright and the Material Object

The distinction between the physical object and the copyrighted work in it is fundamental and applies to any work of authorship, no matter how far down the totem pole of artistic creation the work may lie. Thus, cases dealing with letters written from one person to another have held that, although the property interest in the physical object passes from writer to recipient, the right to reproduce the contents and the copyright generally can be retained by the writer when there is evidence of such an interest. *Folsom v. Marsh* (1841) (No. 4901). Similarly, *Chamberlain v. Feldman* (1949) held that the transferee of a manuscript by Mark Twain, although the legal owner of the manuscript, did not have the right to claim the copyright and thus to reproduce and publish the contents. This distinction is intimately related to the first-sale doctrine which provides that the sale transfers title to the object, but not its underlying copyright. The Ninth Circuit held, in *Mirage Editions, Inc. v. Albuquerque A.R.T. Co.* (1988) that the buyer of a picture book infringed the book author's copyright by cutting out and then mounting the pictures in tiles for resale. But this overlooks the fact, as the Seventh Circuit later observed, in *Lee v. A.R.T. Co.* (1997) that the mounted pictures themselves, being the physical object, were free of any continuing claim by the original author but that there was still no danger to the original author's copyright. This is because the tile-mounted pictures, although the property of the book purchaser, could not be further reproduced without permission of the original author who would profit from any future reproductions she might authorize.

The old rule that the sale of a work of authorship presumptively conveyed not only the physical object itself but also the copyright has been, for all practical purposes, reversed under the 1976 Act. Under section 202, the sale of the tangible object does not impliedly convey the copyright; likewise, the sale of a copyright or of any of the exclusive rights does not imply the sale of the tangible object. Section 204 indicates that any agreement to convey the copyright must explicitly do so in writing to be valid.

## § 24.2 Multiple Claims to Authorship

Copyright ownership becomes somewhat complicated in two basic situations. First, when a work consists of material created by more than one person, or when it consists of various subcomponents (such as melody and lyrics) created by different individuals, the problem of *joint works,* 17 U.S.C.A. § 101, arises. Second, when an author creates a work for publication by another, either as an employee or an independent contractor, the problem of *works for hire,* 17 U.S.C.A. § 101, arises. Some works by multiple authors that are neither joint works nor works for hire may be characterized as either *collective works* or *compilations.* 17 U.S.C.A. § 101. Finally, works that use the work of a prior author may be treated as *derivative works.* 17 U.S.C.A. § 101. In all of these situations, ownership potentially can be clouded and problems arose under the common law and prior statutes. The 1976 Act was designed to resolve them.

The particular label used to characterize multiple claims to authorship determines important legal issues. If a composer authors a musical composition in 1990 and a lyricist authors the lyrics in 2000, the characterization of their status as separate or joint authors or that one or both produced the work for hire may determine when the copyright expires, whether termination of a license of the copyright by one of them effectively will terminate the license of the entire work (or just the part individually authored by that person), and the legal duties, if any, each owes the other. If the musical composition is deemed a new work when the words and music were combined in 2000, and the authors are deemed joint, the copyright in the work will not expire until seventy years after the death of the surviving author. However, if the authors are not deemed joint, the music and lyrics are viewed as separate entities and each will fall into the public domain separately upon the expiration of the copyright (in other words, seventy years after the death of the respective authors of the respective parts).

Previously, the definition of a joint work was somewhat ambiguous, although it focused on the intent of the first author. Thus, if a work was created with the intent that a later author would add either lyrics, music, or any other element that the first author contemplated would be added to produce the final work, then the final collaboration represented a "joint work." This doctrine was expanded by the Supreme Court in *Shapiro, Bernstein & Co. v. Jerry Vogel Music Co.* (1955), to include the intent of an assignee of all the rights in the first work as a determinant of whether the final work is joint or not. Under the current Act, however, the doctrine has been trimmed back to its original form so that according to section 101, a work involving multiple authors is joint if prepared "with the intention that their contributions be merged into inseparable or interdependent parts of a unitary whole." Thus, a joint work must be a "unitary whole" consisting of "inseparable or interdependent parts." It seems, then, that it is the intention of the authors and not of any later assignees that will be determinative. Moreover, it appears that the intent must be fairly concrete, relatively nonspeculative, and, if not definite, at least more than a "hope or expectation," which are the words that the legislative history uses to characterize the impermissibly speculative state of mind of those who do not qualify as joint authors.

The effects of determining that a work is joint on the basis of the authors' intent are numerous. As already stated, although the current Act provides that a copyright usually expires seventy years after the death of the author, a joint work has joint authors and does not expire until seventy years after the last to die. On the other hand, some common law doctrines relating to joint authorship still are viable. The most important of these are those relating to ownership rights and duties. Basically, joint authors become owners in common and their property rights and duties are determined accordingly. See § 24.3, infra.

If two or more authors produce a single work without specifically intending to do so when they prepare their respective contributions, or if the result is not a single, unitary work consisting of inseparable or interdependent parts, the result must be either a compilation or possibly a derivative work. A work may fall into the compilation or derivation category if the conditions of intent or unitary nature fail. If derivative, assuming the second author has been authorized to use the earlier work, he will be the author of the derivative work while the first author will own rights in the earlier work. The preexisting copyrightable elements will fall into the public domain seventy years after the death of the preexisting work's author (assuming it doesn't have the term of a work-for-hire), and the derivative work, with regard to the elements that have been created by the derivative author, will be a matter of public domain seventy years after the second author's death (again assuming a non-work-for-hire).

If a work is not joint and not derivative but nevertheless consists of works of authorship created by more than one person, it is a compilation of some sort except for the possibility that it is a work for hire. A compilation consists of an original work of authorship that incorporates other preexisting material. If the component parts have an independent identity, that is, they are works of authorship, then the compilation is a collective work, a type of compilation. The author who finally assembles the components into a compilation is the owner of the copyright of the compilation—but not of the component parts. Of course, a compilation merely may be an assemblage of data or information produced by others. The individual pieces of data may not qualify as works of authorship and thus would not be copyrightable. However, if the components are independently copyrightable works, such as the individual articles in an encyclopedia or the individual short stories in an anthology, the contributing authors will have independent rights.

Section 201 of the Copyright Act delineates the respective rights of the compiler and of the contributors. The compiler has the right to publish the collective work and owns the copyright in that work; he can revise the collective work and also can publish the contributions in a later collective work if it is part of the same series. However, a computer database of contributions to more than one collective, originally print, work constitutes a new work,

not a later collective work belonging to the same
series, and therefore infringes the individual authors' rights to their contributions. This is so even
though the database "tags" each contribution so
that the original arrangement remains evident on-
line. *New York Times Co., Inc. v. Tasini* (2001). A
contributor owns the copyright in the contribution
subject to the rights of the compiler, unless he
otherwise has expressly transferred the ownership
of it. Under section 404, the contributor will not be
prejudiced by a failure of the compiler to place a
notice of separate copyright for the contribution
apart from the compilation, and in fact there is no
requirement that there be separate notices of copyright for each of the contributors.

A work for hire is either (1) created by an employee within the scope of her employment, or (2)
specially commissioned or ordered. 17 U.S.C.A.
§ 101. The kinds of specially commissioned or ordered works that can qualify as works for hire are
limited by statute to: (a) contributions to collective
works, (b) parts of motion pictures or audiovisual
works, (c) translations, (d) supplementary works
(forewords, afterwords, illustrations, for example),
(e) compilations, (f) instructional texts, (g), tests,
(h) answers for a test, and (i) atlases. The Supreme
Court's decision in *Community for Creative Non–
Violence v. Reid* (1989) supports a literal reading of
the 1976 Act such that other works, even though
specially commissioned or ordered, and even if the
parties expressly agree that they are to be works for

hire, cannot be so treated. It is clear that in only two circumstances can a work be for hire: when one of the nine categories specified in the statute is involved, the work is specially commissioned, and a written agreement exists, or when the author is an employee. Whether an author is an employee is to be determined solely by the traditional common law agency requirement that the employer must have the right to control. *Community for Creative Non– Violence v. Reid,* supra.

The primary importance of the status of a work for hire is (1) all rights of copyright ownership vest in the employer, which expire ninety-five years after publication or 120 years after creation, whichever comes first, and (2) the actual author of a work for hire does not have the right to terminate the ownership rights of the employer, which he otherwise would be able to do if he simply had been a transferor of his own copyright ownership. See § 24.4, infra.

## § 24.3 The Rights of Coauthors

Coauthors of joint works stand in relation to each other much as do coowners in common of any other kind of personal property, with some modifications peculiar to intellectual property. Thus, each owner has the right to use the property for her own purposes, but neither has the right to exclude the other from using the property. Likewise, neither owner can commit waste by depleting, squandering, or otherwise destroying the value of the property.

As a result of these reciprocal rights, each joint author has the duty to account to the other for any benefits if using the property either excluded the other from using it or destroyed any part of the property. This is because intellectual property is not like real property; it is not possible for one person to use it—except in complete privacy—without effectively excluding the other from important uses.

Consequently, the traditional rule forbidding accountings between coowners of commonly owned property is modified in the copyright context. Coowners of other kinds of property are permitted to use the property without accounting because it is assumed that all coowners can use the property in one way or another. But intellectual property is not so amenable to multiple uses. For example, the sale of rights to a song or dramatic composition immediately forecloses coauthors from doing the same. The market, in that sense, is more limited than it is for other forms of property, being less elastic and less amenable to multiple uses, either in space or time. Thus, copyright law has allowed the use of equitable relief, including demands for an accounting, which would be prohibited in other areas of property law.

## § 24.4   Duration of Ownership

The duration of copyright has been consistently increased by Congress since the first copyright statute in 1790. There appears to be little if any constitutional limit upon Congress' power to determine the length of the copyright term. "Calibrating rational economic incentives ... is a task primarily for Congress, not the courts." *Eldred v. Ashcroft* (2003). Under the 1909 Act, copyright ownership vested in the author for an initial period of twenty-eight years. During the final year of copyright protection, the author had the right to renew the term for another twenty-eight years. The maximum period during which an author could exclude others from using the work therefore was fifty-six years. Under the present Act, copyright extends for the lifetime of the author (if the author is an identified natural person and did not produce the work for hire) plus seventy years. 17 U.S.C.A. § 302(a). This is subject to the modification that if the work is joint, the terminal date is seventy years after the death of the last surviving author. 17 U.S.C.A. § 302(b).

In the case of works made for hire, the copyright expires ninety-five years after publication, or 120 years after creation, whichever occurs first. Creation is defined as the date upon which the work is fixed in tangible form. 17 U.S.C.A. § 302(c).

In the case of anonymous and pseudonymous works, the same ninety-five to 120 year scheme applies. 17 U.S.C.A. § 302(c). However, an anonymous or pseudonymous work can be "opted out" of this scheme if, anytime during the ninety-five to 120 year period, a person with an interest in the copyright reveals to the Copyright Office the true identity of at least one of the real authors of the work. In that event, the copyright term reverts to the natural timetable with respect to the author or authors revealed and expires seventy years after death. Thus, if a work were first published and created by a pseudonymous author in 1980 who died in 1981 the copyright would expire at the earliest in 2075. If however, somebody who had an "interest" in the copyright were to reveal the identity of the author in 2051, the work might then lose copyright and enter the public domain. If that person were held not to have an interest, the copyright owner at least theoretically could enjoy copyright protection for an additional twenty-four years in spite of the fact that the true author's identity had been discovered.

On the other hand, if the work were composed and published by a one-year-old child in 1981 who, at the age of ninety-seven, in the year 2077, attempted to preserve the copyright by volunteering the news of his authorship to the Copyright Office the author would be unsuccessful. This is because the Act requires that the filing of such information be completed during the term of copyright, not after its expiration.

Even if the prodigy had authored the work in his own name, he would be in danger of losing copyright if he did not comply with another provision of the Act. According to section 302(e), ninety-five years after publication or 120 years after creation, whichever comes sooner, it is presumed that an author has been dead for seventy years unless an interested person files a statement of the status of the author. Thus, it is becoming increasingly important for copyright owners and their legal advisers to watch out for the possible application of this provision; their objective, obviously, is to prevent others from relying on the statutory presumption. Since section 302 allows recording statements indicating the death and the living status of authors, it will become necessary, to prevent premature expiration of the copyright, for interested persons to file such statements at or around the ninety-five to 120 year points.

## § 24.5   Termination of Transfers

One of the most radical provisions of the 1976 Act allows authors who have sold their rights to others to "recapture" their rights by serving notice that they intend to do so approximately thirty-five years after the rights were sold. 17 U.S.C.A. § 203. Although this termination provision is a major change, it does not apply to every transfer of copyright ownership. The termination-of-transfer provision specifically does not apply to authors who created their works for hire. With respect to virtually all other transfers of copyright ownership, however, an author has the power to regain what might have been sold or otherwise transferred at an inappropriate price when the work originally was created.

The termination-of-transfer provision explicitly is designed to protect authors who have sold their work, perhaps at an early stage of their professional lives, only to find at a later date that their creations have become far more valuable. To avoid the kind of exploitation that it is believed many authors suffered at the hands of those who were (and still are) able to purchase copyrights cheaply before the authors become prominent enough to command sufficient prices for their works, Congress decided to give such authors, except for authors of works for hire, the right to cancel the sale after approximately thirty-five years.

Under section 203, an author can terminate any transfer, whether it is exclusive or not, during the five-year period beginning thirty-five years after the transfer was granted. In the case of a transfer of publication rights, the termination may occur during the five-year period beginning thirty-five years after publication under the grant or forty years after the grant if that occurs sooner. (This is to provide greater protection to an author who may sell the publication rights at an early date but whose work may not actually be published until many years later.) In order to effect a termination sometime during the five-year period, the author must serve a notice upon the grantee. The notice must be served no less than two nor more than ten years before the date within the five-year period chosen by the author for termination.

This right of termination cannot be taken away from the author by any means (although grants that have been devised by the author's will cannot be terminated, apparently because such a testamentary bequest does not seem to be the kind of exploitive transfer with which Congress was concerned). In other words, even if an aggressive publisher attempts to purchase a manuscript from a young author and includes in the purchase agreement that the author waives the right to terminate the grant, the waiver is ineffective.

The Copyright Act contains an elaborate scheme designed to identify relatives who, after the death of an author, are entitled to terminate copyright transfers just as would the author if he still were alive. Basically, a surviving spouse is entitled to half of the ownership and an equal role in the termination right; children or their descendants are entitled to share the remaining half, per stirpes. If there are no children, the spouse takes all; likewise, if there is no surviving spouse, the children share the entire copyright termination right. In order to terminate, however, a total of more than one-half of the termination interests must agree to the termination. 17 U.S.C.A. § 203(a)(2)(A)(B)(C). This is true as well of joint authors, a majority of whom must agree to terminate. 17 U.S.C.A. § 203(a)(1).

If there are three joint authors, two of them must agree to terminate. If a sole author dies, leaving a wife and three children, the three children cannot terminate, since they have only one-half of the termination interest but the wife and any one of the three children can terminate, since any one child will add the required majority to the wife's one-half interest. A similar result would occur if one of two joint authors died, leaving a number of children. The remaining author and any one of the surviving children could combine to achieve a majority interest. On the other hand, all of the surviving children together would not be enough to gain a majority over the remaining coauthor to terminate effectively.

It should be noted that, even under the 1909 Act, authors had the opportunity to regain their copyright interests because a reversionary interest in the second twenty-eight-year term subsisted in the author. In fact, this reversion was more or less automatic so to that extent, the 1976 Act is somewhat regressive because it requires an affirmative notice of termination in order to effect that right. On the other hand, the Act is far more protective and effective in achieving the goal of safeguarding the interests of authors, especially because (1) under the 1909 Act, the second copyright term, although it reverted to the author, automatically was forfeited unless it was affirmatively renewed at the proper time, and (2) the total term was far shorter.

Perhaps most importantly, under the prior Act, an author could assign even the reversionary interest in the second term provided he was alive at the time of the expiration of the first twenty-eight-year term. This was modified somewhat by a Supreme Court opinion that held that "unconscionable" assignments would not be honored. Nevertheless, authors were significantly unprotected from possible harm. *Fred Fisher Music Co. v. M. Witmark & Sons* (1943). Under the current Act, such assignments are impossible, whether unconscionable or not.

Despite section 203, some transfers cannot be terminated. The author of the original work upon which an authorized derivative work is based has no termination right with regard to the derivative. Thus, if a publisher grants to an author the right to dramatize a novel, the original author of the novel may terminate and deprive the publisher of the copyright to the novel thirty-five years after publication. Nevertheless, any dramatization that may be created is immunized from this termination by the original author. 17 U.S.C.A. § 203(b)(1).

Under the 1909 Act, posthumous and most composite works were treated as works for hire. The result of the inclusion of these works with works for hire meant contributors to composite works did not obtain a reversionary interest in the second term and effectively sold the entire two terms of protection to the owner of the composite work; renewal inured to the benefit of the purchaser. The proprietor had the complete rights to the second term just as employers today own the entire work for hire. Under the current Act, except for works for hire, all authors, including contributors to composite works and the representatives of the authors of posthumous works, have the right to terminate a copyright from any purchaser of the work during the relevant five-year period, 17 U.S.C.A. § 203, and to receive copyright protection until seventy years after his death.

## § 24.6 Works for Hire

Works for hire are different than other works, most importantly because they are excepted from the termination provisions. The statute makes it clear that the author of a work for hire does not have the right to terminate her assignment to an employer after thirty-five years. In other words, the employer of an author who produces a work for hire ends up owning the entire copyright, which expires ninety-five years after publication or 120 years after creation, whichever comes first. 17 U.S.C.A. § 302(a).

Although the general concepts of works for hire are discussed under multiple claims to ownership, see § 24.2, supra, there are a number of details growing out of the statutory definition that are notable. A work for hire qualifies as such only under either of two possible circumstances. In true employer-employee situations, any work produced by an author within the scope of employment becomes the work of the employer for all copyright purposes—most importantly for purposes of depriving the author of any right to terminate the ownership by the employer, who owns the work for the ninety-five to 120 year term outright. The second circumstance under which a work can become one for hire requires the conjunction of three essential elements: the work must be "specially ordered or commissioned," it must be described by one of the nine categories of section 101(2), and the parties must agree in writing that the work is one for hire. 17 U.S.C.A. § 101.

The first circumstance is relatively straightforward; determination of a work's status is controlled by relatively well-understood common law doctrines of agency. *Community for Creative Non–Violence v.*

*Reid* (1989). The second circumstance, however, being primarily statutory, requires reference to the statute as a whole and the purpose behind the definition of works for hire. It is clear from the text of the current Act generally and its statutory history that works for hire were meant to be a relatively narrowly defined exception to the general proposition that authors are entitled to a termination interest in their copyrights. Thus, it would be a misinterpretation of the Act to allow publishing organizations or other enterprises to use blanket clauses and boilerplate contracts to convert any purchase of an author's copyright into a work for hire merely by the statement in a contract of sale that the author agrees that the work is one for hire.

It is exactly this kind of unfair bargaining that the termination provisions are designed to prevent. Thus, it is not intended that the mere agreement that a work is to be for hire should decide the work's status. To allow that clearly would be to violate section 203(a)(5), which provides that authors are to have termination rights "notwithstanding any agreement to the contrary." Thus, it is the *status of the work* and the *actual relation of the parties,* not an agreement (which might violate section 203(a)(5)) that determines whether a work is one for hire. It also is essential to realize that the statute's requirement that a work be specially commissioned or ordered is a substantive one—it in fact must be so commissioned or ordered before delivery to the buyer.

As an example, publishers of magazines might desire to purchase the entire copyright term from all their contributors. They might do this by including in their agreements to purchase manuscripts that all work is to be for hire. However, if the manuscripts are sent to the publisher without having been specially commissioned previously, it seems to violate the statute to attempt to convert these works of authorship into works for hire merely by the insertion of such a statement into a contract of sale. In other words, the decision as to the status of the work as one for hire probably should be made at the time of commission, and not later. With respect to manuscripts that were not specially commissioned, and those that were not specially agreed *at the time* of commissioning or ordering to be works for hire, an attempt to convert them to works for hire would be illegitimate. On the other hand, a publisher of magazines or newspapers clearly owns the copyright of the staff members' works as works for hire, since those individuals are employees of the publisher.

## § 24.7  Preexisting Works

A problem that naturally results from the enactment of a new copyright Act with radically different features from the earlier one, is how to treat the terms of preexisting copyrighted works. This becomes an even more serious problem when it is realized that many works that were not even subject to statutory copyright, because they were not "published" within the meaning of the 1909 Act, suddenly were brought within the 1976 Act because they had been fixed in tangible form. Thus, because the present Act so radically diminished the potential area of common law copyright and brought so many previously common law materials into the federal domain, the inevitable problem of how long, if at all, those works should be protected under the 1976 Act also was created.

The two basic problems with respect to preexisting works concern (a) those common law works that never were subject to federal copyright and suddenly were brought into the Copyright Act, and (b) those works that were federally copyrighted but whose terms were to be measured by two twenty-eight-year periods instead of a term related to the lifetime of the author.

Many works that enjoyed common law copyright but were not subject to the 1909 Act—mostly because they were not deemed "published" under that Act's rather narrow conception of that term—theoretically had perpetual common law protection. Whether "published" or not, they were brought under the 1976 Act by their tangible fixation, thereby destroying the author's expectation of perpetual protection. Thus, the problem for Congress was how equitably to grant federal protection that eventually would expire to a work that formerly had unlimited protection. Many of the authors of those works might have been dead for far more than the seventy years of protection now provided by the statute. If they were treated under the literal provisions of the

Act, the effect of the Act could have been simply to cast them into the public domain. Because of this conflict between policy and private expectations, it was decided that the only equitable solution was to treat all these works as all new works would be treated, with protection terminating seventy years after the death of the author. But the statute provides that no protection would expire before twenty-five years elapsed (December 31, 2002)—thus protecting those works whose authors might have died seventy or more years before the Act became effective. 17 U.S.C.A. § 303. Those works, obviously, if treated as any other works under the Act, otherwise would lose all protection and so the guaranteed minimum of twenty-five years was thought to be a fair, although an arbitrary, term.

The term was not entirely arbitrary, however, because the 1976 Act contains the additional provision that if any previously common law works are published before the initial twenty-five-year period expires, they receive a total of seventy years of protection (until December 31, 2047). 17 U.S.C.A. § 303. Thus, in order to encourage publication, with respect to works that would expire either immediately or relatively soon because of the deaths of the authors long before the effective date of the Act, Congress appropriately granted an equivalent seventy years after death provision to all of these works provided that the owner published the work sometime before December 31, 2022.

With respect to other works that already were subject to federal protection under the 1909 Act, the problem was at least as difficult. Some of those works would have been copyrighted shortly before the expiration of the 1909 Act and be in their first term. Others might be nearing the end of the second term. Both of those categories were to be treated alike, naturally, since there was no difference in expectations on behalf of their owners; on the other hand, to treat any of these subsisting copyrights exactly as new works—to expire seventy years after the death of the author—would have upset the expectations of some of the owners who, under the 1909 Act, anticipated two twenty-eight-year terms and who would receive less protection under the new regime.

The solution was to treat the older works copyrighted under the 1909 Act in what might be called a modernized manner. Congress recognized that the total fifty-six year federal protection was, in 1909, a reasonable estimation of average life expectancies of authors. New actuarial figures in the 1970's indicated that an accurate estimation of the life expectancy of a modern author was somewhere between seventy and seventy-six years. Therefore, when it originally chose seventy-five years (altered in 1998 to ninety-five) as a fair estimation of a just term of protection, Congress simply adjusted all subsisting copyrights, whether in their first or second term, so that they would be provided seventy-five (now ninety-five) years of protection. Works that were in their first term and for which there was an expectation that the first term would expire after twenty-eight years were still to expire at that time but would gain an additional forty-seven (now sixty-seven) years as a second term—yielding a total of seventy-five (now ninety-five) years of protection. Works that were in their second term already simply were extended to expire forty-seven (now sixty-seven) years after the beginning of that second term—yielding, again, seventy-five (now ninety-five) years. 17 U.S.C.A. § 304(a)(b).

It should be noted that a termination period has been created for all 1909 works that are still under copyright, consisting of the last thirty-nine years of their extended terms and governed by provisions essentially the same as those for the normal termination right. For those works for whom the termination period had already passed when this provision was enacted, a twenty-year termination period was created. 17 U.S.C.A. § 304(c)(d).

# CHAPTER 25

# FORMAL REQUIREMENTS

## § 25.1  Registration

Unlike patent protection, and markedly different from trademark protection, copyright protection basically is self-executing. An author automatically is protected by federal copyright when he fixes the work in a tangible medium. 17 U.S.C.A. § 102(a). There is no need to obtain approval, conduct a prior art search, or secure registration by any agency. The ease in acquiring protection is related to the nature of copyright: since protection is only against *copying,* not against independent coincidental creation, there is no need for any governmental decision about the propriety of protection, as there is for patent protection, which forbids the duplication of the product or process whether done independently or by copying. Since other authors are free to create whatever they wish as long as they do not copy a protected work, and even to duplicate a protected one so long as they do it independently without copying, there is no need to search prior art to insure that the work has any particular requisite qualities nor to put other authors on notice that a work is protected. Likewise, since there is no defined interest in building up a reservoir of past knowledge, there is no need to collect past art by requiring authors to file their works prior to copyright protection. Thus, copyright differs from patent in both the interest protected and the goal sought; therefore, the need for examination is nonexistent; the need for registration is not terribly significant.

Nevertheless, there still are procedures for registration. There also are deposit requirements that require that copies of the work be presented for possible collection by the Library of Congress three months after publication as well as upon registration.

In a very real sense, both registration and deposit are optional. Copyright protection will exist despite lack of registration and failure to deposit cannot destroy a subsisting copyright. 17 U.S.C.A. § 408(a). However, registration and deposit have significant legal consequences, the most notable of which is that an owner of a "United States work" cannot sue for copyright infringement until he has registered the copyright. 17 U.S.C.A. § 411(a). Importantly, however, as long as registration is accomplished before litigation, there is nothing wrong in most cases with registering a copyright only after discovering an infringement and deciding to sue. Nevertheless, it is a defense to an infringement suit that plaintiff has failed to register a United States work prior to instituting the action.

However, there are some rights that can be permanently lost by failure to register soon enough. Registration is a prerequisite to certain remedies.

First, statutory damages are not recoverable for infringements that occur prior to registration except in the case of first published works if registration is accomplished within three months of first publication. 17 U.S.C.A. § 412(2). Second, attorneys' fees also are unrecoverable under the same circumstances. 17 U.S.C.A. § 412. Another important function of registration is the part it plays under section 405(a)(2) in curing a failure to affix notice of copyright properly to publicly distributed copies, although that is true now only with respect to works distributed prior to March 31, 1989, the effective date of the Berne Convention Implementation Act.

The requirement of registration as a prerequisite to an infringement suit raises two important problems. First, it is possible that registration may be denied by the Copyright Office. In fact, the question of whether an infringement has occurred may turn upon the very same issue that led the Copyright Office to deny copyrightability—for instance, if it were a work based upon a new technology of questionable copyright subject matter. To require registration in such a circumstance prior to suit would pose something in the nature of a Catch–22 situation: one could not sue for infringement of a work whose copyright status was questionable because registration is denied on that very ground. Under earlier acts, the remedy was to sue the Copyright Office to compel registration. *Vacheron & Constantin–Le Coultre Watches, Inc. v. Benrus Watch Co.* (1958). Under section 411 of the 1976 Act, one can sue an infringer despite refusal of the Copyright Office to register, by giving notice to the Office that the suit has been instituted.

The second problem raised by the registration requirement is the growth of new technologies, notably the development of live transmissions. Under section 411(b), such a transmission is protected just as first publications are protected so long as registration is accomplished within three months of the first transmission. However, unlike publications of more tangible works, the transmission of live programming is shorter and the possibility of damages three or more months later is not nearly as important as the availability of injunctive relief before the infringement even takes place. Therefore, with respect to the live transmission of sound with or without visual matter, which by definition cannot be registered prior to initial broadcast, a provision is made for injunctive relief by dispensing with the requirement of prior registration as long as registration is accomplished within three months of transmission *and* notice is served upon the potential infringer at least forty-eight hours prior to the transmission. 17 U.S.C.A. § 411(b).

For instance, in the case of the transmission of a championship game, the owners of the (future) copyright in that program effectively may prevent a threatened transmission of the program over a cable network by sending a notice to the cable company that registration is intended. If the cable company persists in promoting their planned transmission of the game, the owners then are allowed, by section 411, to institute suit prior to registration and, in fact, prior to creation of the work itself (the live transmission of the game) in order to enjoin the threatened infringement. Without this provision, the requirement of prior registration would have made equitable relief impossible.

There are two deposit requirements in the Copyright Act, neither of which imposes severe requirements or even has significant legal effects upon copyright ownership. There is a general deposit requirement for all copyrighted works that mandates deposit of two "best editions" within three months of publication but which explicitly specifies that deposit is not a condition of copyright protection. 17 U.S.C.A. § 407(a). Failure to deposit a copy, but only after a demand for deposit by the Copyright Office, creates a potential liability of no more than $250, 17 U.S.C.A. § 407(d)(1), although a potential $2500 fine exists for those who willfully and repeatedly fail to make deposit after demand is made. 17 U.S.C.A. § 407(d)(3). Thus, at least until demand is made, the requirement of section 407 is in all respects an optional one.

On the other hand, registration itself requires deposit of at least one copy of a work and, with respect to published works, two copies of the "best edition." The Copyright Office, however, has authority to vary these requirements and to adopt substitute requirements, for instance with respect to very expensive works, just as it has under section 407(c) with respect to deposit requirements generally.

## § 25.2 Notice

Because notice is so obviously a formal require-ment, which historically had potentially disastrous consequences for noncompliance, it has been pro-gressively deemphasized in American copyright law. Now, except for foreclosure of the defense of inno-cent infringement, 17 U.S.C.A. § 401(d), all of the notice requirements are completely optional for works distributed on or after March 31, 1989. For those works covered by the 1976 Act distributed prior to March 31, 1989, however, notice require-ments did apply, but with elaborate provisions to allow failure to affix proper notice to be cured within a five-year period. 17 U.S.C.A. § 405(a).

Copyright notice, although minimally relevant under the current Act, serves four functions. First, by warning owners that a failure to affix notice will work an effective abandonment, it assures that works that are unimportant to owners (unimpor-tant enough for them to publish the material with-out notice) will enter the public domain. Second, it serves to inform the public that works are copy-righted. Third, it identifies the copyright owner. Fourth, it serves to determine the date upon which the work was published.

Of course, when notice still is relevant—to pre-clude the defense of innocent infringement—it must comply with the terms of the Copyright Act. The Act requires that, to constitute proper notice, upon any publicly distributed copy of a work of author-ship, a notice must be affixed containing the following information: (1) the emblem C, the letter C in a circle, the word "Copyright," *or* the abbreviation, "Copr.," *and* (2) the date of first publication (except for greeting cards, postcards, stationery, jewelry, dolls, toys, or useful articles), *and* (3) the name of the copyright owner or a recognizable abbreviation or designation thereof. 17 U.S.C.A. § 401(b).

It should be noted that a simple display of a work, such as a photograph or painting, is not necessarily a publication under section 101 of the Act. Therefore, unlike under prior acts, notice is not necessarily required if at all, unless the display is done "publicly." 17 U.S.C.A. § 401(a). Under the 1909 Act, art works exhibited at a semipublic showing, for instance at an art gallery to which the general public was not admitted, nevertheless could be held "published" at that time, especially if there were no notices that reproduction or photography was prohibited, and therefore the lack of copyright notice potentially destroyed all copyright protection. *American Tobacco Co. v. Werckmeister* (1907). Under the current Act, publication, at which time notice must be affixed, does not occur when a work is viewed by some members of the public. Instead, display must be to a *substantial* number of members of the public outside the author's normal circle of family or acquaintances. 17 U.S.C.A. § 101.

One additional wrinkle is worth mentioning. It should be noted that a "copy" of a work includes the original. Thus, if the original artwork is displayed to the public at an art gallery, for instance, that constitutes publication, for the original is itself the copy. If the copy (the original, in this example) does not bear the notice of copyright, innocent infringers who rely on the omission will not be liable for infringement.

# CHAPTER 26

# REMEDIES

## § 26.1  Injunctive Relief

The classic remedy for copyright infringement is equitable relief. This includes both preliminary and permanent injunctive relief. Although in theory the standards applicable to copyright cases with respect to preliminary relief are no different than for other substantive areas of the law, it has been observed that preliminary relief is far more likely than in other contexts, especially when contrasted with patent law. As a matter of evidentiary proof this can be explained by the fact that proof of a valid copyright and of infringement is easier to develop at the pretrial stage than it is to prove comparable elements of other substantive violations of law, such as patent infringement. Perhaps more importantly, copyright infringers, like trademark infringers, but unlike patent infringers, are more likely to be transient entities who, absent injunctive relief, are apt to disappear before judgment is rendered or can be collected.

Another possible explanation for the apparently greater willingness to grant preliminary equitable relief in copyright than in other cases is an ill-articulated assumption that copyright infringement automatically threatens irreparable harm. Since irreparable harm generally is the keystone for obtaining injunctive relief, such an assumption would tend to make injunctions more likely in copyright cases than otherwise might be expected. See *American Metropolitan Enterprises of New York, Inc. v. Warner Brothers Records, Inc.* (1968); *Novelty Textile Mills, Inc. v. Joan Fabrics Corp.* (1977). Thus, although there is no clear rule that copyright carries any such assumption, there is some evidence that courts tend to make one nevertheless.

The Copyright Act expressly provides for injunctive relief, to be fashioned in a way that is "reasonable to prevent or restrain infringement." 17 U.S.C.A. § 502(a). Although a blanket permanent injunction in fact may be the ultimate goal of a plaintiff, especially with respect to continual violations, a court has the power to fashion the relief in a reasonable way. This especially is applicable to the innocent infringer as well as to cases involving new technologies.

## § 26.2  Damages and Profits

Monetary awards in copyright infringement actions are categorized under three headings: damages, profits, and statutory damages. Under the 1909 Act, a plaintiff was entitled to damages "as well as" profits, leading some courts to interpret this as meaning that a plaintiff could recover both. In *Thomas Wilson & Co. v. Irving J. Dorfman Co.*

(1970), the plaintiff recovered his own actual damages (lost profits) and also recovered all of the profits received by the defendant. The present Act clearly is designed to avoid that duplication of damages. Under section 504(a), a plaintiff is entitled to actual damages plus profits that are "additional" to those damages. Section 504(b) makes it clear that profits should be added to actual damages only if they were "not taken into account in computing the actual damages."

Thus, a plaintiff should attempt to prove both actual damages and profits. If plaintiff has difficulty establishing actual damages or any part of them, then to the extent profits have been demonstrated that do not overlap, the plaintiff has a greater chance of recovering a larger and more appropriate award. The 1976 Act makes the plaintiff's task easier by providing that plaintiff need only establish gross profits (similar to the scheme under the Lanham Act, see § 18.2, supra). The defendant has the burden of establishing expenses to reduce gross profit to a net amount.

Another element of damages upon which the defendant has the burden of proof is apportionment of profits. Under section 405(b), if the defendant claims that many of the profits were not due to the infringement but, instead, were due to its own creation, or to public domain material, or in any case, to elements not owned by the plaintiff, defendant must somehow establish how much of the profits are attributable to elements not owned by the plaintiff. In *Sheldon v. Metro–Goldwyn Pictures*

*Corp.* (1940), it was found that defendants had infringed the plaintiff's play when they produced a motion picture partly based on the play and an award of profits was made to the plaintiff. However, the total profits were reduced by eighty per cent because the court also found that only twenty per cent of the profits could be attributed to the plaintiff's creation. The majority of profits were attributable to the fact that a number of famous stars were in the movie, and further reduction was due to the fact that the story itself consisted largely of a plot that was in the public domain. This approach clearly is contemplated under the current Act, but the burden is expressly upon the defendant to reduce gross profits to a smaller net amount.

The third category of monetary awards is statutory damages, which may be elected by the plaintiff anytime prior to final judgment. Under the 1909 Act, statutory damages were "in lieu" damages, which the court, not the plaintiff, had discretion to choose. This discretion led to abuse when courts interpreted "in lieu" to mean that statutory damages could be awarded only if no actual damages could be demonstrated. Thus, in *Shapiro, Bernstein & Co. v. 4636 South Vermont Ave., Inc.* (1966), the court found that profits and damages had been established to be *de minimus* and that, there being no need to grant a statutory award "in lieu" of something already established, plaintiff should take nothing.

Under the 1976 Act, statutory damages are strictly within the plaintiff's discretion. Plaintiff has the right to a minimum of $750 and a maximum of $30,000, according to what the court finds "just." On the other hand, innocent infringers can prove their good faith and have the sum reduced to $200. At the same time, a court has the power to award as much as $150,000 if the infringement is found to be willful. That is, essentially, punitive damages. In certain cases involving a good faith belief that the defendant was exercising a fair use privilege, the court has the power to remit all damages. 17 U.S.C.A. § 504(c)(2). On the other hand, the unreasonable claim of fair use by an establishment providing TV or radio to its customers is subject to twice what the license fee would have been for the previous three years, in addition to any other damages. 17 U.S.C.A. § 504(d). Despite the language in the Act indicating that the court is to decide statutory damages, the Supreme Court determined in *Feltner v. Columbia Pictures Television, Inc.* (1998) that the Seventh Amendment consigns this task to the jury.

## § 26.3  Impoundment

Section 503 of the Copyright Act provides for the impoundment and eventual disposition, including possible destruction, of infringing copies and equipment used to produce them. Subsection (a) provides for impoundment prior to final judgment; subsection (b) provides for permanent disposition including possible destruction after final judgment.

Eventual destruction, or at least confiscation of infringing materials, may be an important part of a plaintiff's goals as a final remedy. However, impoundment prior to final judgment may be a more immediate goal. Certainly with respect to such transient violators as record pirates or fly-by-night paperback book publishers, the immediate goal of a plaintiff may be the confiscation of infringing copies to prevent the necessity of constantly relitigating the case wherever the offensive materials happen to reappear. Thus, section 503(a) is crucial to many infringement suits.

As a form of preliminary injunctive relief, impoundment is governed by basic principles of equity. For many years it was governed, however, by the little-known rules of copyright promulgated by the Supreme Court found at 17 U.S.C.A. following section 501, among which were rules allowing preliminary seizure of allegedly infringing articles. Those rules may have been constitutionally suspect since they authorized seizure prior to notice. This may have been especially true with respect to innocent infringers, a category that has been expanded under the 1976 Act. These Supreme Court rules, however, have now been abolished.

## § 26.4   Criminal Penalties

Copyright infringement if committed willfully is a federal crime punishable by imprisonment for one to ten years, depending upon the particular infringement and whether it is a first offense, and a fine determined by the Federal Sentencing Guidelines. Prosecutions under this and predecessor statutes have been infrequent, except for some recent record, DVD, and tape piracy cases. Nevertheless, it does present a possible deterrent to copyright infringement. Although only willful infringement is subject to criminal penalties and must generally be accompanied by "purposes of commercial advantage or private financial gain," any infringements with a total retail value of $1,000 committed within a six-month period are conclusively commercial in nature. 17 U.S.C.A. § 506(a).

The criminal provisions do provide broader remedies with respect to seizure, forfeiture, and destruction making these procedures mandatory upon conviction rather than discretionary and generally giving the court broad powers with respect to the treatment of infringements as contraband. 17 U.S.C.A. § 506(b). Finally, the current Act also criminalizes the fraudulent use of copyright notices, the fraudulent removal of copyright notices, and the fraudulent representation of material facts with respect to copyright registration applications. 17 U.S.C.A. § 506(c)(d)(e).

## § 26.5  Attorneys' Fees and Costs

Section 505 of the Copyright Act provides that costs shall be awarded in any civil infringement action except one against the government. In addition, the court has discretion to award "reasonable" attorneys' fees to the prevailing party. This differs from patent and trademark law, which provides for attorneys' fees only in special, "exceptional," cases.

On the other hand, it is not clear from some older copyright infringement cases that the courts' views of what are "reasonable" amounts are realistic, perhaps due to the fact that these fees are awarded more often than in patent or trademark cases. See *Davis v. E.I. DuPont de Nemours & Co.* (1966) (only $15,000 for 2,000 hours). However, since the federal courts have been developing experience with attorneys' fees in recent years under numerous other statutes and in class actions, this is less of a problem today. In any event, the Supreme Court has indicated that attorneys' fees are to be awarded on a strictly party-neutral basis. *Fogerty v. Fantasy, Inc.* (1994).

## § 26.6 Eleventh Amendment Immunity

The states are immune from suit for copyright infringement and, along the same lines that such immunity exists in patent and trademark law, §§ 9.5, 10.1, 17.8, supra, it cannot be abrogated pursuant to the Fourteenth Amendment Due Process Clause absent some pattern of state infringement. The attempt by Congress to abrogate the immunity, 17 U.S.C.A. § 511, appears ineffective. *Florida Prepaid Postsecondary Educ. Expense Bd. v. College Savs. Bank* (1999).

# CHAPTER 27

# COPYRIGHT LAWS AND THE IN-TERSECTION OF STATE AND FEDERAL REGULATION

## § 27.1  Preemption

Preemption is the doctrine recognizing that, because of the Constitution's Supremacy Clause, federal copyright protection is superior to any and all other state remedies dealing with the area and that federal law therefore always must be, in the end, the controlling principle. A corollary of this principle, which is far more vague and uncertain, is that to the extent federal copyright law does *not* control matters with respect to which it has potential power, there may be an implied federal intent to leave that area free from both federal and state regulation. Any state law that attempts to control such an area may be held preempted by the federal legislation. Thus, state attempts to control matters already *regulated* by the copyright law potentially are preempted and invalid. Likewise, state attempts to regulate matters that the copyright law could regulate but have been left *free* by federal legislation similarly are potentially preempted and also invalid. The 1976 Act contains an explicit section that addresses the scope of federal preemption with respect to copyright protection, and it is clear that the current Act goes further in that direction than all prior Acts. 17 U.S.C.A. § 301. However, it does not go so far as to preempt everything that arguably is within the possible scope of federal regulation.

Section 301 of the Copyright Act provides that it is the express intent of Congress to preempt all state causes of action that do both of the following two things:

(1) grant rights equivalent to the rights granted by the Copyright Act, which

(2) extend to works that are covered by the subject matter of the Act.

It was the intent of Congress to abrogate any state law that corresponds to the expanded copyright protection afforded by the Act. Thus, any state remedy that is described by the two statements above theoretically is preempted by section 301.

The clearest case of preemption is common law copyright. Any state cause of action securing to an author an exclusive right to copy a tangible expression clearly interferes with federal regulation and is preempted. In this sense, section 301 is what Congress termed the "bedrock" provision of the Copyright Act; it had as a primary goal the destruction of common law copyright protection.

On the other hand, some state statutory or common law protection still is viable to the extent it is not described by the two basic elements: if the cause of action does not secure rights to copy, display, distribute, or perform, it might be a viable state regulation even if it regulates a tangible medium of expression. For instance, laws of theft are not preempted despite the fact that they cover, among other things, tangible means of expression of original works of authorship. To steal a book is not to copy it, necessarily, and a law against theft is not preempted because it does not grant a right equivalent to any of the federal exclusive rights. Similarly, a state cause of action granting protection to a speaker against someone else copying or performing his extemporaneous speech may not be preempted because such intangible expressions are not within the subject matter of copyright. A number of areas of intangible expressions therefore are still viable candidates for state protection. These include unrecorded choreography, conversation, live unrecorded broadcasts, and improvisational theatre. Thus, with respect to all cases that do not involve copyright subject matter, state law in fact can grant rights equivalent to copyrights, just as with respect to cases that do involve copyright subject matter, state law can grant rights that differ from copyright.

Only when a state tries to do both—to grant *rights* equivalent to federal copyright *and* to extend those rights to *subject matter* included within federal copyright—are state laws preempted and invalidated. This has the appearance of greater simplicity than is actually the case, however, because it is not really an easy matter to decide how to define these equivalent rights nor is it clear how far the subject matter of copyright extends.

For instance, copyrightable subject matter is defined in terms of tangible media. Section 102(b) of the Copyright Act explicitly excludes ideas, as opposed to expressions, from copyright subject matter. However, Congress did not intend to allow states to grant the equivalent of copyright protection to ideas (disregarding the obvious First Amendment problems this raises) by defining preemption solely in terms of those things that are included within copyright subject matter. The statute itself militates in favor of this conclusion, because it identifies as an example of permissible state regulation subject matter that "is not fixed in any tangible medium of *expression*" (emphasis supplied).

Rights of a personal nature that are centered on the relationships of parties seem to be sufficiently dissimilar to those granted by copyright—which focus on the nature of the work itself—to escape preemption. Thus, causes of action that protect those relations rather than prohibit the copying *per se* of works of authorship should not be preempted. Included in this are relationships of trust and confidence, and interests in privacy and reputation. Thus, although the line is not absolutely clear, a workable treatment of preemption certainly is possible in the vast majority of cases under section 301.

An early draft of what is now section 301 of the Act enumerated some specific examples of state doctrine that would not be preempted. Included were breaches of contract, violations of trust, trespass, conversion, invasion of privacy, defamation, deceptive trade practices such as passing off and false representation, and misappropriation not equivalent to the federal exclusive rights. Even though this version of the section was not included in the final version of the Act, it probably represents an accurate list of nonpreempted areas. Merely listing the labels of those causes of action, however, does not tell how far those doctrines may extend. For example, misappropriation is not preempted but only insofar as it does not grant rights equivalent to federal copyright. This, of course, still leaves unanswered which misappropriation rights may be preempted and which are not. Similarly, deceptive trade practices may not be preempted but perhaps only to the extent they are similar to passing off or false representation. And, the extent to which the common law tort of unfair trade practices is preempted because it is unlike passing off or is not primarily deceptive but more like copyright is unclear.

Section 301's preemption provisions are meant to codify the Supreme Court's holdings in *Sears, Roebuck & Co. v. Stiffel Co.* (1964) and *Compco Corp. v. Day–Brite Lighting, Inc.* (1964), which generally stand for the proposition that preemption does not extend to causes of action dissimilar to copyright nor to subject matter outside the scope of copyright. Simple copying, without more, cannot be regulated by the states because that is the very essence of federal copyright legislation. If the copying, however, is accompanied by deception or some other tortious element, a state may regulate that conduct since what is being controlled is not the copying itself but the conduct—the unfair business practice.

In *Int'l. News Service v. Associated Press* (1918), see § 27.2, infra, the plaintiff's interest in being free from systematic piracy of its news information by the defendant was protected by the Supreme Court under a state doctrine of misappropriation. The tort of misappropriation comes dangerously close to that of copyright because it deals with subject matter that is a fixed and tangible form of expression—wire service news reports—and because the right is very close to one of copying—the exclusive right to sell and distribute the information at least while the news is still "hot." Nevertheless, it can be distinguished from copyright by carefully identifying the nature of the wrong and the remedy sought. The complaint was not so much that defendant was copying but that the copying was being done in a particular way so as to deprive the plaintiff of the value of the news information it had collected.

## § 27.2  State Remedies

Many state common law doctrines function in a way that is comparable to federal copyright in protecting interests and subject matter similar to those governed by the federal copyright laws. These state doctrines are described in a variety of ways. They can be included under the rubrics of unfair competition, unfair trade practices, misappropriation, and trade secrets. Some of them can be called moral rights, see § 27.4, infra. They relate to the law of intellectual property to the extent that they grant remedies for interferences with intangible property rights. The common law torts of defamation and invasion of privacy also affect and interact with interests related to copyright protection. They will not be extensively discussed in this volume (see McManis, *Unfair Trade Practices in a Nutshell, 5th ed.*) because they comprise a substantial and independent body of common law doctrine. However, it is important to recognize the overlapping of federal and state regulation of these similar interests for at least two major reasons.

First, the availability of another substantial body of law offers the possibility that a state remedy may be available despite the failure of copyright law to offer protection or that a state remedy may be available even in addition to federal protection. Thus, merely because a work is not fixed in a tangible medium of expression—for instance, a circus act that has not been recorded but is distinctive enough to be of value to the performer—does not mean that others are free to copy it just because it does not qualify for federal copyright. *Zacchini v. Scripps–Howard Broadcasting Co.* (1977). One cannot conclude that there is not a viable cause of action simply because a copyright remedy is unavailable or insufficient. One must always consult the battery of state remedies.

Second, because of the doctrine of preemption, it always is possible that an apparently viable state tort action, for example, may have been abrogated due to the fact that it too closely resembles federal copyright to coexist with it. Knowledge of the nature and scope of these state tort doctrines is a necessary prerequisite to a decision as to whether federal copyright protection is legally relevant.

The tort of passing off is characterized by some kind of fraudulent conduct and, unlike copyright, focuses primarily on the defendant's intent. It bears more resemblance to trademark than to copyright protection because its essence is that the defendant is attempting to sell its goods under the pretense that they are plaintiff's—passing them off as someone else's. To the extent, however, that the remedy sought is to forbid the defendant from selling a work that resembles the plaintiff's—that is, to forbid defendant from deceptively imitating the works of the plaintiff—the similarity to copyright protection is obvious. In order to avoid federal preemption, the state remedy must turn on some kind of deceptive conduct. *Sears, Roebuck & Co. v. Stiffel Co.* (1964).

Thus, *Dior v. Milton* (1956), declared that the fraudulent practice of spying on rival fashion designers to gain access to new designs that then could be copied in order to undercut the original dress designers unfairly might constitute an independent state tort. The court reached that result despite the fact the relief requested would restrict the otherwise free right to copy due to the fact that there is no federal copyright protection for dress designs.

The tort of misappropriation is similar in that the remedy can bear a marked resemblance to an injunction against copying. In *Int'l. News Service v. Associated Press* (1918), the Supreme Court held that the defendant could be enjoined from using the plaintiff's wire service news items during the period the information constituted "hot" news and had commercial value. For the defendant to use this information without paying for it was to misappropriate to itself property that belonged to the plaintiff. That the defendant was acting in bad faith was important, although the case also focused on the property rights of the respective parties. The result in *INS* was to prohibit the defendant from copying the plaintiff's uncopyrighted news items. To the extent *INS* is viewed in that way, it might represent an impermissible encroachment upon federal copyright protection by state law. However, the Court found that the essence of the suit and of the remedy awarded was not a restriction on copying "but only postpones participation by complainant's competitor in the processes of distribution and reproduction of news that it has not gathered, and only to the extent necessary to prevent that competitor from reaping the fruits" of the plaintiff's efforts. Thus, *INS* still may be good law because the nature of the right protected—not the exclusive right to copy, which would be equivalent to federal copyright but the right to be free from unfair competitive conduct—was one in which copying played a significant but not a defining role.

## § 27.3  Other Federal Remedies

In addition to state remedies potentially available to the plaintiff in a copyright action, there also may exist other federal remedies. Obviously, it is important to be aware of this possibility but equally important is the fact that these additional federal remedies are not threatened, as are state remedies, by the problem of federal preemption since, as federal creations, it cannot convincingly be argued that they conflict with congressional intent, although they might conflict with constitutional limits by intruding on the public domain that the Copyright Clause intends to be free.

Thus, attempted state protection of certain kinds of works or state provision of certain rights that federal copyright does not protect or provide might be ineffective under the argument that Congress, by leaving those works unprotected or by failing to provide those rights, intended that the public have free access to them. Under the Supremacy Clause, that perceived congressional intent would become the law of the land; those state statutes would be held preempted and unconstitutional. Clearly, however, if federal instead of state statutes attempt to protect those works or provide those rights, a Supremacy Clause argument would be a *non sequitur.* Assuming the federal statutes were otherwise constitutional, there is no reason why Congress could not afford certain works protection or grant certain rights even though it did not do so under the copyright laws.

That is roughly the situation under section 43(a) of the Lanham Act which has been held to give authors certain rights that the Copyright Act does not provide. In *Gilliam v. American Broadcasting Cos.* (1976), the plaintiffs, authors of the "Monty Python" British Broadcasting Corporation noncommercial television series, claimed that the defendant had "mutilated" their work by grossly editing it in order to insert commercial interruptions. Although European copyright law specifically protects the "moral rights" of authors against distortions of their works, American law does not expressly do so, although there is reason to believe that there will be considerable doctrinal growth in this area in the future. See § 27.4, infra.

Nevertheless, the court held that the Lanham Act might provide a remedy. The injury to the plaintiffs' reputations by the broadcast, which presented the edited version as a fair representation of plaintiff's own work, could be actionable, said the court, since it might create "a false impression of the product's origin," in violation of section 43(a). See § 16.8, supra. It seems clear that a state attempt to provide this kind of protection, which historically has been alien to American copyright law, would have faced a serious and probably fatal preemption argument.

## § 27.4  Moral Rights and the Berne Convention

Moral rights refers to those inherent rights of authorship recognized in many other countries, that exist in individuals who create intellectual works separate and apart from the property rights created by copyright law. These rights allow authors to object to a use or distortion of their works, even if they no longer own or even never owned, the copyright, if it would injure their reputation or honor. Issues such as film colorization, see 2 U.S.C.A. § 178, defacement, or removal of artistic works, *Serra v. United States General Services Admin.* (1988), and selective distortion or commercialization of a work, *Gilliam v. American Broadcasting Cos.* (1976), commonly implicate moral rights. Other elements of moral rights include the right to be identified as the author of a work—the "paternity" or "maternity" right—and the right to recapture or suppress the work. Note that in all those instances, the person claiming the moral right typically no longer owns the work itself or the copyright. The claim is thus based on a different, inherent right that is part of authorship itself.

American law fairly consistently over the years has refused to recognize moral rights, as such, but through various common law doctrines, such as defamation, misrepresentation, unfair competition, and even contract, and federal claims such as section 43(a) of the Lanham Act, courts frequently have upheld claims that superficially resemble but fall far short of moral rights. See § 16.8, supra. Now, however, the United States has joined the Berne Convention, which demands that its signatories recognize these rights. Berne Convention for the Protection of Literary and Artistic Works, Art. 6 bis (Paris 1971).

However, the federal legislation by which we acceded to the Berne Convention specifically states that the Treaty itself is not self-executing, meaning that the terms of the Convention are not binding absent legislation implementing specific provisions of the Convention. And the issue of moral rights was debated vigorously before accession. Although authors' groups urged that we expressly adopt moral rights, opponents argued for a specific rejection of them. The opponents' position was that we could qualify for Berne on the basis of existing state and federal remedies, and no additional remedies, express or otherwise, were needed or desirable. Importantly, the opponents insisted that existing, expanding, common law doctrines already protect moral rights.

The result was a compromise by which Congress asserted that the terms of the Berne Convention "do not expand or reduce any right of an author of a work, whether claimed under Federal, State, or the common law—(1) to claim authorship of the work; or (2) to object to any distortion, mutilation, or other modification of, or other derogatory action in relation to, the work, that would prejudice the author's honor or reputation." Thus, it remains to be seen whether further federal or state legislation will adopt specific moral rights or whether federal and state courts will take Berne as a signal that the common law should expansively protect moral rights. Several states have enacted "moral rights" statutes protecting various categories of fine and graphic art and a federal statute, the Visual Artists Rights Act of 1990, has been enacted. Any further expansion that does occur would not be based on the Implementation Act, which prohibits the use of Berne as the basis for recognizing more moral rights, but on the emerging common law of moral rights which the Act identified as one of the very reasons its prohibition would not violate the very Convention to which it acceded. Indeed, the Implementation Act states that the requirements of Berne are to be satisfied by, among other things, "any other relevant provision of Federal or State law, including the common law...." Berne Convention Implementation Act of 1988, Pub.L. 100–568, § 3(a)(1), 102 Stat. 2853.

The Visual Artists Rights Act of 1990 is an attempt to create moral rights but it, too, falls short of the mark for reasons of both coverage and substance. First, it applies only to "works of visual art"—which is technically defined as only a very small part of copyrightable works of authorship— only works of essentially fine art that, if distributed in copies such as prints, may not be issued in quantities greater than 200, numbered and signed. Traditionally, moral rights cover virtually all copyrightable works of authorship. Second, and more importantly, the substantive distinction between moral rights and economic rights is that moral rights cannot be bargained away and authors, as a result, can never lose them. (In fact, the copyright termination right—being nontransferrable even by agreement—seems the only United States right that can be characterized as a moral right.) The Visual Artists Rights Act specifically allows authors to "waive" the rights safeguarded by the Act and, being therefore transferrable, do not constitute the moral rights that the Berne Convention demands, unless such "waivers" were limited to waivers of past violations. 17 U.S.C.A. § 106A.

# PART IV

# GLOBAL IP

## CHAPTER 28

## INTERNATIONAL AGREEMENTS

### § 28.1 Overview

There are only a handful of important multilateral international agreements to which the United States is a party that directly affect intellectual property. The major agreements are the Paris Convention (addressing patent and trademark), the Patent Cooperation Treaty, or PCT (addressing patent), the Trademark Law Treaty, or TLT (addressing trademark), the Berne Convention (addressing copyright), The Universal Copyright Convention, or UCC (addressing copyright), NAFTA (addressing all three), and the Trade Related Aspects of Intellectual Property Rights, or TRIPS (also addressing all three). Although all differ in more than just their subject matter, they share certain characteristics that have historical and continuing significance. In 2003, the United States acceded to the Madrid Protocol of the Madrid Agreement, governing trademark, and is now a part of the so-called Madrid system of international trademark registrations.

## § 28.2  National Treatment and Minimum Standards

The oldest and most well-established characteristic of intellectual property agreements is that of national treatment, which can best be understood historically. When the first intellectual property treaties were proposed in the nineteenth century, different countries, at different levels of economic and cultural development, favored different coverage, treatment, and terms. Because it appeared impossible to reach an agreement on the level of protection that should be guaranteed in all signatory countries, a compromise was reached.

Unable to agree on one substantive standard that would be enforceable transnationally, the signatories were left with two possibilities. The first was that of reciprocity under which one country could grant to a second's citizens what that second citizen's country would grant to the first. That, of course, was an impossible choice for the same reason that a transnational standard could not be reached: each country valued its own substantive law over that of the others. The second possibility was that of national treatment under which a country would grant to a second's citizens the treatment the first gave to its own nationals. The result of this, of course, is that such a treaty guarantees no minimum treatment, but only that which is enjoyed by the nationals of each country. That approach could, in fact, be no protection at all (for years, Switzerland, for instance, had no patent protection but was in full compliance with the Paris Convention which demanded nothing but national treatment).

The undemanding approach of national treatment has been the stated rubric of international intellectual property treaties even as, in fact, they depart from that approach in favor of agreement upon transnational minimum provisions. Thus, even NAFTA and TRIPS, which create important transnational norms of substantive intellectual property purport to be documents incorporating national treatment.

## § 28.3   Non–Self–Executing Force and Reservations

Although treaties can have legal force on their own, many, including most intellectual property treaties, are not self-executing. The legal force of a treaty derives from the terms of its implementing legislation. Thus, a party generally cannot rely on the terms of a treaty, but must rely, instead, on the language of the statute that implements the treaty. For instance, the Berne Convention by itself cannot be used as a source of legal rights, but the Berne Convention Implementation Statute may serve that role. Additionally, one feature of international treaties is that signatories can opt out of portions of treaties (short of being incompatible with the "object and purpose of the treaty") through what is called a reservation.

## § 28.4   Copyright Treaties

Although Berne is considered a typically national treatment agreement, it has always had some minimum standards that have increased through each new revision of the treaty over the years. Despite its national treatment, it now demands that signatory countries assure certain terms to various categories, guarantee moral rights, and maintain a fairly clear idea/expression dichotomy. Many, although not all, of these provisions allow for considerable latitude to signatory countries in enacting statutes that implement the treaty's terms.

For many years before accession to Berne, United States publishers nevertheless gained "back door" entry to Berne by simultaneously publishing in the United States and a Berne signatory country (most often Canada), since Berne protection attaches to works that are first-published in Berne countries and simultaneous publication constitutes first publication in each country. Another feature of Berne is the "rule of the shorter term" which allows a Berne signatory, despite national treatment, to apply the shorter term of a work's country of origin if there is such a difference in terms.

The Universal Copyright Convention was created as an alternative to Berne, largely by the United States with the assistance of UNESCO. It is a very unintrusive national treatment treaty, more similar to the Paris Convention for patents than Berne for copyrights, requiring very little more than national treatment and making liberal allowances for formal requirements like notice and registration. It has little significance now that the United States has acceded to and implemented the Berne Convention.

## § 28.5 Patent Treaties

There is no international patent treaty—outside the European Union—by which inventors can gain anything like an international patent. The major patent treaty is the Paris Convention, which is a true national treatment document but whose major characteristic and advantage is the priority—twelve months—it provides for applicants intending to file in other Paris Convention signatory countries. This is an important procedural right, however, because in many countries simply filing an application publicizes the invention, making it ineligible in other countries, many of which demand absolute novelty (including lack of publication) at the time of application. Beyond that, the Paris Convention imposes no particular term, or rights, or disclosure, or any substantive standard of patentability. It does, however, guarantee that signatory countries have the right to impose compulsory licenses and working requirements—insisting that an invention be practiced in the country upon penalty of forfeiture.

The Patent Cooperation Treaty ("PCT") is a purely procedural treaty by which applicants can preserve their priority and gain a head start on filing in other countries. By utilizing the PCT, applicants can file one patent application and, in successive national and international "stages," have patent applications filed in as many signatory countries as desired. The initial application is examined by a central authority, but merely for a limited scope of prior art, resulting in an assessment of, rather than a decision about, patentability. The ultimate decision of patentability is made by each member country relying, only in part, on the PCT examination process results.

Members of the European Union have something approaching a true multinational patent, since, pursuant to the European Patent Convention, applicants can choose to be examined by a central authority that makes a decision on patentability and issues a European patent. Nevertheless, it is still necessary to register formally for a separate patent in each EU member country.

## § 28.6   Trademark Treaties

The major international document relating to trademarks is the Paris Convention, which offers to applicants the same basic priority advantage—although of only six instead of twelve months—enjoyed by patent applicants, under a similar mostly procedural regime. A second, more recent agreement is the Trademark Law Treaty, which for the most part simply harmonizes and simplifies several international procedural and formal features such as recordations of assignment, application minimums, and even the physical dimensions of specimens.

Besides those two treaties, the Madrid Protocol to the Madrid Agreement represents a substantial international regime to which the United States now belongs. Though couched in procedural terms, the Madrid Agreement, and the Protocol in an improved form, offer the equivalent of an international trademark, since the major achievement of the agreement is an automatic registration in all member countries upon a home country registration. For many years the United States opposed Madrid because, among other things, registration in most other countries requires little more than application. Because United States law, however, does not grant registration simply upon application but requires actual use, United States applicants were disadvantaged. Similarly, the multiple registrations pursuant to Madrid were vulnerable to "central attack," losing their registrations if the original home registration was cancelled. The Madrid Protocol was proposed as a solution, and allows Madrid international registrations simply upon application, not registration, and also ends "central attack." Upon its accession to the Madrid Protocol in 2003, the United States became a part of this international Madrid system.

## § 28.7   GATT, NAFTA, and TRIPS

GATT and NAFTA are departures from the tradition of national treatment with few substantive minimums. Despite being trade, not intellectual property, agreements, both NAFTA and GATT adopted substantive terms addressing intellectual property. NAFTA, comprising only Canada, the United States, and Mexico, although with provisions for extensions throughout the Western Hemisphere, was in many ways a precursor to TRIPS. Under the banner of globalization, both NAFTA and TRIPS member signatory countries have agreed upon substantive minimum standards for patent, trademark, and copyright—as well as trade secrets and unfair competition—with various although severely limited opportunities for developing countries to delay compliance temporarily. GATT, which has been absorbed into an umbrella organization, the World Trade Organization, or WTO, includes TRIPS as part of its overall terms. TRIPS, in turn, imposes upon its members most of the provisions of the Paris and Berne Conventions, with some important exceptions, in addition to imposing quite substantial minimum requirements for patent, trademark, and copyright coverage. Among the most important of these are mandatory patent coverage in almost all areas of technology, severe restrictions on compulsory licenses and working requirements, and protection for computer programs and databases.

## § 28.8    Trade Act Special Section 301

All of the international treaties governing intellectual property leave enforcement vague, at best. Although some of the agreements have enforcement provisions, they are either undefined, untested, or awkward to apply. In almost all instances, enforcement is left up to each individual state pursuant to its own legislative scheme.

Perhaps as a result, the United States has reserved to itself the right to address international legal disputes over intellectual property in a unilateral fashion. The Trade Act of 1974, as amended, includes a provision, Special Section 301 of that Act which authorizes sanctions against foreign countries in violation of trade agreements or even, absent such violations, when they unfairly restrict our foreign trade. Amendments in 1988 produced so-called "Super 301," which enhances these penalties and also includes the creation of various watch and priority lists and, ultimately, trade sanctions. What is most surprising is that even when a state is in full compliance with international agreements to which we adhere—such as TRIPS, for instance—the United States reserves, under section 301 of the Trade Act the right to impose penalties upon countries that, in its view, do not provide "adequate and effective" intellectual property protection. There is some doubt whether the application of section 301 in those cases is in violation of the letter of TRIPS but it seems certainly a violation of its spirit.

# INDEX

---

**References are to Pages**

---

445

†